THE WORK H(AT)OME BALANCING ACT

THE
WORK
H AT OME
BALANCING ACT

THE PROFESSIONAL RESOURCE GUIDE FOR MANAGING YOURSELF, YOUR WORK, AND YOUR FAMILY AT HOME

SANDY ANDERSON

AVON BOOKS  NEW YORK

AVON BOOKS, INC.
1350 Avenue of the Americas
New York, New York 10019

Copyright © 1998 by Sandy Anderson, Ph.D.
Front cover illustration by Nick Catano
Published by arrangement with the author
Visit our website at **http://www.AvonBooks.com**
ISBN: 0-380-79801-8

Library of Congress Cataloging in Publication Data:
Anderson, Sandy.
   The work-at-home balancing act : the professional resource guide for managing yourself, your work, and your family at home / Sandy Anderson.
      p.   cm.
   Includes bibliographical references (p. 260).
   1. Home-based business. 2. Self-employed. 3. Home labor. 4. Telecommuting. 5. Work and family. I. Title.
HD62.38.A53   1998   98-20230
658'.041—dc21   CIP

First Avon Books Trade Paperback Printing: September 1998

AVON TRADEMARK REG. U.S. PAT. OFF. AND IN OTHER COUNTRIES, MARCA REGISTRADA, HECHO EN U.S.A.

Printed in the U.S.A.

OPM   10   9   8   7   6   5   4   3   2   1

CONTENTS

INTRODUCTION

One of the biggest reasons I enjoy working at home is that I don't have to commute. In fact, my husband, Bob (who also works at home), and I take a four-mile walk each morning, while the majority of the work force is on their way to work, with radios blaring and coffee cups and car phones gripped firmly in hand. (I sure don't miss spilling hot coffee on *my* lap in a mad rush to get to work on time.)

Just this morning we took a path that ran parallel to a busy freeway, which was unusually backed up for miles. As we walked in our shorts enjoying the morning sun, we couldn't help but notice the looks of frustration and despair on the faces of the drivers. We remembered being there not long ago, and took a moment to count our blessings. Because we work at home, we didn't have to be among those upset, frazzled drivers who were probably running so late for work that their only thought was how the delay would throw their whole day (and evening) off. Would they work through lunch or stay late at the office to get caught up?

Just imagine how many lives could be saved if more people worked at home and stayed off of congested roads during traffic hours, not to mention what that could do for the air we breathe.

On a personal level, working at home presents the opportunity to take control of your life and be your own boss. When you work at home, you are in charge of how you spend your time and whom you spend it with. If you want to work a couple of hours and take a half-hour break to catch up on a good book, take a walk, or spend time with your kids, you have the flexibility to do so. You'll also have more time because you no longer have to make that *dreaded* commute.

I am amazed at the difference in my attitude and stress level since I left the corporate world to work at home. I am free and in control with no one telling me what to do, how to do it, or when. It's a powerful, exhilarating place to be. But at the same time, it can be overwhelming and frightening if you enter the situation unprepared.

WHAT'S IN THIS BOOK FOR YOU?

That's why I wrote this book—to prepare you. Working at home is dramatically different from going to work at an office every day. You're cut off from the rest of the world in many ways. There's no more office gossip (okay, you won't miss *that* . . . at first, anyway), no one to go to lunch with, no one to schmooze with by the water cooler, no one to bounce ideas off of, no administrative support, and in many instances, no one but yourself to manage—need I go on?

Unfortunately, the media has a tendency to oversimplify and glamorize a home office arrangement. A recent cover story of a popular magazine described how you can earn $100,000 working at home. What grabbed my attention was the photo on the cover. It portrayed a woman on the phone doing business while taking a bubble bath—with a smile on her face, a glass of wine and Daytimer by her side. Certainly one could argue that conducting business and taking a bath simultaneously is effective time management, but such images are unrealistic.

While other books on working at home focus primarily on business aspects (e.g., marketing, finances, equipment), this book focuses on personal aspects. What are the personal aspects and why do they matter? They involve knowing your own needs: Are you suited for this? What line of work will you choose? How can you be happy? How can you be productive? How will you handle isolation, motivation, stress?

The personal aspects also involve communicating and negotiating on family-related issues and needs: How will your home office impact your family? How will your family impact your work? How will you manage children, pets, household responsibilities, distractions? Will your family be supportive of your efforts? What can you do to gain their support? My goal is to help you make a smooth and successful transition. If you already work at home, you'll find examples and exercises to help you improve your existing arrangement.

The anecdotes presented are based on interviews I conducted

with over one hundred homeworkers. I interviewed women and men who are self-employed, have work that requires a high level of concentration (e.g., writer, bookkeeper, graphic designer, medical transcriptionist), and have at least one child under the age of thirteen living at home. These challenged individuals were anxious to share their stories because there is so little information available to help people and their families make the necessary emotional and physical adjustments to working at home. Their support and enthusiasm were the main source of motivation for writing this book.

Whether your family consists of your partner, your children, your parents, your pets, your plants, your friends, your visiting nieces, nephews, grandchildren, or any or all of the above, you will find information to help you establish a satisfying arrangement. At times I aim this book toward individuals who are flying solo in a home business, but if you're a telecommuter or an independent contractor working for a company, you will also benefit. Plus, you can determine whether you're willing and able to start your own home-based company.

Studies reveal that about 90 percent of success with anything first involves mentally preparing yourself to win. You will do just that when you conduct an honest evaluation of yourself and your situation in Chapters 1 through 3. This will allow you to knowledgeably choose suitable strategies from those presented in Chapters 4 through 9. You'll then create a plan for making a smooth transition to a home business or telecommuting arrangement in Chapter 10. Finally, you'll focus on managing and growing your home business in Chapter 11. These last two chapters are filled with valuable business tips and resources (plenty of "nuts and bolts") to help you get up and running in your home office quickly and efficiently.

THE WORK-AT-HOME MOVEMENT

Home-based work is rapidly becoming a widespread phenomenon in the United States. According to marketing researchers IDC/ Link of New York City, in the past six years the number of homeworkers has grown from about 26 million to 40 million— representing roughly one third of the entire labor force. This estimate includes 9.6 million telecommuters, 14.9 million full-time home business owners, and 15.8 million who run part-time home businesses to supplement full-time jobs. Some experts predict that if the work-at-home movement continues at its current pace, it won't be long before more Americans will be working out of their homes than in offices and factories.

Ironically, a little more than one hundred years ago, about 90 percent of all Americans were self-employed, with most working on farms and many working from their homes. At that time, shared work and family space was the norm. It was the industrial age that launched the physical separation and differentiation of work and family, and gender roles. Women stayed home, taking full responsibility for household management and child rearing, and men went to work to provide financially for their families.

Currently, people are opting to combine work and family in their homes, similar to (but also very much different from) earlier times. What are the reasons? In recent years several factors have led to the resurgence of home-based work, with an emphasis on home business.

First, the unstable economy of the 1970s and 1980s, combined with strong competition from abroad, has forced U.S. businesses toward a leaner labor force, in an effort to cut costs while trying to maintain quality and remain competitive in a world market. As a result, American companies are turning to a *just-in-time* workforce—hiring workers as independent contractors rather than employees. Such a strategy allows a company maximum flexibility, and saves from 30 to 40 percent on each worker. Because the worker is self-employed, the employer pays only for the work done, not for any lag time between projects. Furthermore, the company is not responsible for contributing to the worker's Social Security account, or providing health insurance or pension coverage.

The second factor contributing to the rise in home-based work is technological change. The U.S. economy is being transformed from an industrial base to an information/service base. Advanced telecommunication equipment allows for the transport of service-related work away from a centralized work site to the home. This phenomenon has opened up vast opportunities, making exciting career options like home business and telecommuting more feasible than ever before.

There are also personal reasons that contribute to the rise in the work-at-home movement. *U.S. News & World Report* editor Amy Saltzman refers to one as "downshifting"—the deliberate pursuit of greater personal fulfillment on a slower, more private, professional track. Simply put, women and men desire to spend more quality time with their families. Consequently, there is a pressing need for creative lifestyle alternatives that offer more flexibility for partners seeking to balance paid employment, parenthood, and household work.

The fourth factor contributing to the work-at-home movement involves changes in family structure, and the traditional allocation of work and family roles between men and women. The norm of the sole-provider husband and at-home wife has given way to the dual-career family in which both spouses have paying jobs. Although men still earn more income than women on average and hold most of the positions of power and leadership in society, home business offers women the opportunity to achieve equality in these areas.

The number of women starting small businesses is on the rise—an occurrence that is not at all surprising. In a business of her own, a woman has no "glass ceiling" to prevent her from reaching her potential. She is the boss, and she decides what is satisfactory in terms of salary and career growth.

On a similar note, home business offers men the ability to become more involved with family. Employers' policies continue to reflect a traditional culture in which women with children leave the workplace, and men with children are not perceived as accountable for family responsibilities or desiring of time with their families.

On the contrary, recent surveys reflect that nearly one third of working fathers have refused a new job, a promotion, or a transfer that threatened to reduce their family time. Half the men polled by the largest executive recruiting firm in the financial field reported that they'd be willing to reduce their hours and salary by up to 25 percent in order to have more family time.

The number of stay-at-home dads is on the rise. While newsletters, organizations, and resources catering to stay-at-home moms are commonplace, there now exists a national newsletter focusing on dads who stay home with their children, either full- or part-time. According to the publisher of the *At-Home Dad* newsletter, Peter Baylies, the idea is gradually gaining acceptance.

Many entrepreneurial couples are home-based, where they can creatively integrate work and family. These ''copreneurs'' represent the fastest-growing segment of the business population, showing an increase of 83.9 percent from 1980 to 1989.

Obviously, working at home makes sense for a lot of people, and for a variety of reasons. The important question is, does it make sense for you? And if it does, how can you get started on the right foot? With these questions in mind, please read on.

PART I

SIZING UP YOURSELF AND YOUR SITUATION FOR A WORK-AT-HOME LIFESTYLE

CHAPTER ONE

Why Work at Home?

 Homeworker Hint

You never realize how much of your life is wasted in your car—away from the people you love—until you go to work at home.

Greg, Cartoonist

Everybody's doing it: tech-savvy twentysomethings and baby boomers who are reluctant to ride the corporate treadmill, people who are laid off, retired people, empty nesters, people who want more personal time, people with kids, people without kids, people who want a sense of purpose and passion, and more quality in their work and personal lives. People who are value-driven. Yes! People like you.

Working at home can be a viable alternative for many, but is it right for you? In this chapter and the two that follow, you will size up your own compatibility with a work-at-home lifestyle. Think of this process as an adventurous journey.

You will read excerpts from interviews with homeworkers offering insight on the realities of what it takes to successfully work from home. Along the way you'll find questions that will stimulate your thoughts and help you understand your goals and dreams. What are your overpowering reasons for wanting to work at home? In what ways will you benefit from making this transition? How does your personality compare to that of the typical homeworker? What occupation or business do you feel passionate about? What kind of business image is most appropriate and comfortable for you? What are the potential pitfalls of working at home that are unique to you and your situation? What are the perks?

These may seem like basic questions, but if you can provide clear, honest, in-depth answers to them, your chances of working happily and productively from home are much better. The questions will encourage you to tune in to your internal desires and identify potential obstacles. You will then be in a prime position to create your own work-at-home strategy.

Be honest with yourself and take whatever time you need to answer the questions posed throughout the chapters. This is a perfect opportunity for journaling. If you keep a spiral notebook handy, you can write down your thoughts while you read. You might want to separate your journaling by chapters so you can go back and review particular areas, or see how you've progressed.

Whether you're considering a transition to a home office environment or have already taken the plunge, these first three chapters will help you do some serious introspection about where you are currently, in relation to where you want to be. If you're already working at home, these chapters will allow you to reaffirm your reasons for choosing to do so. They'll also help you identify overlooked obstacles that may be impeding your performance so you can work on those in the strategy chapters.

IDENTIFYING YOUR REASONS FOR WORKING AT HOME

Many people are striking out on their own, apparently with much satisfaction. The results from a regional research project revealed that 85 percent of individuals interviewed receive "a lot of satisfaction" from their work-at-home lifestyle. Why are vast numbers of people opting to work at home? Even more important, why do you want to work at home?

VISUALIZING YOUR WORK-AT-HOME FANTASY

Sit back for a moment and fantasize about working in your home office. What do you envision? Nine years ago, before I made the leap, I imagined my ultimate home office environment. My office would have a panoramic ocean view, all the latest high-tech equipment, custom furniture, and plenty of space and storage. Because there would be few to no interruptions (ha!), I could accomplish a full day of work (or more) in half the time. There would be plenty of free time (and lots and lots of money) to accomplish personal goals, begin new projects, take exotic vacations, teach my dog new tricks, and spend time with people I care about.

Sound too good to be true? Well, I'll admit that many aspects of what I originally imagined haven't been realized. Am I sorry? Not for a minute. For one thing, my fantasy changes and evolves as I do. What was a priority for me nine years ago isn't necessarily a priority for me today.

Regardless of whether my fantasy changes, however, it never fails to pull me through when the going gets tough. It serves as a tremendous source of comfort and motivation. My vision reconfirms my dreams and my reasons for working at home. Besides, when it comes to realizing your dreams, half the fun is in the process of making things happen—the thrill of the chase. "We create a lot of dreams," says Paul, an environmental product distributor. "On our refrigerator, we have a picture of a motor coach, and my wife cut out a picture of our family and put it in the cab. If I don't have something to motivate me, I tend to lose my focus."

In this chapter you will establish your own reasons for working at home and create a vision that soothes, comforts, or humors you during difficult periods. When you are in a slump or your business is in a slump, when you've lost a good client or a deal falls through, when your family or friends don't understand why you're home but not available, when you miss having co-workers to bounce ideas off of, when you've taken so much rejection that you can stomach no more, you can call on your vision to come to your rescue. It will not only validate your choice to work at home, but it will revitalize you so that you can stay centered, focused, and moving forward.

WHAT EXCITES YOU ABOUT WORKING AT HOME?

Instead of me simply itemizing the advantages of working at home, it's important that you identify them for yourself based on your individual needs, values, and personal qualities. If you want to work at home to have the freedom to indulge in spontaneous and passionate lovemaking in the afternoon, then plug it into your vision. We are all unique, and it's critical that you tune in to your desires. I love the fact that I no longer have to commute to work, but you might value commuting as a chance to relax or unwind. Even though not having to commute is an advantage for me, you would most likely label it as a disadvantage because you'd no longer have that desired transitional time to yourself when you work at home. Similarly, I might despise the isolation of working at home while you might consider it a definite plus, especially if you value significant amounts of alone time.

As you read the following anecdotes from the interviews I conducted, it is critical that you write down your reasons for wanting to work at home in detail. If you see yourself in these stories, make a note of it in your journal. Remember, your dreams and vision will keep you inspired when the going gets tough. The more you can articulate your desire to work at home, the sooner you'll make the transition.

CONTROL AND FLEXIBILITY

Ask people why they enjoy working at home, and chances are, most will mention flexibility or the ability to control so many aspects of life. Try it. Ask anyone, and I'll bet that nine out of ten times the answer you'll receive falls into one of those two categories.

Most homeworkers say that working at home has improved the quality of their life. They feel more balanced than when they worked for someone in an office. Interestingly, prior research reflects that individuals who express the greatest satisfaction with life express feelings of competence and a sense of control. Having control is what working at home is all about.

Control over Time

Would you like to have more control over how you spend your time? When you work at home and no longer have to commute, you automatically have more personal time. Instead of driving to work, you can get in some daily exercise at the gym. You can work on that personal project you've had on the back burner for months. You can take a cooking class or meet a friend for coffee while the rest of the world sits in traffic. Of course, if you really love your work, you can put an extra hour in at the office. With a twenty-second commute, you can even work at 3:00 A.M. in your "jammies."

A work-at-home lifestyle also offers the ability to spend more time with those you care about. It provides the golden opportunity to be there for your children—to transport them to and from activities, or nurture them when they're sick. "When my son is sick, I don't have to take time off from a job," says Jill, a desktop publisher. "It's easy for me to work because he sleeps most of the day. Actually, I get more work done." Many parents also find that working at home provides a great opportunity to home-school their kids because their schedules are so flexible.

Flexibility—the Double-Edged Sword

Homeworker Hint

The pluses and minuses of working at home are very closely interwoven—like an ice cream swirl.

Jim, Fund-Raising Consultant

Before we go further, it's important to say a few words about the highly touted "flexibility" of a work-at-home lifestyle. There's no denying that working at home offers tremendous personal freedom. It's very seductive in that way. However, it's not all peaches and cream. Chris, a magazine publisher, refers to the flexibility of a home office arrangement as a "double-edged sword." "Having the ability to work any hour of the day can work for you or against you," she cautions. Most homeworkers, for example, struggle with the tendency to overwork, but losing motivation and not working enough can certainly be issues as well.

I remember when Bob and I left our not-so-secure jobs as computer analysts to become work-at-home real estate agents. Unknowingly or unthinkingly, we jumped into a business that was in a negative spiral without a plan. The stress and frustration of our situation often felt unbearable. Our "coping strategies" temporarily eased our pain but didn't do wonders for our business. Instead of making our morning work calls, we found ourselves at the beach watching dolphins and drinking coffee. With so much flexibility, you have to be careful not to go to extremes. Bob and I quickly realized that with our newfound freedom, it was necessary to establish boundaries and schedules, or we might end up sleeping at the beach with the dolphins.

I have come to respect working at home as a delicate "high-wire act" that takes tremendous concentration and balance, not to mention enduring persistence. Jean, a computer research analyst, refers to the "give and take" or "heaven and hell" inherent to working at home. Homeworkers are pulled in opposing directions because of the flexibilities and freedoms so readily available. Striking that perfect balance is an ongoing, relentless challenge:

> The flexibility is nice, but with so much freedom, it's easy to work too little or too much, spend too much time with your family or not enough. I don't have to dress up, which is nice, but since I started working at home, I don't seem to worry as much about how I look. I get lonely sometimes, but I wouldn't give up my solitude for anything. When I boil it all down, I know I'm in control, and no matter what, that makes it all worthwhile.

Pat, a newspaper publisher, decided to work at home to be close to her kids—a value judgment she made, but not without sacrifice. "I think I'd get further in my career and I'd get more done if I worked in an office," she says. "But I'd also miss out on being with my kids, which I wouldn't like. It's a give and take."

Strong Family Ties

Homeworker Hint

The ten minutes you used to spend having a soda with somebody in the office is the ten minutes you can now spend with your kids. If it's a beautiful day outside, you can have lunch outside with them. You can't do that when you work in an outside office. With Daddy out of town, I'm a single mom Monday through Thursday, so it allows me to keep my finger on the pulse at home. Essentially, your trade-off is your co-workers for your family.

Val, Travel Agent

Do you want to work at home in order to be closer to your family, or be there to care for your children? Many homeworkers feel they chose the best possible lifestyle for themselves and their family. Whatever the trade-offs were in leaving the corporate world behind, the ability to stay close as a family and be there for one another makes it all worthwhile.

Ron, a pet product distributor, was having an intimate champagne dinner with his wife in the hospital after their son was born. At the time, Ron was pulling down twelve-hour days working for a corporation, and he was exhausted. He leaned back against the wall and fell sound asleep in the midst of celebrating the happiest moment of their lives. "When I started snoring, you can better believe it was the last straw," he remembers. "We had to do some pretty heavy talking to work through that episode." Ron and his wife decided to work at home together so they could share in the raising of their son. They wanted to create an environment that would support his growth and allow him to know both parents. "That was six years ago, and it was the best move we've ever made," Ron says.

Starting a home business usually means a cut in income (unless you already have established clients), so making this decision forces you to closely examine your values and the level of income your family requires. "I would go to work for someone else if I had to—for my son or to pay the mortgage, but not to buy a nicer car," says Jan, a property manager. "People think they need the money," says Ted, a market researcher. "It's amazing what you can economize on, and the kids don't care. They don't care about having new things. They care about having Mom or Dad close."

Control over Income Level and Job Security

Would you like having control over your income level and job security? Although working at home initially results in less income, a recent survey revealed that 75 percent of home business owners believe they make adequate or good money. In fact, many women who work in a home business stress that they make more money than they did working for someone. "When I'm working six hours a day, feasibly making what I would in nine hours working outside for somebody else, it does work out great," says Sue, a medical transcriptionist.

Ironically, job security is another advantage of operating a home business. Many men, in particular, decided to start their own business because they were tired of working for companies that downsized them right out of a job. As Paul, an environmental product distributor, puts it:

> I've earned my security because of relationships I have with clients. I have 560 bosses, so I have 560 jobs. If I had one boss and he had a bad day, I'd feel insecure. With 560 bosses, if one of them has a bad day, I've got 559 more I can call up and feel okay about.

Control over Your Schedule— Ability to Be Your Own Boss

While Paul may have 560 clients, he ultimately answers to only one boss—himself. Would you like to be your own boss? Imagine not having to pull out your list of 101 excuses to find a "good one" for being late. Imagine having the ability to take charge of your own work schedule. If you want to take an impromptu vacation, you don't have to ask for permission.

Control over Stress Level

Can you imagine having control over your level of stress? Most homeworkers will tell you that being your own boss is a definite challenge, but it allows you to have control over so many aspects of your life and work that you may notice a considerable drop in your stress level. "Having to go to work and keep the boss happy and keep your co-workers peaceful is a lot more stressful than sitting at home for eight hours focused on one job, doing one thing," explains Jill, a desktop publisher. "I'm totally in control. There's nobody for me to be angry at, and nobody's yelling at me."

Control over Working Relationships

Would you like to be in a position to pick and choose who you work with? "When I don't want to deal with people, I don't," asserts Ann, a personal image consultant. "In an office situation I don't have a choice. Here, I can choose who I want to be around, and I can choose not to open the door. I don't have to deal with undesirable clients or negative associates."

Control over Career Destiny

A number of women, in particular, express that a home business allows them to take control of their career destiny, and avoid unfair hiring practices used by corporations. "It has been my experience that you're not hired if you aren't young and pretty," says Lynn, a bookkeeper. "Working at home, I'm judged on what I produce. It doesn't matter what I look like, it's what I give them that matters." Liz, a computer programmer, had trouble finding a professional job in her field that would allow her to work on a part-time basis. "They'll let me work part-time running errands or answering phones, but they're not going to let me do something that uses my brain,'' she says. In a home business you can work part-time one week and full-time the next. It's entirely up to you.

Control over Attire

Ever fantasize about what it's like to work at home naked? Or in your bathing suit in between dips in the pool? Now is your chance to partake. When you work at home, you don't have to wait for ''dress-down Friday.'' You can dress down any day.

I'm one of those people who used to hate dressing up for work. What can I say? I'm a sucker for comfort. Unless I have an appointment or a meeting, shorts, T-shirts, and sneakers are my favorite work attire. The cost savings on clothes alone can be substantial. Now when I shop, it's for clothes I really love to wear, rather than have to wear to make an impression.

Control over Your Environment

Mary, an insurance agent, loves having the ability to control her work environment. She feels more relaxed and even safer working at home because she no longer has to walk through a dark parking lot when she works late into the night. ''Everything in my home office was created and prepared by me,'' she says. ''It's an identification process. I thrive on working in an environment that's pleasing to me. What could be better than the comfort of your own home?''

No More Office Politics and Gossip

If you're leaving a corporate setting to work at home, will you miss the office politics and gossip? Most homeworkers are happy to leave *that* scene behind. The time wasted at the office on power struggles and keeping up with daily rumors is time that can be channeled into work, leaving even more time left over for family, friends, and personal pursuits.

Increased Work Productivity

The majority of homeworkers stress that they're much more productive working out of their home than they were in an office setting. The few who experience decreased productivity have difficulty with self-discipline and dealing with distractions, two issues we'll cover in Chapters 2 and 7.

Mentally Stimulating and Confidence Building

Jan, a property manager, decided to work at home because she wanted to spend time with her son but realized she needed something more to think about besides "Barney." Starting a home business proved to be the perfect solution. Not only is it mentally stimulating (because you learn how to juggle and master so many things at once), it's a great confidence builder as well. Carol, an architectural illustrator, always had the yearning to work on her own at home, and finally took the leap just to see if she could really do it. She not only did it, she did it with tremendous success. "My home business is a real source of pride for me," she says, beaming.

Financial Benefits

Want to save money? Many find the financial benefits of running a business from home very appealing:

- Low overhead
- Tax breaks
- Less wear and tear on your car
- Savings on gasoline
- Savings on food expenses
- Savings on the purchase of an elaborate wardrobe
- Savings on child care expenses

Advantages for You and Your Partner

Will your partner be supportive of your home office arrangement? If so, your experience will be all the more rewarding. Wendy, a newspaper editor, says her husband loves the fact that she works at home because she can handle personal matters that need taking care of. "My husband can't just leave his job and run to the bank," she says. "I, on the other hand, have total freedom and have become a master at weaving those nagging personal responsibilities into my workday. I like it because it breaks things up."

Jack, a copywriter, reveals that when he started his business at home, he wasn't bringing any money in, and he appreciates that his wife took on the role of "sole breadwinner" in the family. Jack takes pride in the fact that working at home allows him to be a tremendous support to his wife and son. "I like being home and available to take care of my son, and it enables my wife to be totally into what she does," he says. "I support her in that way, and she has really advanced in her career." We'll talk about strategies for gaining the support of your partner in later chapters, but most homeworkers say that their partner also benefits from their choice to work at home.

Do you value working at home as a way to be closer to your partner? I talked to a number of homeworkers who stress that working at home is advantageous to their relationship. Ann, a personal image consultant, winds down her workday while talking to her husband as he cooks dinner. Amy, a computer software distributor who works with her husband, says working together has improved their relationship because it gives them a lot more common ground and alone time together.

Advantages for Your Children

Do you realize how much your children can benefit from seeing you in action in your home office? The children of parents who work at home automatically benefit because they gain a true understanding of what it means to work firsthand. Work isn't some mysterious unknown duty that their parent leaves the house to perform five days a week. "My daughter gets to see a woman in action having everything that she has ever wanted, knowing that she can make those decisions for herself as well," says Sara, a fitness trainer. "If she wants something badly enough, maybe it's time she creates it for herself."

In the August 1991 issue of *Home Office Computing,* a survey of some of the magazine's readers—nearly four hundred parents—revealed that in general they had no major dissatisfactions with their home office arrangement. The results suggested that a work-at-home lifestyle has several advantages for parents and children alike. Among those surveyed: 90 percent believed they better balance their family and career; 85 percent said that their children like the arrangement better; 84 percent felt that they were better parents; 81 percent indicated that their children better understand and appreciate their work, and that their children are more likely to be entrepreneurial adults; 76 percent believed that their children are less likely to use drugs and alcohol; 72 percent said that they are more involved with their children's school activities.

A previous study on homeworking families supports the results of this survey. Children of all ages verbalized "parental access and availability" as the major advantage of having parents who work at home.

GETTING CLEAR

It's extremely important that you clearly identify your reasons for wanting to work at home. Now is a good time to write down any goals you have in making this transition. What will you do with the additional time and freedom? If your goal is to spend more time with your partner, children, or pets, write it down. If you desire to work at home so you can take breaks and do some gardening during the day, or swim laps in the pool, write it down.

Elaborate as much as you can why these goals are important to you. Be specific. How will you benefit? How will the people you care about benefit? How will your relationships benefit? As I mentioned earlier, your goals will keep you afloat when it feels like your boat is sinking. They're important visualization tools, and they'll be a great help when you're coming up with a strategy to make this lifestyle work for you.

● **Your Reasons for Working at Home**

Which of the following do you value in relation to working at home? Write these values down in your journal and expand on them in detail as much as possible.

Having Control Over . . .

____ Scheduling of your time (e.g., personal, family, and work roles)
____ Your income level
____ Job security
____ How you dress
____ Your level of stress
____ Whom you work with
____ Your environment
____ Your career destiny

Additional Goals . . .

____ To obtain a better quality of life
____ To create a more balanced existence
____ To spend more time with family and/or friends
____ To be a good role model for your kids
____ To have more personal time
____ To be your own boss
____ To be more productive in your work
____ To build confidence
____ Financial savings (e.g., clothes, gas, car wear and tear, low overhead, tax breaks, child care)

CHAPTER TWO

Are You Suited for Working at Home?

 Homeworker Hint

Look at your personality. Are you suited for it? You can't be too shy or you won't reach out. Strive to be a confident expert at what you do—organized, independent, a self-starter, a realist but an optimist at the same time, highly creative, and able to roll with the good and the bad. You won't survive if you're a constant worrier.

Mary, Insurance Agent

Is there a certain personality type characteristic of successful homeworkers? Must you be a hermit who loves to hide out most of the time, or so self-disciplined that tuning in to "Oprah" during the middle of the day is unthinkable? No formal research has explored the personality of individuals who work at home, to see if certain qualities might be typical of those who feel satisfied with their lifestyle choice.

THE HOMEMAKER PERSONALITY INVENTORY

One goal during the course of my interviews with homeworkers was to inquire about personality traits they possess that enhance or hinder their ability to work at home. I will present the top twelve traits revealed in a brief personality inventory, and question you on where you stand in relation to each trait. Rate yourself on a scale of one to five, with one indicating that you do not believe you possess the trait, and five indicating that you strongly believe you do possess the trait. To gain even more insight, ask a friend or loved one to give you feedback on how they perceive you in these areas as well.

This is a good time to pull out your journal and make notes to yourself. Jot down your strengths and the areas where you feel weak. If you have any thoughts on how you'd resolve potential problem areas, write down those as well. This self-knowledge will lay the groundwork for choosing appropriate strategies in later chapters.

Self-Motivated

Most homeworkers describe themselves as extremely "self-motivated." Pat, who publishes a local newspaper, says people are amazed at how she does so much at once. "My friends tell me I'm the most driven person they know," she says. "They think I'm psychotic, running from a childhood of abuse or something, trying to fill up every bit of time. That's pretty much the way I like it."

Pat's behavior may be a little extreme, but in general, are you self-motivated? Do you tend to get things going on your own or do you prefer to be directed by others? You may be thinking that it depends on the task you're performing, right? I'll admit that my motivation for doing administrative work, such as setting up files, is not so hot. On the other hand, when it comes to writing a challenging proposal on a book I'm excited about, my motivation soars.

Lisa, a medical transcriptionist, stood out because of her lack of motivation, a constant theme throughout her interview. "I'm the queen of prolonging agony," she confesses. "My lack of motivation is a hindrance. I procrastinate. I wait till the very last minute." Lisa refers to her work as "agony" and admits that money is her only source of motivation, but it isn't enough to trigger her into action. As a result, she constantly struggles with trying to push herself to work more hours when she just doesn't feel like it. Unlike Lisa, most successful homeworkers are passionate about their work and have strong reasons for working at home. Many want to be close to their family or have more time for personal interests.

Consider your behavior in your current or previous work environments. Are you a self-starter? Val, a travel agent, offers tips on determining your level of self-motivation:

> *Anyone who works in a self-motivating job like a consultant, a salesperson, a project manager . . . anyone who has autonomous responsibilities, has a thinking job, and is responsible at organizing stuff . . . if you're the type of person that when someone says, "Here's this project, go figure out how to do it, the deadline's here," and you get it done, you have what it takes to do this. It might take some transition time at first and some adjustment, but once you make the mind-set change, you can do it!*

● **Personality Trait #1**
On a scale of 1–5, how do you rate your level of self-motivation?_____

People who work in highly structured jobs directed by others may have the most difficulty striking out on their own. In listening to homeworkers talk about self-motivation, however, it became clear that this trait can be developed. "I've learned how to be self-motivated. It's a muscle I never knew I had," says Ron, a pet product distributor. "In the beginning, it was a battle for me to stay motivated because I was so used to having someone tell me what to do. I didn't know how to create my own agenda." Ron gradually worked through his struggle until finally he became comfortable and self-sufficient on his own.

Self-Disciplined

If self-motivation is the fuel that propels you to get work done, then self-discipline can be thought of as the imaginary "seat belt" that straps you to your chair long enough to achieve your goals. How can you stay focused if you're subject to frequent interruptions from family, friends, neighbors, or pets during work time? "It can get nasty at points," says Ben, a marketing consultant. "The dog barks as the doorbell rings, and I can't conduct business. That's when I kick the door shut, but it's just not effective."

Distractions are everywhere when you work at home—household chores, TV, your favorite magazines, that great book you've been dying to read, the refrigerator—and they are a constant threat to self-discipline. "Actually sitting down and working, that's my major hurdle," says Lynn, a bookkeeper. "The bathroom has to be cleaned. I have to do something with my daughter. *Anything,* even abstract noise, throws me off."

A previous study conducted by Betty Beach (1989) on a small group of homeworkers revealed that those who didn't use childcare services attended to preschool children (to age six) an average of 8.3 times per two-hour work period, and school-age children (ages seven to eighteen) an average of 2.71 times per two-hour work period. Furthermore, they interrupted their workday an average of 5.8 times to do an average of 2.2 hours worth of household chores. Many work-at-home occupations would be difficult, if not impossible, to perform with such frequent interruptions and distractions.

How are you in the self-discipline department? When you start a task, are you good about seeing it through? Are you able to focus with noise and activity going on around you, or do you require peace and quiet? Can you handle interruptions and get back on track? "I don't have a problem shutting my office door and tuning out the fact that there's a house around me," says Val, a travel agent. "The vacuuming can wait. I grew up in a family of six kids, so I know how to focus. Some people find that very difficult."

Overworking also poses a major challenge to self-discipline. "If I worked at an office during the day and then picked up the kids at day care and came home, at least I wouldn't feel like I should be working," says Jean, a computer research analyst. "Now I don't have a quitting time and it's hard for me to leave unfinished business—it's constantly in my face."

Having an accessible office creates a nagging invitation to work any hour of the day. Obviously this arrangement can be unhealthy if you tend to be a workaholic. According to Ben, a marketing consultant, the biggest challenge of working at home is figuring out how to strike a balance between underworking and overworking:

You have to have a certain amount of discipline to survive at home. You need to learn how to stay focused. It's tempting to walk twenty feet to the couch and call it a day. Lord knows, it's all available. But don't be hard on yourself either. You can't sit chained to your desk. You've got to strive for a happy medium.

● **Personality Trait #2**
   On a scale of 1–5, how do you rate your level of self-discipline?_____

Write down in detail what you believe are potential threats to your ability to be self-disciplined.

• Interruptions (kids, pets, personal calls)
• Household distractions (housework, TV, hobbies)
• Managing yourself (sticking to a schedule)
• Office accessibility (overworking)

In Chapter 7 we'll discuss strategies for overcoming these obstacles.

Enjoy Solitude

Homeworker Hint
   In order to run a successful home business, it helps if you're a little older because you don't require as much social contact. The thirty-and-over

crowd are more established in their careers. Make sure you know your area of expertise before you venture out on your own.

Wendy, Newspaper Editor

I was surprised to find that many homeworkers enjoy being alone and refer to themselves as a "loner" or "solitary person." They not only spend a lot of time alone in their work, but in their personal time they participate in activities such as reading and making crafts, or spending time with their families. "I feel really in tune with myself when no one is around," says Laura, a freelance writer. "My greatest insights come when I'm alone. That's actually when I experience the most personal growth."

Other homeworkers, a group I refer to as the "networkers," are outgoing and like interacting with people in their work and personal time. "I look forward to getting together with my girl-friends for lunch," says Wendy, a newspaper editor. "I love to talk, and we can dish for hours."

Where do you fall on the continuum of personality styles? Are you a loner or a networker, or somewhere in between? Are you more comfortable working alone, or do you thrive on having frequent contact with others? Regardless of the type of work you do, you'll have large amounts of alone time when you work at home.

I found the isolation nearly intolerable when I began working at home. It interfered with my ability to work. I gravitated toward excessive telephone talking and running menial errands just to get out of the house. I soon realized that I needed to schedule regular interaction with people into my work week or I wouldn't survive. We'll discuss strategies for overcoming isolation in Chapter 8, but be aware that this can be a major struggle.

- **Personality Trait #3**
  On a scale of 1–5, how much do you enjoy spending time alone while you work?_____

Thrive on Control

Would you like having the flexibility to set your own hours? Do you resent micromanagement, or any supervision at all? Because they are in total control, home business owners make decisions constantly. Can you make quick decisions under pressure without consulting others? "I like having the ability to control, to choose or not to choose," notes Phil, an attorney.

Control is a big issue for many because there is so much in life that we, as individuals, can't control. With the world in a constant state of flux, the more we adopt lifestyles that can roll with the punches, the better off we'll be. Operating a home business is one way to shelter yourself from corporate dictation and downsizings. Does this line of thinking appeal to you?

- ### Personality Trait #4
  On a scale of 1–5, how much do you thrive on having control?_____

If having complete control doesn't feel comfortable, one option is telecommuting, whereby you can continue to work for someone, stay connected to a company, and satisfy your desire to work at home. In Chapter 10 we'll discuss the creation of telecommuting arrangements in depth.

Organized

Do you like to start your workday with a clean, organized desk? Being organized isn't everything, but it helps when you work at home. Unless you have an overabundance of space, having a place for everything will go a long way toward helping you maintain sanity in your work and personal lives. When you waste time looking for a phone number for the third time in one day, your business suffers. Good organizational skills will allow you to be more productive. Efficiency is the key.

● **Personality Trait #5**

On a scale of 1–5, how organized are you?_____

As a side note, being organized is not necessarily synonymous with being a perfectionist, but it could point toward that tendency. "I'm a perfectionist, and that gets in my way sometimes," reveals Carol, an architectural illustrator. While perfectionist qualities may be difficult for homeworkers to wrestle with (and many do), their high standards contribute to their success and commitment to the business.

But perfectionism can also be a hindrance when carried to extremes. As a writer, I can always read my work and find something that could have been said a little more clearly. If I get caught up in an infinite proofreading and editing loop, however, I will eventually become counterproductive. No matter what line of work you pursue, it's important to identify the point at which discontinuing your investment of time will not compromise the quality of your work.

Committed

Do you desire to have a real sense of passion and purpose in your work? Are you value-driven rather than having to work just for the money? "I love money, but that's not the driving force behind me," says Sara, a fitness trainer. "I want to be able to check out at the end of my eighty-nine years and say, 'I've done a good thing on this planet.'"

Are you willing to go the extra mile to succeed? Homeworkers tend to be extremely passionate about their work, and willing to do whatever it takes to get the job done. They thrive on the sense of accomplishment. It's their enduring persistence that sets them apart from those who give up during difficult times.

You'll find that *retirement* is not a word in the vocabulary of many homeworkers. "I'm a writer," says Jack. "I'm a writer when I'm writing, and I'm a writer when I'm not writing. So when I'm eighty years old, I'll probably still have the compulsion to write things down, whether it's for me or somebody else."

Work is a strong source of self-identification that doesn't cease simply because one reaches retirement age.

- **Personality Trait #6**
  On a scale of 1–5, how do you rate your level of commitment to your work?_____

Self-Confident

"If I work hard enough at it, I can do almost anything," says Pat, a newspaper publisher. Do you believe in your abilities to make things happen? A self-confident attitude is critical when you work at home and have little or no diversion from your own thoughts. You have no co-workers or managers to praise and comfort you. Therefore, you must learn to praise and comfort yourself.

"I haven't made any money so far, but the potential is there, and I can see the potential," says Chris, a magazine publisher. Are you generally an optimist? Do you tend to have faith that everything will work out even in the worst of situations, or are you a worrier?

Effective homeworkers maintain a lighthearted attitude about what they do, and don't allow the little things to get them down. They frequently use humor to cope, often laughing at stressful predicaments rather than giving up.

- **Personality Trait #7**
  On a scale of 1–5, how self-confident are you?_____

Risk Takers

How do you feel about stepping out of your comfort zone to take risks? Not just financial risks, but emotional risks as well? Do you visualize yourself as a go-getter? An adventurer? Willing to put your all into your passion?

Working at home involves certain financial and emotional

risks. If you're starting a new business, you'll most likely work excessive hours with little or no money coming in initially. "I was working fourteen-hour days when we first started," recalls Jim, a fund-raising consultant. "It was an intense time—very nerve-racking, very scary. Were we going to make it? There was a lot of pressure, and a lot of stress."

Even after the business is up and running, many men say they make less money than they did while working for someone. "A lot of my peers who work for companies are two to three times ahead of me in the money they're making," explains Ron, a pet product distributor. "I haven't been able to sock the money away like I wanted."

The lack of traditional employer-paid benefits such as health insurance and paid Social Security contributes to the decrease in income. Also, there is no disability insurance or availability of parental leave. "When you work for yourself, there's no such thing as maternity leave," reveals Jan, a property manager. "I had my son on a Saturday over Labor Day weekend, so I got Monday off, but I had to start back to work right away. The first six weeks were really hard, just the logistics of it all."

Businesses tend to run in sporadic cycles of highs and lows, which is a challenge not only to your morale but to your cash-flow situation. According to the U.S. Small Business Administration (SBA), 80 percent of people who start a business from scratch have no financial cushion to fall back on. Homeworkers who don't have a financial cushion or their partner's income to rely on experience increased stress. Also, individuals who leave their jobs not only cut their household income in half, but the majority have to take out some type of loan or dip into their savings or retirement accounts to get their business established. Many have to adjust to a lower standard of living or put family assets at risk.

Unfortunately, it can be difficult to establish credit and get loans for start-up capital, as Amy, a computer software distributor, experienced:

We wanted a MasterCard/Visa for the business, and we were told no because we're a home business. That same week the Wall Street Journal *had this powerful article about home businesses. We took the article in to the bank man-*

*ager and said, "We're long-standing customers. You know
what's in our accounts, and you know we can do this." We
got one, but we were turned down initially because we're
a home business.*

Besides financial risks, working at home poses personal challenges. Some homeworkers indicate that their spouse, kids, and
friends don't support or respect their efforts to work on their
own because the first few years of the business start-up are so
demanding on personal relationships.

● **Will You Have the Support of Others?**
   ____ Your partner (Will you have your partner's physical, financial,
       emotional support?)
   ____ Children (Will your children interrupt? Will they understand you
       are working?)
   ____ Friends and extended family (Will friends and extended family
       respect your work hours? Will they support your efforts?)
   ____ Clients (Will clients support and respect your work-at-home
       arrangement?)

Think about your situation in the areas of emotional and financial backing and support. If you don't already have what you
need, are you prepared to do what it takes to fill any voids?
Being aware of the risks involved in working from home is para-
mount because you'll be better able to deal with the challenges
if you know what to expect.

● **Personality Trait #8**
On a scale of 1–5, how much of a risk taker are you?_____

For many who work a nine-to-five job outside the home, regular increases of pay, benefits, and seniority serve to discourage
them from making transitions to opportunities that could better
challenge their potential—a situation that, unfortunately, stifles

risk-taking behavior. A home business, on the other hand, encourages risk taking.

Knowledge Seekers

Homeworker Hint

I spent a fortune on books before getting started—a couple hundred dollars every time we went to the bookstore. I invested a lot of time into researching my home business before I opened the doors. I was determined to start off on the right foot.

Ted, Market Researcher

Do you thrive on learning new things? If so, a home business provides the opportunity to use multiple talents, and learn new talents when needed. If you happen to be the investigative type, you'll love the variety.

Jenny, who recently started a secretarial service, enjoys having the ability to "wear numerous hats" but realizes she doesn't have the time or energy to keep it up for long. After a mere six months her business is starting to thrive, a phenomenon she credits to her willingness to learn:

I am the marketer, the financial planner, the boss, the administrator. I handle everything. I am very hungry for information. I attend a lot of classes and seminars. I read books and listen to tapes. I want to know what I'm doing in all capacities so that when I hire someone to fill in, I can knowingly tell them what I expect.

Homeworkers constantly adapt and change in order to live in accordance with their values, rather than allowing their destinies to be determined by others. Their constant search for challenge and knowledge reflects their desire to grow and develop as individuals. Does this strike a chord with you?

- **Personality Trait #9**
  On a scale of 1–5, how much of a knowledge seeker are you?_____

Support Elicitors

You've done all your homework, you've set up your office, and you're ready to take on the world. It's important to be able to work independently and self-sufficiently; however, successful homeworkers know their limits, and they know when to ask for help.

Running a business can wear you down. How long can you tolerate twelve-hour workdays six or seven days a week? Because everything is up to you, you need to seriously evaluate what you can and cannot comfortably take on. Are there aspects of your business that you're not qualified or willing to do (e.g., marketing, bookkeeping, administrative details, accounting, or legal functions)? Will you get help with family and/or household responsibilities (e.g., child care, housecleaning)?

How will you handle times when business is booming? Will you delegate certain aspects of the business in order to free yourself to do what you do best, and are happiest doing? If you absolutely hate keeping the books, and it takes you three times longer than it should, you'll be better off hiring someone to do it for you.

- **Personality Trait #10**
  On a scale of 1–5, how much of a support elicitor are you?_____

Good Communicators

It's common knowledge that good communication is key to most jobs. Conversing with clients, defining the scope of projects, marketing for business, collecting money owed, and solving problems are actions that require good oral and written communication skills that you'll be using in your business.

How well do you get along with different personalities? Home business owners need to develop working relationships with a variety of people, including customers, vendors, bankers, and professionals such as lawyers and accountants. Can you deal with a demanding client or an unreliable vendor in the best interest of your business?

It's equally important to maintain good communication with those you love. Your family and friends will be affected by your decision to work at home. There will be times when they won't understand what you're doing, especially when it takes away from their time with you or upsets their routine (e.g., clients coming to your home, working odd hours). They might unknowingly stand in the way of your efforts to succeed. You will need to ask for their support up front, and keep an ongoing dialog that stresses compromise.

- **Personality Trait #11**
  On a scale of 1–5, how do you rate your ability to communicate?_____

Creative

Are you a creative person? Are you imaginative? Do you bubble over with ideas? Do you like to express your originality? If so, there are infinite ways to channel your creative energies when you work at home. "I've always had a creative side," says Liz. "Can you believe I used to work at home doing cake decorating and floral design, and now I write computer programs?"

Creativity is a valuable quality to possess in a home office arrangement because it helps you find unique solutions to the unique problems you encounter. Creative problem-solving abilities really came in handy for Pat when she started her newspaper publishing business on a shoestring budget:

> I just started a newspaper from scratch, and didn't know anything about it. I hadn't worked on a computer in ten years. Fortunately, someone donated one to me, and I was given new software programs to learn. I also talked to people in the business. Whatever I didn't know, I contacted people who did know and bartered for services. Eventually I learned how to do those things myself.

Typically, when you work for someone in an outside office, many things are taken care of and you can work on autopilot. Not so when you work at home (at least not until after you read this book and utilize the advice and strategies offered). When you go to work for someone, your office is usually set up, your schedule and breaks are generally given, and your co-workers are minding their own business in offices of their own (okay, most of the time). You aren't inundated with kids, pets, friends, or extended family members dropping in unannounced (unless, of course, you work in a pet store or the local zoo). The more you can think openly, creatively, and be quick on your feet, the better off you'll be.

● **Personality Trait #12**
On a scale of 1–5, how creative are you?_____

Humanistic psychology is concerned with self-actualization, intentionality, and creativity. According to Abraham Maslow, we need to be in touch with those resources that lie deep within us. These include imagination and creativity, and our ability to experience great joy and to make total use of our potential. Most homeworkers strive to achieve these higher-order needs. Is this true for you?

THE BOTTOM LINE

There! Wasn't that personality inventory quick and painless? When you totaled your points, how did you score? Record in your journal the areas where you scored two or less. Also put the areas where you scored a three on probation. These may or may not hinder you. Just keep these weak areas in mind as we continue designing your personalized work-at-home system.

● **Personality Inventory Recap**
Self-Motivated _____
Self-Disciplined _____
Enjoy Solitude _____
Thrive on Control _____
Strive for Perfection _____

Committed	_____
Self-Confident	_____
Risk Taker	_____
Knowledge Seeker	_____
Support Elicitor	_____
Good Communicator	_____
Creative	_____
Total Score	_____

Concerning the overall picture, if you scored forty-eight or above, you are definitely well suited for working at home. If you scored anywhere from thirty to forty-seven, you are likely to succeed but may have some struggles. If you scored less than thirty, consider what I have to say next, and then make your decision.

The personal qualities I described throughout this chapter make working from home easier and less stressful, but are they prerequisites for success? My belief is that a rewarding and successful work-at-home arrangement is not necessarily dependent on being personally suited for it.

While there are particular qualities that enhance a person's ability to excel in a home office lifestyle, two necessary ingredients seem to prevail: desire and self-discipline. Desire is defined as: a longing or craving—passion. Self-discipline is defined as: training of oneself and one's conduct, usually for personal improvement.

If you feel uncertain about some of the qualities discussed in relation to your ability to work at home, do an honesty check. Do you have a burning desire to work at home (based on your input in the last chapter)? Do you possess the self-discipline? Are you willing to do whatever it takes to make the arrangement work?

It may reassure you to know that the homeworkers I interviewed were very enthusiastic about the tremendous personal growth they had experienced since starting a home business. Remember Ron and his self-motivation muscles? Many were very skeptical and lacked confidence in the beginning. However, a home business put them to the challenge in multiple areas, and each time they rose to the occasion, they felt that much better about themselves, and more complete as individuals.

The bottom line? If you have the desire and self-discipline, a work-at-home future looks bright for you too.

CHAPTER THREE

Choosing a Fitting
Line of Work

Homeworker Hint

If you want to be successful working at home, you've got to do
something you really know. I looked at the things I needed to satisfy me
as an individual.

Wendy, Newspaper Editor

Now that you've determined you are personally suited for working at home, you may be wondering what line of work to pursue.
On the other hand, you may know exactly what you want to do
but are unsure of how to get started. In this chapter we'll discuss
the process of choosing a fitting line of work, and pose some
preliminary questions for developing your plan of action.

ESTABLISHING YOUR
MOTIVATION FOR WORKING

Everyone works for a reason, and it's important to clearly define
your reasons. Is making money your top priority? Does work

provide a source of identity? Self-esteem? Self-confidence? Is being recognized in your work important? Perhaps you want to work to keep busy. Is your goal to have adult interaction? Are you interested in new learning opportunities? Are you looking for a challenge? Intellectual stimulation? Do you want to work so you can contribute to society at large?

In your journal, establish your list of reasons for working. Jot down what automatically comes to mind as your true burning desire. Put your number one goal at the top of the list, then number two, number three, and so on. You may have one goal or ten.

As much as possible, elaborate on each goal so your reasons are clear and precise. If your number one reason for wanting to work is to make money, write down how much you want to make and what you plan to do with it. Perhaps you're the sole breadwinner in your family and you need money to pay the bills. Or you may want money to supplement your spouse's income so you can take more vacations, put more money away for retirement, or have more "fun money."

Once you've elaborated on each goal, go back over your list and put a star (*) next to those goals that are an absolute must for you to accomplish in your work. These are your "necessities." Any goals that you don't set off with a star will be considered "nice to have" but not necessary. If you prioritized your list according to your true desires, your necessities would all be at the top. This list is an important tool, so keep it handy. We'll be coming back to review it later in this chapter after we complete some "searching within" exercises.

TARGETING YOUR COMFORT ZONE

What are you willing to do in your work? How far will you stretch your comfort zone to do what may not come naturally? In the last chapter I introduced the loner and networker personalities that surfaced in my interviews.

Not so ironically, most of the loners do not like the act of marketing a service or product, and don't consider themselves good at this skill. "I'm okay one on one, but I'm not good at going out and selling, so I knew I'd be working at home doing something where I didn't have to be involved with a lot of people," explains Beth, an accountant. Beth created an ideal business arrangement that suits her personality. She partnered with a man who handles most of the client meetings and marketing aspects of the business, while Beth handles all the technical aspects. Each partner manages an area the other is weak in.

In contrast, the networkers like selling and consider themselves good at it. "I have a degree in marketing, so I really know how to sell," asserts Bob, a financial adviser. "I use a lot of different methods to get the word out."

Not everyone is strictly a loner or a networker, but many homeworkers have strong tendencies in one direction or another. Loners tend to choose occupations such as writing or transcription, whereby they can have fewer clients and less interaction with people. This allows them to avoid the selling process as much as possible.

Networkers, on the other hand, tend to choose occupations involving high-volume sales with multiple clients, requiring a high level of interaction with people (mostly over the phone). They are confident in their abilities to market their products and services, and thrive on the selling process. They are more apt to participate in networking organizations, and socialize as a family with other families in their free time.

DESIGNING YOUR PERFECT CAREER

Do you like the act of selling? Does networking with others come naturally to you? If so, you might consider sales, consulting, or public speaking. On the other hand, if you enjoy large amounts of alone time, perhaps bookkeeping, writing, or desktop publishing may be your forte.

If, however, you happen to fall somewhere in the middle, and enjoy equal amounts of networking and solitude, you can create a career that suits both of your needs. I worked at home as a writer for some time and found I needed to balance my writing with another activity that provided more interaction with people. Also, I thrive on variety and tend to get bored doing one thing.

Portfolio Career

The solution I came up with is one that many people are adopting—a portfolio career. Much like a financial portfolio, a portfolio career consists of two or more income-earning pursuits. In my career portfolio, I can earn a living from writing, consulting, public speaking, and conducting workshops.

The beauty of this arrangement is the ability to diversify. When you put all your energies into one career pursuit, you're in trouble when that pursuit hits a financial low point or disappears altogether. With multiple income sources, you're better able to combat the high and low cycles characteristic of working on your own.

This is emphasized when your multiple careers complement each other. If I conduct a workshop or give a talk, I can also sell books or pick up new clients. My marketing efforts produce synergy when I'm able to sell more than one product or service at a time. This is an exciting phenomenon, especially when you see the results in your bank account.

Hot Work-at-Home Careers for the 1990s and Beyond

Financial Services
Personal Investment Planner
Expense-Reduction
  Consultant

Personal Services
Gift Buying/Gift Baskets
Party Coordinator
Personal Coach/Instructor

Specialized Services
Web Site Developer

Computer Consultant
Client-Prospecting Marketer
Desktop Publisher
Copywriter
Interior Designer
Paralegal
Detailed Vacation Arranger

Caregiving Services
Child Care
Elder Care
Speech Pathologist

Challenging Your Opposite Personality

What if you are a loner by nature but have the desire to expand your comfort zone to pursue a career that challenges your networking capabilities? Maybe you're tired of programming computers and want to sell them. On the other hand, what if you are a networker by nature and desire to pursue a solitary career as a fiction writer?

By default, we tend to operate in our comfort zones, pursuing avenues that come naturally to us. However, each of us has a "displaced" opposite personality just waiting to bust through. Can you think of people who left comfortable occupations to pursue work that challenged their opposite hidden selves? I know a successful insurance salesman who left his job to become a writer. I know a woman who left her ten-year nursing career to become an accountant. There's nothing like the feeling you get when you break through fear barriers and allow your hidden desires and talents to surface and shine through.

Career Inventories and Vocational Tests

If you're interested in exploring suitable careers based on your personality type, I recommend *Do What You Are* (Little, Brown and Co.), by Paul Tieger and Barbara Barron-Tieger. This personality assessment can also be found on the Internet. It's fun, informative, and the best I've encountered in terms of helping you match your personality with your career interests.

There are numerous career inventories and instruments available through career counselors and centers to help you choose a desirable career based on your interests, abilities, and values. They are one source of self-assessment worth tapping into. However, it is not wise to rely on these instruments entirely because the results can be misleading.

When I graduated from high school I was confused about what career direction to take. I knew I loved doing anything creative—writing, music, drama—but I didn't believe I could make a decent living at it. When I enrolled in college I was given a personality inventory to see what my "right" occupational fit was. My answers closely matched those of "Computer Analysts" and "Physical Therapists"—not the most creative lines of work. I ended up pursuing a career in computers because I believed the test instead of my internal desires. Although I was financially successful and went far in my career, I wasn't happy.

Much like statistics, tests can be deceptive because the results are generalized. You are an individual who may or may not fall into the norm. Pay close attention to career aspirations that come through you, in addition to assessment information that comes to you from outside sources.

"Yeah Buts" and "What Ifs?"

This is a good time to mention two phrases you must dismiss from your vocabulary. "Yeah buts" and "what ifs" can spoil your dreams, and they're energy drainers. If I dream of working as a fabulous gourmet cook and the best things I've ever made for dinner are reservations, I can hang on to 101 excuses for not moving toward my dream. "*Yeah, but* I've never really cooked before." "I know I can take classes or practice on my own, but *what if* I spend lots of time and money and wind up hating it?" Negative self-talk is nothing more than fear of change in disguise. We all fear change, and that fear is normal and healthy. It motivates us and propels us forward. The good news is that about 98 percent of what we worry about never transpires.

📎 Homeworker Hint

The first thing I would do before starting a home business is to write out a list of what I am and what I'm not—"I can't get up in the morning. I love to sleep." Don't go into situations where you have to be up at the crack of dawn. You're going to check out after four months of doing that. Be true to yourself. Then look to answer one question: "If I knew that no matter what happens in my life, I could not fail at this particular business, what would it be?" Then go from your gut, versus trying to rationalize.

Sara, Fitness Trainer and Educator

Mining for Ore—the Search Within

If you're struggling with what line of work to choose for your work-at-home career, I have the perfect exercise for you. While attending graduate school, I had to turn in a twenty-five-page paper filled with potential ideas for research that might eventually develop into my dissertation. The only requirement was that I had to allow my thoughts and ideas to flow freely on paper with no regard for how I was presenting the material.

This exercise was extremely fruitful, as it not only turned up my eventual dissertation topic, but it also provided ideas for the topics of several papers I submitted throughout the remainder of my educational journey. Even more important, I learned that creative expression is a fun, easy, and nonthreatening way to explore your interests. This "mining for ore" exercise offers a way to explore your interests in the career arena as well.

Much like the research ideas I carried around in my head that were part of my motivation for enrolling in graduate school, you carry ideas in your head that motivate you to find a fitting work-at-home career. Now is the time to explore those ideas on paper. Pick up your journal and write down anything that interests or excites you. This could be anything from your passion for teaching your child something new to a specific occupation you may wish to pursue. The object is to allow your mind to relax. Dismiss your internal judge. Don't think, "I can't do this because of this, this, and this." Pretend you can do anything and allow yourself the luxury of free creative expression. Here are some questions to help you get started.

- What do you enjoy doing with your personal time?
- What are your talents?
- What are your hobbies?
- What do you love to talk about?
- What do people say you are good at?
- What do you enjoy doing around the house?
- What do you like doing in your current line of work?
- What have you enjoyed doing in previous work capacities?
- As a child, what did you have the most fun doing?
- What did you dream of becoming?
- How do you visualize yourself in the future?

The Art of Clustering

The next step in this exercise is for you to brainstorm possible work-at-home careers that might be suitable based on the ideas you noted in your journal. Pat stresses the importance of keeping your talents and desired work patterns in mind. "One of the reasons I'm doing publishing is my personality type. I'm very good at starting businesses and getting them going. I like short-term projects with deadlines. That's why publishing is perfect for me."

● **Best Work-at-Home Careers for Parents**

1. Bill Auditor	13. Mail-Order Business
2. Bookkeeper	14. Medical Billing Service
3. Computer Programmer	15. Medical Transcription Service
4. Copywriter	16. Newsletter Publishing
5. Child-Care Provider	17. Proposal and Grant Writer
6. Desktop Publisher	18. Public Relations Specialist
7. Editorial Service	19. Résumé-Writing Service
8. Freelance Writer	20. Reunion Planner
9. Home Tutoring	21. Tax Preparation Service
10. Gift Basket Business	22. Technical Writer
11. Information Broker	23. Transcript-Digesting Service
12. Mailing List Service	24. Word-Processing Service

When I did my mining-for-ore assignment, I performed a task called "clustering" before I sat down to write my paper. If you are a visual person, I highly recommend clustering for this brainstorming task. Start with a big blank sheet of paper—the bigger the better. Transfer your interests from your journal to your cluster sheet, allowing lots of space in between each interest. Put circles around all your interests.

Write down ideas for any related work-at-home opportunities at the end of a line extended from each circle of interest. For example, if my interest is "working with computers," I would write that down on my big sheet and draw a circle around it. I would then draw lines to work-at-home careers such as computer programmer, computer trainer, Web site developer.

If another one of my circled interests is "investing money and watching it grow," I can branch off from there to financial planner, stockbroker, personal investment counselor, and so on. These financial careers also satisfy my desire to work with computers, so you may have careers attached to multiple interest circles. You can have a lot of fun with this exercise. It's even more productive when you get ideas for potential work-at-home careers from a friend or loved one.

For additional ideas, consult one of the many books available that present all sorts of work-at-home opportunities. The infinite possibilities listed can be mind-boggling. Instead of trying to narrow down your choice, start with a few hunches and look for occupations or businesses that satisfy what interests or excites you. You might turn up ideas you hadn't thought of.

Comparing Your Results with Your Reasons

When you've exhausted all your ideas on paper, highlight or put a star next to the work-at-home careers that stand out as your top choices. Look for careers that satisfy multiple interests. In the opening section of this chapter I asked you to prioritize your goals in your journal. Now is a good time to glance over your goals and bounce them against your top career choices. Do your top career choices satisfy your necessary goals? How about the goals that would be nice to have? You may want to put two or three stars next to the career choices that satisfy the most goals.

Take a close look at your primary career alternatives. Is there one (or more) that satisfies your necessary goals and incorporates one (or more) of your interests? Sometimes the picture is so clear you have no doubt about which way to go. Sometimes, with just a little thought, the decision comes easily. If the decision is unclear, list the pros and cons of each alternative. If you're still stumped after this process, give voice to your intuition. At some deeper level, you usually know which choice feels right for you.

If after much thought and weighing of alternatives you're still confused about which avenue to take, I recommend a little information gathering. Even if you're 100 percent positive you want to start a home-based desktop publishing service, I strongly advise you to do some research first to learn the ins and outs of what you're about to commit to.

RESEARCH, RESEARCH, AND MORE RESEARCH

Now that you've identified your top work-at-home career(s), the next step is to conduct your research. Please don't cringe at the thought of doing research. When you've targeted one or two career areas you feel passionate about, the research process takes on a whole different meaning. It becomes more like detective work. As you follow the clues to unravel the mystery surrounding your top career choices, it's highly satisfying. After all, you're that much closer to making your work-at-home dream a reality. The research process becomes a learning and growing experience in itself.

At your local library you'll find career manuals, such as the *Dictionary of Occupational Titles* (DOT), which offers brief job descriptions on over twenty thousand occupations. There are books that introduce numerous work-at-home career opportunities as well. Unfortunately, these resources only scratch the surface. The best way to find out whether a particular work-at-home career is for you is by conducting informational interviews.

Informational Interviews

📎 **Homeworker Hint**

Talk to people who are doing it. They can tell you the pros and cons. Make sure it's something you're passionate about. If it's something you hate, you may as well work for someone else.

Chris, Magazine Publisher

People who are successful in their work-at-home careers like to talk about it. After all, they've been in your position at some point in time.

Informational interviews give you the opportunity to get feedback on specific questions you have in relation to your top career choices. They can be done briefly by phone, E-mail, fax, and regular mail, as well as in person.

I have conducted hundreds of informational interviews for a variety of reasons, and they are an excellent vehicle for learning and networking, not to mention a lot of fun. When you show a genuine interest in someone's work, you get a positive response. In fact, if the experience is positive, people don't hesitate to refer you to other people you can talk to, who may also be working at home in similar lines of work. Just ask.

The best way to get started doing informational interviews is to write down in your journal all the people you know who work at home in your top career choices. If you can't think of people, ask your friends or loved ones. The average person has at least 350 people in his or her circle of influence, so you're bound to find someone who qualifies.

If your career choice is uncommon or you have difficulty gathering names of people who fall within your parameters, take out your local Yellow Pages and search by business type (or a related business if your interest is new or unusual). In my area, I can spot the businesses that are conducted at home because they often have a P.O. box, a street address that I know is residential, or they have no address listed at all. These are clues that the work is done at home.

Another way to find people working at home in different capacities is by attending a meeting put on by a professional organization geared toward working at home. Call the organization's membership services and leave a message. When you get a return call, ask for a referral to members who work at home in your career(s) of interest. The representative will most likely give you names and numbers and, if the group meets regularly, invite you to attend one of their upcoming meetings. This will give you a chance to talk to people face-to-face.

If you have access to the Internet, you can join news groups and mailing lists that are geared toward working at home. You can E-mail your questions to the group and wait for responses. You can also participate in on-line discussions. The beauty of this type of research is that you only have to ask the question once, and it's posed to a targeted audience. Plus, these groups are free to join. (See Chapter 13 for a list of on-line resources and professional organizations geared toward working at home.) Just be on the lookout for people trying to make a quick buck off of you. Some will prey on people who are in transition and try to sell you the business opportunity of a lifetime. We'll discuss the issue of avoiding scams in more detail shortly.

"Call people and ask what you need to do," advises Jenny, a secretarial service provider. "That's how I got started. I called everyone in the phone book. Call your competitors. See what they're doing." When you cold-call people from the phone book, be yourself. Generally, if you're friendly, you'll get a warm response. Always remember to smile. Have a script in front of you so you exude confidence. Also, have your questions handy in case the person has time to talk when you call. I have found this to be the case about 25 percent of the time.

You might start the phone call with something like this: "Hi, my name is _____, and I'm interested in working at home in the field of _____. I saw your ad in the Yellow Pages (or I was referred to you by _____) and wondered if I could possibly ask you a few questions about your work at a time that's convenient for you." If you make it clear that you are interested in working at home in your opening line, people will usually let you know whether they operate out of their home. If people are quick, gruff, or disinterested, don't push. Just move on to the next person. You want to talk to people who are as enthused as you are.

Once you establish a rapport with the person, set up a time for the informational interview or proceed with your questions if the time is right. Keep the interview brief (ten to fifteen minutes) unless your interviewee has enough time for a longer period. When you're done, let the person know how much you appreciate his or her valuable time and willingness to share. Confirm the person's address and immediately send out a handwritten thank-you note. This kind gesture will be remembered, and you will have established a warm contact with someone you may want to touch base with down the road. Some people will tell you to call again if you have questions, or to keep them posted on your progress. Do keep in touch. You may get a referral someday, or even a job.

● **Informational Interview Questions**

Here's a list of typical informational interview questions you can modify or add to:

How did you get started in your work-at-home career?

What kind of training do you recommend to get started?

What is the estimated cost to get started?

What do you enjoy most about your work?

What do you enjoy least about your work?

What is a realistic income for this line of work?

What is your average monthly overhead expense?

How much competition is in this field?

What marketing strategies do you recommend to a newcomer?

What professional organizations can I join or visit?

What journals or magazines do you recommend?

● What advice would you give to someone just starting out?

Volunteering

If you exhaust all your informational interview efforts and still feel unsure about which of your top work-at-home careers to pursue, you might try volunteering your time to help someone who works at home in a capacity you're interested in. This will give you an opportunity to get into the trenches and experience the real thing.

Sue, a medical transcriptionist, started her business this way. She cold-called medical transcriptionists listed in the Yellow Pages to conduct informational interviews. One woman she called had too much work on her hands, and asked Sue if she would be interested in helping her on a part-time basis to familiarize herself with the business.

What started as volunteer work became a part-time job. Sue was able to learn the medical transcription business under an experienced mentor, and was paid in the process. Eventually she went to work at home on her own, taking her knowledge base and a couple of clients with her. See what can happen when you conduct informational interviews?

Invent a Career

When all else fails in your efforts to find a suitable career, you can always invent one. Sometimes when you're stumped and have ideas but don't know which direction to take, the answer may be right in front of you.

What do you like to do that other people dislike? Turn your talents into a business that can benefit others. Have you solved any problems around the house or on the job? Chances are, others could benefit from your solutions as well. One person I interviewed developed a unique product for motor homes that is now selling nationwide. If you can make life easier for others, consider turning your product or service into a moneymaking home business. This is your opportunity to create your own niche and fill a void in the marketplace. A little creativity can go a long way.

Still Stumped?

If your self-exploration, research, and volunteer efforts have still not turned up career paths of interest, or if you have so many career paths to choose from, you don't know which way to turn, I highly recommend *I Could Do Anything If I Only Knew What It Was* (Delacorte Press), by Barbara Sher. It's a wonderful book, filled with exercises and insights to help in your decision process.

DEVELOPING YOUR PLAN OF ACTION

Now that you've targeted the line of work you're interested in pursuing, it's time to ask a few critical questions to help you develop your plan of action. Jot down your answers as you go along under appropriate headings in your journal.

Knowledge or Skills Needed

Does your chosen work-at-home career require additional knowledge or skills beyond what you presently possess? Does it require a special license or state certification? How wide is the gap between where you are currently and where you need to be to get started? Are you willing to do what it takes to fill the gap?

There are a variety of ways to acquire knowledge and sharpen your skills. You might consider taking adult education courses at a local university or junior college. Many universities have certification programs designed for adults making a career transition. Some require internship experience whereby you work in the field for a few hours a week to display your competence.

If getting experience is all you need, and you require no additional education or formal training, create your own internship much as Sue did before starting her medical transcription service. Find a mentor who will take you under his or her wing and teach you the ropes in exchange for your assistance in the business for as many hours as you can spare each week. Maybe you can even get paid in the process.

How do you find a mentor? Ask people you know. Contact professional organizations. Call people in the Yellow Pages. Start with a quick informational interview to feel things out. Ask if volunteering your time is a good way to get exposure to the business. If you get a positive response, offer to volunteer your services in exchange for an opportunity to learn the business. You'll be surprised at what you'll find just by reaching out and asking.

One of the advantages of operating a home-based business is that you can work in a variety of fields without a college degree. If finances are tight, there are many ways to get started in a work-at-home career without spending lots of time and money on formal education and training.

In my area we have free educational training courses offered through the Regional Occupational Program (ROP). In fact, Sue got her initial training in medical transcription that way. "I went to the ROP office to sign up, but the classes were all full, so I just showed up the first day of class and took the place of someone who didn't show and forgot to cancel," she explains. Check with your local school district or junior college for information on ROP in your area. If ROP doesn't exist, someone may be able to refer you to similar educational opportunities.

Finally, brainstorm your options. If you can't spare a few hours each week volunteering your time to get training or acquire education, look into partnering with someone who already has the expertise. Remember Beth, the accountant who teamed up with a partner who specializes in marketing while she handles the technical aspects of the business? Maybe you offer talents and expertise that can complement a potential partner, creating a win-win situation for both of you.

Investment of Time

How many hours do you desire to invest each week in your work-at-home career? Do you want to work part-time or full-time? When starting a business from scratch, the demands on time and energy can be tremendous. "It's more demanding on me than my newborn," says Ted, a market researcher.

Think about the amount of time you are realistically willing to invest in your work. This will be important when we discuss schedules and time management in subsequent chapters.

On Your Own vs. Having a Boss

Do you prefer to work on your own or for someone else? Do you desire having co-workers to mingle with? Ponder these questions as you consider the following work-at-home options to find the best fit for you.

TELECOMMUTERS

At one end of the spectrum are *telecommuters*. A telecommuter is an employed individual who works part-time or full-time at home. These homeworkers communicate with their places of employment via computer, fax, and phone. Telecommuting offers the ability to stay connected with a company, as well as the ability to keep a finger on the pulse at home. Although most telecommuters work during regular business hours, this arrangement still offers tremendous flexibility in terms of balancing work and family commitments. Telecommuting is a desirable option that is growing faster than all other types of home-based work.

ENTREPRENEURS

On the other end of the spectrum are *entrepreneurs* or home-based business owners. These self-employed individuals are the boss of their own company.

There are a variety of options available to the work-at-home entrepreneur. The most popular are service-oriented and commission sales businesses because the start-up investment is relatively low. Plus, service and sales businesses do not usually require employees initially, which is a definite consideration when working out of the home. They also don't generally require the purchase and storage of inventory, so your ongoing investment in the business remains low, as does your need for storage space.

The downside of a service business is that your income is limited by what you can do with your time unless you take on a partner or hire additional help. To overcome this, you can diversify and multiply your efforts on your own. Remember the portfolio career option we discussed earlier? There are infinite ways to create a satisfying work-at-home career, aimed at producing a synergistic effect from varied occupational roles (and income sources) that ideally complement each other.

What about a manufacturing business? It is possible to start your own manufacturing business out of the home; however, the financial investment is usually much higher than a service or commission sales business. Also, unless you have a lot of space and are willing to hire employees, such a business does not lend itself well to the constraints of a home environment.

Two other options are franchises and multilevel marketing businesses, which can be comfortably operated out of the home. While you give up a certain amount of control because you did not create the service or manufacture the product, if the service or product you're selling is proven or established, your chances of success are higher. One downfall of these types of businesses is that your initial capital investment can be sizable. Be sure to look before you leap!

● **Top Ten Home-Based Businesses**

1. Business consulting and services
2. Computer services and programming
3. Financial consulting and services

4. Marketing and advertising
5. Medical practice and services
6. Graphics and visual arts
7. Public relations and publicity
8. Real estate
9. Writing
10. Independent sales

INTRAPRENEURS

Somewhere in the middle of the spectrum are work-at-home *intrapreneurs*. Intrapreneurs may have the best of both worlds because they remain company employees while contracting their services to their employer. Using company resources and support, they often develop services or products that their company is unwilling to commit to with large-scale expenditures.

In this situation, the company benefits by retaining its employee as an independent contractor and not having to pay regular employee benefits. The individual benefits by having the freedom to work at home as his or her own boss, while remaining connected to the company. Intrapreneurship may require some capital, but generally involves less risk than entrepreneurship. If you're currently employed, look around your workplace for potential intrapreneurial opportunities.

Avoiding Scams

 Homeworker Hint

There are a lot of scams out there. They draw you in with all those business opportunities, sell you the package, and it's a joke. Be careful. That's the biggest thing—avoid the scams.

Jean, Computer Research Analyst

Be sure you thoroughly research the line of work you choose, and the capacity you choose to conduct it in. If you plan to buy a business opportunity such as a franchise or multilevel marketing business, check it out. Call your local Better Business Bureau (BBB) or the BBB located in the state where the company selling the opportunity resides. Also, call the National Fraud Information Center Consumer Assistance Hotline at (800) 876-7060.

Always look for a thirty-day money-back guarantee with the opportunity you purchase. Any company offering a desirable commodity will offer a guarantee. Finally, if the opportunity sounds too good to be true, it probably is, and in this event it may be best to steer clear.

If you wish to purchase an already-established business, examine the financial records. Be on the lookout for possible tax liens, impending competition, or laws that could adversely affect the business. Do as much research as you can on your own. Before you make the purchase, hire an attorney or accountant to conduct a thorough study of the business. Gaining awareness will definitely lower the risk factor because you'll know exactly what you're getting into.

Designing Your Perfect Business Image

Some homeworkers choose to tell their clients they work at home, while others do not. Most are comfortable with making their clients aware, and receive a positive response. "I'm very proud to say that my business is *homegrown*," says Sara, a fitness trainer. Some are hesitant in the beginning, concerned that clients might not take their business seriously if they find that it's run out of the home. "At first I acted as if I had a real office," says Lisa, a medical transcriptionist. "I tried to make it sound very professional. Gradually, as time went on, I dropped the facade, and now everyone knows this is a 'rinky-dink' thing—just me and this computer."

Other homeworkers do not let their clients know they work at home. They describe how the "illusion" they create—of being a full-fledged, professionally run company—is so strong, the issue of whether they're home-based never comes up. Amy and Don, computer software distributors, could teach a class on how to create the illusion:

> We tell clients that this is the marketing office, and our production facility is downtown. We make a joke, "Why should we spend forty-five minutes in traffic when we can

spend more time working?" I can't think of one company that knows we're a home-based business. It's part of the structure we set up. We spent a lot of money on graphics for advertising, and 800 numbers, and fax numbers. We've got multiple lines going into our office. When we moved here, we knew what we were doing. We designed the entire office so two people could work in it, with a possible third. We both have titles that make it look like people are above us or below us. We'll even put someone's initials on the bottom of something typewritten to make it look like someone else did it. We pay to use an executive suite address rather than a post office box because our image matters. We don't have a baby crying beside our phone, but when that has happened, we make excuses like, "Oh, someone just brought our son into the office." You become quick with things like that. You have to when you service big clients.

The big-company illusion is not for everyone. "I used to hide in the pantry and talk on the phone in the kitchen just so clients couldn't hear my kids playing in the background," reveals Pat, a newspaper publisher and mother of four. "I gave up pretending long ago. It wasn't worth the stress."

How do you desire to present yourself and your business? Do you prefer a strict professional image or are you more comfortable with a loosely run approach? Do you want or need to be high-tech, furnishing your office with state-of-the art equipment (e.g., computer, fax, copier, modem, pager, mobile phone), or do you prefer something more basic? Will you dress up for work every day, or go casual?

These questions are important in terms of visualizing how you wish to present yourself and your business. Consider your personal inclinations as well as the type of business you're running. I found that loners who have less interaction with clients lean more toward the casual freelance approach. On the other hand, networkers who have frequent interaction with clients are more concerned with maintaining a strict professional image. When we discuss issues such as the presence of children, boundaries, and setting up your office, it is critical that you are clear about the kind of image you're comfortable with and confident in. This will allow you to select strategies that protect and preserve your image accordingly.

The next eight chapters present strategies you'll need to deal with the challenges of working at home. Your goal is to channel the work you've done in the first three chapters into a work-at-home system tailored to your needs. Keep your journal close so you can jot down ideas that interest you along the way. With this valuable insight in hand, there is no doubt that you, too, will master the "work-at-home balancing act."

PART II

COPING STRATEGIES— KEYS TO CREATING BALANCE

(HONESTY, COMMUNICATION, NEGOTIATION)

CHAPTER FOUR

Managing Children

Homeworker Hint

If you have small kids, you need to have someone come in so you can devote a certain number of hours to your work. All you do is drive yourself crazy without child care. It's not good for your family, it's not good for your business, and it's horrible for your stress level.

Laura, Freelance Writer

The ability to care for their children is the primary motivator for most women and some men to work at home. Is that what motivates you? When you work at home and have children, it's critical that you create an arrangement that works positively for you and your kids. Because you are combining work and family roles, your work will have a direct impact on your children, and your children will have a direct impact on your work.

CHILD CARE—TO HAVE OR NOT TO HAVE?

Let's determine whether your particular situation lends itself to working without paid child care. Then we can look at creative strategies that enable you to work when your children are present in the home. We'll wrap up the chapter with an exploration of the variety of child-care options available (paid and unpaid), depending on your needs and budget.

Can You Work Without Paid Child Care?

 Homeworker Hint

We haven't had any need for child care. We designed everything to fit our daughter first, even before the business. Day care has never been something we've done in the seven years she has been with us. That's the number one reason I work at home.

Sara, Fitness Trainer

A minority of homeworkers do not rely on any form of paid child care. How do they do it? Most express that their decision to do so was value-based rather than an effort to keep expenses down. "My daughter didn't like child care, and that was what motivated us to start a business in the home," says Lynn, a bookkeeper and mother of two. "She cried whenever we'd leave, and it just wasn't good."

OPTING FOR NO CHILD CARE—A QUESTION OF MONEY OR VALUES?

This raises an important question. If you wish to not rely on paid child care while you work, does your desire tend to be more value-driven or financially driven? Deep-seated values are likely to sustain you through difficulties far better than efforts to save on child-care costs. In their efforts to save money, the parents avoiding child care sabotage their ability to make money. "I tried to watch my son and work at the same time to save on child-care costs," remembers Kevin, a real estate agent and single father of three-year-old Bobby. "Every day was a constant struggle with no money coming in until I finally broke down and got someone to come in and watch him on a part-time basis. Since then, my production has really taken off."

In contrast, the homeworkers who don't use any form of paid child care because it's entirely against their values (and primary reasons for working at home to begin with) are succeeding because of their strong beliefs. Among those who are value-driven, there's a willingness to do whatever it takes to create a workable situation. When faced with challenges, frustration is not a state they entertain for long. They are determined to make it work, even if it means choosing a career that allows them to achieve their goal of not using child care. "One of the reasons I've always been attracted to freelance is because I never wanted to use child care," says Mike, a screenplay writer and father of two. "We totally focus on the kids. We've always arranged our schedules around their needs."

If your choice to not use child care is primarily based on your values, you have much in your favor, and all the other following variables that you have working for you will only enhance your situation. On the other hand, if your motivation is financially driven, it is imperative that you have the majority of the following factors working for you to increase your chances of success and satisfaction.

CONSIDER THE AGES AND DISPOSITIONS OF YOUR CHILDREN

Homeworker Hint

When you work at home, it's easier if your children are little because they just lie there. They're very contained. It's when they start crawling that it gets a little dicey. And when they begin to walk, you might as well forget trying to work. They get into *everything*. When the second one came along, and started to crawl and walk, my hours went down to nothing. My income dropped to $2,000 that year.

Jill, Desktop Publisher

Whether you can work when your children are present is highly dependent on their ages. "I can work while the kids are doing something and they don't need my constant supervision," says Lynn, a bookkeeper. "With them being older and more calm, it's a lot easier."

Ann, a personal image consultant, found that working with your kids present also depends on their personalities. "I like to describe my daughter as a little volcano because we never know when she's going to erupt," she says. "I try to schedule my business when she's in school or busy. I've had to work it around her much more than my son. He's very easy."

What are the ages and dispositions of your children? Are they good at entertaining themselves while you're busy doing something else? Are they fairly cooperative? "My kids are independent," says Wendy, a newspaper editor and mother of two young boys. "If you have clingy' kids, you're definitely going to have a problem." It's critical that your children are somewhat autonomous in order for you to effectively focus on your work.

Are your kids in school? "If you have school-age kids or older, you're probably in a prime situation," says Bob, a financial adviser and father of four. "It's too hard with young kids. Whatever you're trying to accomplish, it will take twice as long if you have young children around."

CAN YOU BE PRODUCTIVE WITH CONSTANT INTERRUPTIONS?

Working at home with children present and unsupervised takes a lot of patience and discipline. Parents who work without child care put their children first. They integrate their children's schedules and needs into their workday on an as-needed basis. Can you easily drop what you're doing at frequent intervals throughout your workday and quickly get back on track? Before you make the decision to forgo child care, be sure of your desire and ability to work in a back-and-forth fashion.

CONSIDER THE NATURE OF YOUR WORK

Another important consideration in determining your need for child care is the nature of your work. Is your work detail-oriented? Does it require a high level of concentration? Will you be doing a lot of phone work? Will you meet frequently with clients face-to-face?

If you answered yes to any of the preceding questions, your work does not lend itself well to the presence of children in need of supervision. Strongly consider whether you'll be able to accomplish your work goals and, at the same time, be available to your children when they need you. If your work requires total focus, your children will most likely be safer and more content with another caregiver.

CONSIDER YOUR WORK HOURS AND SCHEDULE

How many hours will you be working per week? What are the ideal times of the day or night for you to work? If you'll be working at home on a part-time basis, and the majority of your work can be done during the evenings or early mornings when your children are occupied or sleeping, you have a workable situation—as long as you find enough time to sleep. On the other hand, if you'll be pulling down long days during business hours when your children are present and longing for your attention, you'll definitely need some kind of child-care support.

WHAT ABOUT YOUR BUSINESS IMAGE?

We talked in the last chapter about establishing a business image. Obviously it would be difficult to maintain a strict professional image for your clients if your children can bounce in and out of your work area unannounced while you're talking on the phone. If you're comfortable with a more loosely run approach (and your clients don't mind), your situation will be more conducive to working without child care.

The word *comfortable* is important when we talk about business image. Some homeworkers are fine with letting clients know they work at home. They even warn their clients that they may hear children in the background at times because they work at home to be near their children.

Whether you maintain a strict professional image or a more relaxed approach is not important. What matters is that the approach you choose comes naturally and feels right, and that you establish yourself accordingly with family, friends, clients, and associates. The goal is to work in a capacity that minimizes your level of stress and maximizes your ability to work productively.

IDENTIFY YOUR BUILT-IN SUPPORT SYSTEMS

Homeworker Hint

I tell a joke that I could quit my job and spend forty hours a week working on these kids. I would like my wife to be home more to help. I'm not as productive as I could be because I get caught up in child-care issues, which detracts from the time I could be on the phone following up on new leads.

Bob, Financial Adviser

Unfortunately, the truth is that Bob's situation is unusual among most dual-income couples working outside the home. Research suggests that child care is still the responsibility of women in terms of planning and implementing decisions regarding a child's care, and in the overall commitment of time. Although fathers desire to spend more time with their children, their involvement in child care increases with the prestige and importance of their wife's career and her earned income.

Whether the man views parenting as costly to his career achievement, and whether the woman perceives his involvement in child care as important, also affect the roles fathers play in their children's lives. The "assistance" husbands offer is helpful, but without taking responsibility for children—freeing women from solely having to anticipate needs, remember schedules, and so forth—men's contribution may do little to relieve the strain women feel.

What about a home-office arrangement? I found that parents who work at home, regardless of their gender, take equal responsibility for the care of their children. A home office appears to represent a step forward in evening out work and family roles and responsibilities. This is especially true when husbands work at home and their wives work elsewhere. We will be touching on this exciting phenomenon in more depth in the next chapter.

Do you have a partner who is willing to share child-care responsibilities equally? Do you have extended family members, older children, or friends who are available and willing to help with child care on a regular basis?

If your situation doesn't meet all of the preceding criteria, you still may be able to pull off working without paid child care if you have a strong support system and use some of the creative strategies that follow.

CREATIVE STRATEGIES FOR WORKING WITHOUT PAID CHILD CARE

If you've decided that your situation lends itself to working without paid child care at least some of the time, here's a general idea of how much work you can expect to accomplish with the presence of unsupervised children at home: if your baby is four months or younger—one and a half hours a day; from five to eighteen months—about two and a half hours a day; from nineteen months to three years—about three hours a day; from four to five years—about three and a half hours a day (maybe more); and above five years when children are in school—five to eight hours a day. These general guidelines are also dependent on your child's temperament and sleep schedule, as well as your work style and habits.

It's obvious that the bulk of most parents' child-care needs take place before their kids start school (unless they decide to home-school them, which many homeworking parents do). Regardless of the ages of your children, however, through the use of creative strategies you can beef up the number of hours you can effectively work without paid child care. You can never have too many tricks up your sleeve, and the more clever they are, the better.

Before All Else Fails—Communicate

Homeworker Hint

Keep in constant communication with your family. Let them know you love them, that you're trying hard to achieve something, and you'll be there as soon as you can. Talk about it before you get into it . . . the difficulties and the benefits.

Sue, Medical Transcriptionist

If your children are at an age at which you can talk and reason with them to any degree, the earlier you begin to foster empathy and respect toward your home office arrangement, the better. In order to get cooperation from your children, however, it is crucial that the lines of communication stay open and that they be two-way.

Establish Rules of Behavior

Teach your children to respect your home office. Establish rules of behavior as early as possible. You want your children to be children, but it's important that you clearly convey what is expected of them in terms of chores, responsibilities, and behavior. This becomes increasingly important when you work at home without child care. As you teach your children to respect your work obligations, you are transferring the skills and values you wish to pass on to them. Keep your kids informed and explain why you need rules so that they'll be much more likely to work with you, rather than against you, in your efforts to succeed. We will discuss effective communication and establishing rules with children in more depth in Chapter 7.

Arrange Play Dates

If your children get along well with other kids in the neighborhood, regular play dates are an excellent strategy that will allow you extra work time. Liz, a computer programmer and single mother of two, puts concentrated effort into her work until seven o'clock each night because she has a daily play date set up for her kids:

> We know everybody in the neighborhood . . . It's so safe. Most of the time, all the kids are here. There are probably fourteen or fifteen kids here from 4:00 until 7:00 P.M. every day, in the front and back yards. I'll stop and give everyone a snack and something to drink—this is the place to come. One fight or one dirty word, though, and they're out. It's much easier with a house full than just two because they keep each other occupied.

Pat, a newspaper publisher, has a similar situation to Liz's, but she is paid to take care of four children on a regular basis—chosen playmates who are roughly the same age as her four children. Not only do the children play together and keep each other occupied, but the older kids watch the younger ones so Pat can get her work done. Her office is set up in a converted two-car garage that has two doors, both exiting into the backyard where the kids play. If they need her, or if an argument starts or someone gets hurt, she's right there. The kids play together, occupying themselves for hours.

Offer an Incentive

If you run errands and plan to take your children along, make it fun for them. Give them something to look forward to. Ann, a personal image consultant, rewards her five-year-old son for being good at the end of her weekly product-delivery rounds. "We play this game when we're running around doing deliveries," she says. "If he's good, we spend 10 percent of whatever I sell that day on him on the way home, or he can save it—he usually spends it."

The incentive or reward doesn't have to be expensive. The idea is to make it fun for your kids so they feel special. When Ann takes her son on an appointment, she makes sure her client has a VCR handy. On the way to the appointment she and her son stop at the video store and he picks a video. This form of "cheap child care," as Ann refers to it, allows her to spend time with her son and work at the same time.

Obviously, many lines of work do not lend themselves to bringing a child along to watch videos on client appointments— especially new clients you're trying to impress. If your clients are regulars, however, and are family-friendly, they may be very supportive. You never know unless you ask.

Reward Their Independence

Another option is to reward your children for taking care of themselves while you work. This can be something simple like a favorite treat or an extra story at bedtime. If they're of the age when money captures their interest, pay them a nominal amount. They will learn how to take care of themselves and respect your work time.

Tire Them Out First

Carol, an architectural illustrator, uses a strategy with her two-year-old son that is more physical and a bit more time-consuming, but effective in allowing her to focus on her work. "I devote attention to my son in the mornings, and I find that it gets him good and tired so he'll take a better nap,'' she explains. ''Then I can work rather than try to work and keep him occupied. I tried that for a while and it didn't make him happy, and I couldn't get anything done.''

Keep Them Occupied

The easiest time to get work done is when your children are constructively occupied. This can be a difficult challenge with babies and toddlers. Phil, an attorney and father of a one-year-old, installed a window between his home office and an adjoining room so that he can keep an eye on his daughter while she naps or plays in her playpen.

"This window has been a lifesaver," Phil claims. "When Tammy couldn't see me, she would cry and fuss a lot, and I was up and down all the time. If I just look up every so often and smile and wave, she feels secure knowing and seeing I'm right here. Every work-at-home parent with little ones should give this a try." Greg, a cartoonist, found a similar solution to Phil's. He placed a large sandbox in the backyard next to the window of his home office. He's able to put in a good two hours of uninterrupted work while his four-year-old son keeps himself occupied.

Meanwhile, Lisa, a medical transcriptionist, finds that home-schooling her five-year-old daughter provides the opportunity to work while her daughter completes her ''homework'' assignments. Can you afford a second computer in your home? If so, keep it loaded with educational software or shareware, and your children will stay busy for hours. This is highly effective for children ages three and up. Constantly be on the lookout for ways to positively keep your kids occupied, and you'll be able to put regular blocks of time into your work.

Involve Your Kids in Your Work

Homeworker Hint

For children who display a natural curiosity about your work, the way to start teaching them how to do certain tasks is to first show them how to do the task. Immediately afterward, you let them do it while you do

it with them, and then you let them do it while you watch. The final
step is to let them do it by themselves, and you check it later.

Jenny, Secretarial Service Provider

Since a distinct advantage of working at home is the benefit of
having your children witness what it means to work, why not
involve them? Unlike parents working outside the home, homeworking parents actively assume a principal role in their children's socialization for the world of work. Furthermore, they
offer what appears to be a gender-neutral mentoring process.
Research suggests that children of work-at-home parents display
knowledge of, and participate in, their parents' work (regardless
of the type of work, or gender of the parent).

Can you arrange a spot within your work space where your
children can have a desk with their own supplies and file folders
so they can "work" alongside of you? Do you typically have
mundane work in your business like folding mailing materials or
stuffing envelopes that your kids can help you with? Kids typically display an active curiosity and desire to become involved
in their parents' work, starting with imitation and later possibly
working for pay, as Beth, an accountant, has found:

*My daughter imitates me at work. She has all of her own
little office supplies, and her own little desk and briefcase,
the same as mine. I color-code them so she knows which
ones are hers. She helps me with organizing, and as she
gets older she'll be doing more. She's getting a good intro-
duction to business.*

Liz, a computer programmer, is proud of the fact that she pays
her children to work for her, and they love it. "Instead of TV,
they would rather come in here and help me," she says. "But I
never let it interfere with their school or playtime."

Children's involvement in their parents' work activities tends
to occur on four different levels, in developmentally appropriate
ways: play, watch, help; simple tasks; assistance with work on a
regular basis, paid or unpaid; regular paid work.

A previous study conducted by Betty Beach (1989) on work-
at-home parents revealed that the concrete knowledge of parental

work demonstrated by children in the early stages formed a base from which they moved into participation in their parents' work. This lengthy and natural process was unanticipated by parents who were not coercing their children but simply responding to their interests. Parents extended their availability to children beyond the parental role to incorporate children into their worker role as well.

Try the Barter System

Do you know other people with children in your neighborhood who work at home? If so, try what Ben, a marketing consultant and father of two, does on a regular basis. "We have a real supportive community," he explains. "At least five houses in our neighborhood have people working at home. We trade back and forth and watch each other's kids. That allows us more concentrated work time."

Chris, a magazine publisher and mother of two-year-old Jessica, exchanges child care with a work-at-home dad in her neighborhood. "I have many friends with kids the same age as mine, so we exchange child-care services all the time," she says. And if you don't have neighbors or friends with kids the same age as yours who live close? You might try bartering your work services in exchange for child care.

If you have a line of work or special talent that someone is in need of in your neighborhood, you might be able to do an exchange. If you're a bookkeeper, lend your services to someone close who is willing to watch your child regularly. Perhaps you can cook or run errands while you're out for someone who is retired and wouldn't mind watching your child while you work.

Baby-sitting Co-ops

Baby-sitting co-ops consist of a group of families who exchange child-care services. Basically, you receive as many child-care hours as you provide in trade. It's best if the group is large enough to meet everyone's sitting needs. A membership of at least fifteen families is optimum, but fewer can work if the group tends to have opposite work schedules.

If you join a co-op that consists of parents who work from nine to five, you will have little chance of covering your child-care needs during the day. On the other hand, if you regularly need evening or weekend child care, such a co-op would be desirable. In fact, you would be in high demand with parents working outside the home during the day, who are in a position to care for your children during their off hours at night while you work. Ask around for a co-op in your neighborhood, or advertise on local bulletin boards.

Choose Kid-Friendly Work

Some homeworkers find it easy to integrate child care and work activities. If you perform work that is more physically than intellectually demanding (e.g., day-care provider, knitter), you may be able to work with your children present and unsupervised. This is the vehicle of choice for many parents desiring to forgo paid child care.

Because more physically demanding work does not usually require such a high level of concentration, it is possible to care for children in a back-and-forth orientation—interrupting work to tend to children on an as-needed basis. If your work can be performed at any hour of the day or night, and doesn't require much phone activity, it's even more conducive to such an arrangement.

Work in Short Spurts of Time

"I get the most work done during my daughter's nap time," says John, a graphic designer. "I always have a 'to do' list made up ahead of time so I can go like a jet when she's down." John finds himself consistently working odd or late hours because he takes time to entertain his daughter in the mornings.

If you desire to work without child care, you must be flexible with your time. Whenever possible, parents work while their children are occupied, asleep, or in school. Especially with young children, it's less stressful if you learn how to work your schedule around them. Otherwise, it's difficult (if not impossible) to concentrate on work when you know your child needs you. We'll be talking about choosing an ideal schedule in Chapter 7.

Elicit Support from Family Members

Do you have supportive family members who will regularly pitch in and help with child care while you work? While many homeworkers rely on their spouses for support, a few rely on older children at home, and a small minority rely on extended family members. Having child-care support from extended family is becoming less and less common because family members frequently move about and often go their separate ways. Also, couples who delay childbearing may have parents who are no longer physically able to care for their small grandchildren. Furthermore, people tend to lead full lives with plans that don't necessarily include caring for children.

If you're lucky enough to foster a system of support among extended family members, by all means do it. Your children will be loved and cared for by someone who is more likely to share your values than an outside child-care provider. If there are strings attached, feelings of guilt, or huge differences, however, it may not be worth it unless you can resolve these issues.

Whether to pay family members for child care is an optional matter. If you feel you're imposing and can't afford to pay, offer your services or talents instead (e.g., a home-cooked meal, home repairs), similar to the barter system.

PAID CHILD-CARE OPTIONS

 Homeworker Hint

Anyone who tells you they can work and do child care at the same time is not really working.

Val, Travel Agent

Most homeworkers make attempts to work without paid child care, and quickly learn, as did Amy a computer software distributor, that their attempts are frustrating and futile:

Since the baby, for the first six months I tried to do child care and work. It was very hard. I was doing an hour of work whenever he slept. I would breast-feed while I was on the phone. I would do anything so I could work. Once he got more mobile, I couldn't do it anymore.

Think of paid child care as an investment in the future success of your business, as well as an opportunity to separate your work and family lives so that the time spent with your family can be focused, and vice versa. If you're a telecommuter, a formal child-care arrangement will most likely be required, depending on the agreement you have with your company. In this section we will explore in-home and out-of-home paid child-care options.

● **Choosing Quality Child Care**

Quality child care can be determined by certain characteristics:

A Caregiver who provides warm, loving care and guidance for your child and works with you to make sure your child develops and learns in the best way possible.

A Setting, whether a home or center, that keeps your child safe, secure, enriched, and healthy.

A License by the appropriate agency.

Activities that help your child develop mentally, physically, socially, and emotionally.

●

Examining Your Needs and the Needs of Your Child

Most homeworkers use paid child care on a part-time basis and supplement that with creative diversion tactics (previously mentioned) and working odd hours while children are occupied. In terms of the type of care used, about 50 percent of homeworkers use in-home care, and the other half rely on care outside the home. Homeworkers who use full-time care tend to have in-home caregivers.

The YMCA Child Care Resource Service suggests that you examine your needs as well as the needs of your child to determine what kind of child care is best for your situation. Ask yourself the following questions:

- Do you need care during regular working hours, or for nights or weekends?
- Do you need care close to home?
- Do you need irregular drop-in care or care on a consistent schedule?
- Do you need subsidized care?
- Will you need any transportation for your children?
- Will you need meals or just snacks provided?
- Do you have children of different ages whom you would like to place together?
- Does your child feel comfortable in large groups of children or with just a few other children around?
- Does your child need a lot of one-on-one attention?
- Is your child comfortable with other adults?
- Does your child become bored easily, and need a lot of stimulation?
- Does your child prefer spending time with children the same age or with children of different ages?
- Does your child have any special needs?

In-Home Child Care

Homeworker Hint

I hired a woman who comes to the home and takes care of my daughter. What I love about this arrangement is that I can have lunch with my daughter. I can take a ten-minute break and go down to the park and see them. If she wakes up from her nap, I can go in and say hello. She knows Mommy is working, but if she's having an "I need Mommy" day, she can come up and see me.

Candace, Small Business Consultant

With an in-home care arrangement, a caregiver comes to the parents' home. The cost of full-time in-home care can range anywhere from $125 to $450 per week depending on which part of the country you live in and the level of the caregiver's training. Generally, in-home care consists of one of the following:

Baby-sitters provide in-home supervisory care for children, with no special training expected.

Nannies are employed by a family to live in or out of the home and provide child care on a full- or part-time basis. Nannies may or may not have formal training.

Au Pairs usually live in a family's home and help with child care and light housework. Au pairs tend to come from Europe or various parts of the United States.

Sharing Care with another family is an excellent option to consider if you can't afford (or don't need) to hire an in-home care provider full-time. Val, a travel agent who requires part-time child care, shares her nanny with her business partner, who also works out of her home. "My partner and I alternate three days a week that we actually work with child care," says Val. "Our nanny is happy with the arrangement because she needs full-time employment. Fortunately, she loves both of our kids, so it works out great."

The Positive Aspects of In-Home Care

- You save time not having to drive to and from care centers outside your home.
- You and your children have more flexibility because outside centers are only open certain hours. If your children are asleep, you don't have to awaken them to drive to group care. Also, they can follow their own eating and sleeping routines, rather than have to conform to a schedule in group care.
- Your schedule doesn't have to be altered when your child is sick.
- Your children won't be exposed to the germs of other kids.
- Your children will get individual attention.
- Your caregiver can accommodate children of different ages, unlike most group settings.
- Your caregiver may perform other household duties.

Will In-Home Care Work for You?

In order to decide whether in-home child care is the best option for you, consider the positive aspects of this type of arrangement, and weigh them against the positive aspects of out-of-home child-care options covered in the next section. Even more important, ask yourself whether you and your children have the discipline to be under the same roof and not be together.

As much as having your children at home in someone else's care can allow you the opportunity to be close and take little breaks with them during your workday, it can also be a constant invitation begging you not to work. At the same time, it can be a tease for your children knowing that you're home but not available to them.

Will your children cooperate with an in-home caregiver so that you'll have the freedom to focus 100 percent of your attention on your work? In most cases it takes time and practice, but kids learn to let go, allowing you to work while the caregiver is in charge. This is easiest when children learn early on in their lives.

Jill, whose children were a bit older when she began working at home, found that it takes a bit of outsmarting at first to get kids acclimated. She offers a clever yet helpful hint for parents whose children are having a tough time adjusting to an in-home caregiver while their parent is working at home.

🖉 Homeworker Hint

When I had an in-home sitter, I would walk out the front door, wave and kiss the kids good-bye, and sneak in the back door to my office, making sure I went to the bathroom first—four hours is a long time without going to the bathroom. If they know I'm in there, they won't stay with the sitter. I was so quiet, they didn't even know I was there. It worked like a charm.

Jill, Desktop Publisher

It's critical that you be clear on how much interaction you want with your kids during your workday, and set up a routine accordingly. It's actually easier on children when you respect their time with the in-home caregiver. If you randomly pop in and out, it can be disruptive, especially if your child has difficulty separating from you. Also, if you have that kind of freedom, shouldn't your child be able to come into your office at random? Establish regular visiting times during breaks or lunch to provide a sense of predictability to your child's day. This will make your child feel more secure and less apt to demand to be with you at other times.

The Search

Although quality in-home child care is often scarce, there are several ways to search for a good provider. The goal is to find someone with whom you feel a mutual sense of trust and respect. This is a reciprocal relationship, and it's critical that you develop it that way from the start.

ASK EVERYONE YOU KNOW

An excellent way to find a good in-home caregiver is by asking everyone you know. Talk to your neighbors, friends, and colleagues. Other sources include your pediatrician, church, and other caregivers at local playgrounds. The best referrals come from people you know and trust.

CHECK ADS

Check the local papers for caregiver ads. Check the bulletin boards at schools, doctors' offices, supermarkets, libraries, gyms, and churches. Take a look at community newsletters. You can also call local community colleges to see if any recent graduates are looking for work as a caregiver.

ADVERTISE

There are several ways to advertise for caregivers, and many don't cost a cent. While placing ads in the local newspapers is the most obvious approach, seek out the not-so-obvious ways such as posting ads on free bulletin boards. Talk to real estate agents who send out monthly newsletters in your area. Many are receptive to placing free ads. The benefit of this approach is that you'll be targeting potential caregivers right in your neighborhood. Also, if you belong to a homeowners' association, call to see if you can place a free ad in their monthly newsletter.

Depending on whether you're looking for a caregiver who is younger or more mature, it is wise to place your ads accordingly. You might try posting ads on bulletin boards at local high schools and colleges if you're looking for someone younger. If you're looking for someone more mature, the local papers, church bulletins, and community newsletters are likely to be your best bets for advertising. Or you might place an ad in the newsletter of a local senior citizens community. Many experienced seniors would love to spend their time caring for young children. If they're on a fixed income, the extra money will certainly be appreciated.

CONSIDER A PLACEMENT AGENCY

Placement agencies can be a helpful resource in your search for an appropriate caregiver. However, agencies charge fees ranging anywhere from $400 to $2,600. While they basically save you some of the legwork in terms of finding prescreened candidates, you still have to do the interviewing, and often your own reference checks, as well. One problem with agencies is that anyone can hang a shingle and start making placements. The industry is not regulated, so be careful about which one you choose. Asking your friends for recommendations is usually the best way to find a credible agency.

The Interview

Before you conduct face-to-face interviews with potential caregiver candidates, tell them you work at home. Prequalify them over the phone by asking if they would be comfortable having you in the home while they work.

It's usually best to invite candidates to your home so they can meet your children, and see the environment they'll be working in. This will give you an opportunity to see the interaction that takes place. If you're married or living with someone, it is best if both of you are present to make sure you're comfortable with the person you hire. Make up a list of questions you want to ask, and information you want to provide during the interviews.

SAMPLE INTERVIEW QUESTIONS

General Information:

- What is your employment background (especially in reference to caring for children)?
- What are the age ranges of children you have cared for?
- What do you enjoy about working with children?
- What is your level of education?
- Do you smoke?
- Do you have a valid driver's license?
- Can you show proof of American citizenship or eligibility to work in this country?

Specific Questions:

- What types of activities do you like to do with kids? (e.g., indoor and out-of-door activities)
- What is your style for handling discipline?
- How would you keep the children from interrupting me?
- Should they get too noisy, how would you quiet the children down?
- How would you handle a trying situation, such as . . . ? (Offer an example from a recent experience you encountered with your child.)
- When the children nap, how would you spend your time?
- What questions can we answer for you?
- Whom can we contact for references?

JOB DESCRIPTION

It's also wise to provide applicants with a thorough job description. Include detailed information on the desired starting date, salary, hours and breaks, as well as any benefits offered (e.g., insurance, vacation, holidays, sick days).

Also include a list of responsibilities such as what you expect in terms of child care, and anything additional (e.g., transporting children, care of children who regularly play with yours). Clarify any household responsibilities required such as meal preparation, shopping, errands, housework, or pet care.

If you have any house rules (e.g., telephone or TV usage) you wish to convey, put them in the job description so applicants will know exactly what to expect. Be honest up front and you will prevent misunderstandings down the road.

BACKGROUND CHECKS

If you're not working with a placement agency, thoroughly screen all candidates who spark your interest by checking their references. Talk to as many prior employers as possible. Ask about candidates' reliability, strengths and weaknesses, reason for leaving, and how they resolved problems. You may want to see if a potential caregiver has a criminal record. Contact your state police office for more information on background checks.

The Decision

What if you wind up with three suitable candidates? If everything checks out with each candidate, ask yourself who gave you the best feeling. Trust your gut instincts.

Will your child be upset knowing that you're nearby but occupied? If so, hire a caregiver who shows interest in taking your child to the park or on long walks. Overall, it's best to hire a caregiver who is a go-getter and who will take charge even when you're around.

The Written Agreement

In an effort to avoid confusion or misunderstandings, put things in writing. Establish a written agreement between you and your caregiver. Remember the job description you created? You can use your word processor to transfer the information it conveys on salary, hours, benefits, responsibilities, and rules to a written agreement that should be signed by both parties.

Taxes

Under certain conditions you are obligated to pay Social Security and Medicare taxes for household employees. For more information on this, call (800) TAX-FORM. You may also be subject to the tax for federal and state unemployment, as well as any state-required workers' compensation and disability insurance. Check with your state unemployment office for information about your state obligations.

Out-of-Home Child Care

If you decide to use out-of-home child care, there are many options to consider, depending on your children's ages and dispositions. The cost of out-of-home care varies widely, and can range anywhere from $75 to $400 per week for full-time care.

DAY-CARE CENTERS AND PRESCHOOLS

In day-care centers and preschools, children tend to be grouped according to age. The centers can be privately owned or operated by nonprofit organizations such as churches, schools, or community groups. Good day-care centers or preschools offer age-appropriate educational activities.

The Positive Aspects of Day-Care Centers and Preschools

- There's a wide range of activities for your child.
- The staff is generally trained in child development.
- Your child can interact with other kids.
- You don't have to worry about turnover of caregivers.
- Unlike caregivers, centers don't call in sick.
- Most centers are regulated and must meet certain standards.
- You can work peacefully without children at home.
- You don't have to deal with the responsibilities of being an employer.

FAMILY DAY CARE

Generally, family day-care providers consist of moms who want to earn extra income watching other people's kids while they care for their own. They may also be moms whose children have already left the nest. Typically they care for a small group of children ranging from four to six kids including their own. They usually hire an assistant to help out when watching six kids or more. Family day care is best suited for infants, toddlers, and preschoolers.

The Positive Aspects of Family Day Care

- Usually it's economical.
- Your child can interact with other kids.
- Providers may be flexible with their hours.
- The atmosphere is more intimate than a day-care center.
- You can work peacefully without children at home.
- You don't have to deal with the responsibilities of being an employer.

SUBSIDIZED CHILD CARE

Subsidized child care provides free or low-cost care to eligible low-income families. Subsidized child-care centers such as state preschools and Head Start receive funding from government sources to serve eligible families. A sliding-scale fee is used, with rates based on the family's income. There are a variety of private and public child-care providers that participate in subsidized child-care programs (including family day care and licensed exempt providers). Check with your local YMCA or YWCA for more information.

SCHOOL-AGE PROGRAMS

If your kids are school age and older, look into the variety of after-school activities available. Check out the local YMCA and YWCA where kids can do their homework as well as participate in activities such as swimming lessons, dance classes, Scouts, and all types of sports. Also look into local churches, community centers, parks and recreation, and private facilities that offer instruction in your child's interest areas (e.g., music, dance, karate).

SUMMER CAMPS

During the summer there are day camps available where your child can be around other kids and be exposed to a variety of recreational activities. If your child is older, sleep-away camp is a possibility for a portion of the summer. Look into what is available in your community through private schools, community centers, and large day-care center chains.

Resource and Referral Agencies

There are more than five hundred government-funded resource and referral agencies across the country that can provide the names of licensed day-care centers and family day-care providers in your community. They also have listings for available school-age programs and summer camps. Check your local Yellow Pages for the nearest agency, or call Child Care Aware at (800) 424-2246.

Choosing the Best Out-of-Home Child-Care Option

In making your decision about which out-of-home child-care option is best, consider not only what you can afford but what type of environment your children will be most comfortable in. If you're interested in family day care or a day-care center, make a visit and check things out first.

WHAT DO YOU LOOK FOR?
When doing your research on potential out-of-home child-care providers, the YMCA Child Care Resource Service suggests that you focus on the following:

Licensing

Check to see if the facility is licensed and that the license is displayed. If licensing is not required, check references. See if there is an enrollment capacity.

Registration and Fees

Is there a waiting list? How much are the fees and when are they due? Is there a late fee? See if there is a fee for absent days due to illness or vacation. Find out what is required of parents, and ask if there is a written contract.

Providers/Teachers

Look into what kind of training or experience the caregiver has. Is the caregiver accredited or certified? How many adults are present during child-care hours, and what is the adult/child ratio? Make sure there are enough adults present to ensure the basic safety of the group and to help individual children who need it.

Is the provider or teacher patient, warm, and sensitive to the needs of children? Does he or she encourage natural curiosity and exploration as well as the desire to learn? You want someone who enjoys the job and is caring but at the same time firm with the children. Question the person's values and disciplinary methods to see if they are similar to yours.

Home/Center

Are the rooms and play areas large enough to accommodate the number of children and activities offered? Ensure that the home or center is clean, and that it offers a safe and inviting outdoor space.

Materials/Equipment

Make sure that there are a variety of materials and equipment to allow your children many different choices and experiences. Check to see that the materials and equipment are appropriate for your child's age level. Also, look for any signs of neglect or wear and tear that may be a safety hazard.

Programs and Activities

Is there a regular daily schedule? Is the schedule flexible enough to handle the needs of all children? Investigate the types of activities offered, and whether the caregiver focuses on all areas of child development (i.e., social, emotional, physical, cognitive). Some programs provide an ongoing assessment for each child.

Meals

Is there an extra charge for meals? Do meals meet nutritional requirements? You may be expected to provide food for meals, snacks, or formula. Check to see if the provider participates in a federally funded food program.

Health and Safety

Ensure that someone is present in the home or center who has first aid/CPR training. Check to see that there is a fire emergency plan posted, as well as an earthquake/disaster plan. Also, does the provider offer a nonsmoking environment?

MAINTAINING A GOOD RELATIONSHIP WITH YOUR CHILD-CARE PROVIDER

Whether your child-care provider is in or out of your home, always strive for an open and honest relationship. Schedule regular meetings with your caregiver. If there is a problem, speak up about it immediately, and encourage your caregiver to do the same.

Mutual respect, trust, and display of appreciation are key to maintaining a healthy relationship. Small and unexpected tokens of gratitude can go a long way. Jean, a computer research analyst and mother of two, is so happy with her day-care center that she sends "appreciation" cards periodically to let the staff know. "I think people go the extra mile when you show you care," she says. "My kids get a lot of special attention, and I think my extra efforts have a lot to do with it."

It's wise to monitor your child-care arrangement on a regular basis. Jean occasionally volunteers to work at her children's day-care center, especially when the kids go on field trips (another way she shows that she cares). This also gives her an opportunity to periodically keep an eye on things. In the beginning she dropped in unannounced to have lunch with her children and get to know the staff better.

It's also important to monitor in-home caregivers, always asking how the day went and whether they have any suggestions or issues they'd like to discuss. Although you're at home working, don't be tempted to hover. Give your caregiver the latitude and trust you would want in the same situation. You want your children to sense your confidence so they feel comfortable being cared for by someone else while you're at home. Otherwise, like Jill who sneaks in through the back door, you'll constantly be searching for clever ways to outsmart your kids into thinking you're not home just so you can get *any* work done.

EXPERIMENT TO FIND WHAT WORKS

Don't be afraid to experiment with the many child-care options available until you find what works for you and your children. Most homeworkers wind up with a "piecemeal" approach, consisting of paid part-time care either in or out of their home, supplemented with the selected strategies presented in the beginning of this chapter. If you discover that something doesn't work, move on until you find the right fit.

CHAPTER FIVE

Dividing and Conquering the Household Load

Homeworker Hint

In order to work at home, you've got to have help with the housecleaning. If you don't get help from your partner and kids, hire someone, because you're not going to have time. It's cost-effective for me to pay someone to clean the house so I can do what I need to do.

Carol, Architectural Illustrator

Setting up a system for sharing the workload around the house will do wonders for your relationship with your partner and children, and it will preserve your sanity as well. I'm addressing this chapter to women, men, and children in an effort to convey how critical teamwork is, especially in a home-office environment.

Where do we stand today in terms of how household labor is divvied up among dual-career families? Since children learn by example, we'll talk about them pitching in a little later. For now, let's focus on husbands and wives.

Little research has been conducted on couples in which one or both partners work at home. However, among dual-career couples working outside the home, wives spend six hours per day in household work (including meal preparation, care of family members, and housecleaning), while husbands spend an hour and a half per day contributing to household work.

In her book *The Second Shift* (Viking), Arlie Hochschild, who studied dual-career couples, conveys why women feel more strain than men even when their husbands share the household responsibilities. She found that women did two thirds of the daily chores (e.g., cooking meals, tidying up), while men did the chores that are done periodically (e.g., household repairs, taking out the garbage). Furthermore, men's total time devoted to domestic tasks was weighted more toward child care, while women's was weighted more toward housework. The women tended to do the undesirable chores such as cleaning ovens and toilets, while men did more of what they wanted to do. Also, women tended to do two or more things at once, such as laundry, cooking, and child care, while men performed their tasks sequentially, focusing on one task at a time.

In reference to time spent on child care, women performed more of the caretaking functions such as bathing and feeding, while men were more involved in playing with the kids. The women also acted as household managers, constantly keeping their families on schedule (for commitments, appointments, etc.), all the while feeling like the "bad guy." The bottom line, according to Hochschild, is that some marriages have disintegrated because of divisiveness over household responsibilities. Obviously this is not an issue to be taken lightly.

WHO CARRIES THE LOAD IN A WORK-AT-HOME ARRANGEMENT?

Does any of this change when one or both partners work at home? As I mentioned in the last chapter, women and men who work at home tend to handle child care equally, which is a refreshing and welcome change. On the other hand, the issue of feeling responsible for household tasks is a recurring theme that surfaced in my interviews with women but not men. Men exhibit more financial concerns about being able to provide a certain standard of living for their family. Some are discouraged with their drop in income since they left the corporate world to work at home.

This suggests that homeworkers still tend to be preoccupied with the responsibilities associated with traditional gender roles—wherein men are the "breadwinners" and women are the "homemakers." A work-at-home lifestyle doesn't necessarily result in a disappearance of these defined roles but more of an evening out of gender roles, whereby couples are not strictly "egalitarian" or strictly "traditional," but somewhere in between.

A work-at-home arrangement offers a unique challenge in the form of a continuous confrontation with the responsibilities of both gender roles (breadwinner and homemaker) simultaneously. In order to be productive in their work, women can't allow themselves to succumb entirely to their stereotyped gender role responsibilities. Similarly, in order to spend more time with their wives and children, men need to reexamine their role in the family.

The upside to this continuous confrontation is that it allows homeworkers to decide where they want to direct their energies. The decision about the definition of roles is entirely up to the couple, and is less influenced by workplace and societal structures and norms that tend to foster and support traditional gender roles. Hence, a work-at-home lifestyle offers women a chance to work for equal pay and have equal opportunity to exercise their potential. It also allows men the opportunity to spend more time with their family than working for a company outside the home typically supports.

Among the couples I interviewed, women tend to invest more time handling household responsibilities than their husbands, while men invest more time in their careers than their wives. This held true whether the husband or the wife worked at home, or both partners worked at home. The busy work schedules of the husbands weighed heavily on the division of labor in the household. Val, a travel agent, explains:

The division of household labor is 90 percent me and 10 percent him, and that's by choice. I run the household. My husband is gone Monday through Thursday, and he works at home on Friday. He works a lot of hours. His chores around here are minimal, and that's a value decision we made wanting to spend time with our daughter, and all of us as a family on the weekends. We sat down and hashed things out from the beginning so we could create a fair arrangement we'd both be happy with.

In general, homeworkers express satisfaction with the decided division of labor between themselves and their partner. They commonly refer to the decision as a "value judgment" or "personal preference," rather than being "gender-driven." As Val's scenario suggests, communication is the key to creating a satisfying arrangement for everyone involved.

OVERCOMING A LACK OF SPOUSAL SUPPORT

Many working couples' disagreements arise from a feeling that one partner isn't pulling his or her fair share of the household load. Support from your partner can be emotional, physical, or financial. Each partner's perception of the balance created is what matters. As long as each partner perceives the situation as fair, then for that particular couple it is fair.

But doesn't it all come down to the fact that each partner has only twenty-four hours in a day? If a couple figures out that between them they have X number of hours of work to do in order to run the household and earn enough income to sustain a comfortable living, doesn't it make sense that those hours should be split fifty-fifty?

If both spouses work an eight-hour day but the husband makes more money, that doesn't mean the wife should be expected to handle the majority of the child care or domestic chores. Unless the husband spends an excessive amount of time in work travel in order to make more money, they both have equal time remaining in the day. If the husband invests more time in his work to make more money so his wife can work less, it makes sense that his wife would handle proportionately more domestic tasks (and vice versa), *if* that is what they *agree* upon.

What steps can you take to encourage a team approach with your spouse? Because research suggests that men are less involved in domestic and child-care tasks than women, I will present strategies primarily aimed at gaining the support of husbands; however, the situation can and sometimes does work in reverse. Therefore, men who feel that their wives are not contributing their fair share will also benefit from these strategies.

Communication! Communication! Communication!

Sit down with your partner and decide who will be responsible for what in the domestic and work arenas. This will prevent disagreements and misunderstandings that could sabotage your relationship and ability to succeed.

Liz, a computer programmer, claims that her biggest mistake was not discussing with her husband who would do what when they first started a home business together. As a result, Liz worked her fair share in the business in addition to handling all the child care and domestic chores. At the time I spoke to her, she was separated from her husband because the inequities of the situation created a negative spiral of resentment that only deepened in the silence between them. Liz felt that the differences were irreconcilable.

Don't wait for your partner to read your mind. When you feel anger brewing because of inequities, immediately open a dialogue and calmly present your position in a nonaccusatory fashion. If you feel overburdened, ask for your partner's cooperation in finding a solution to the problem. Always take a team approach by presenting your feelings without casting blame. If you put your partner on the defensive, you'll only aggravate the situation. In Chapter 6 we'll discuss strategies for resolving conflicts and getting along with your partner in a work-at-home arrangement.

Involve Your Partner By Stepping Back

If your husband or wife is reluctant to share domestic responsibilities, you may need to give yourself permission to step back so your partner can get involved. Because women form a close bond with their babies through the experience of pregnancy and child-birth, society has deemed them the primary caretakers. Even if women know nothing more about child care than their husbands, they're still placed in the primary position by default. Perhaps it's because of this conditioning that, although women may resent the imbalance of roles and say they want help, they are often reluctant to relinquish child care responsibilities to their husbands.

Phil, an attorney, relates how his wife's reluctance shines through in her criticism of his parental skills. "When I try to take charge of caring for my daughter, my wife hovers over like she doesn't trust me," he says. "She doesn't like the way I diaper her or prepare her food because my approach isn't exactly the same as hers. It really frustrates me."

Men can be just as effective parents as women if they are given the opportunity. An experimental study conducted with monkeys illustrates this beautifully. A male and female monkey were placed together in a cage with an unfamiliar infant. When the female was present, she performed 100 percent of the nurturing and caretaking of the infant. When she was removed from the cage, however, the male took over and assumed all of the "mothering" responsibilities. This illuminating study suggests that the nurturing potential present in males is only expressed in the absence of their female partner.

And how does this play out in terms of who does what in relation to domestic chores? It was once believed that women's employment would "liberate" them from unending responsibilities on the home front. While this view is optimistic, the pessimistic expectation of an inevitable "second shift" is also exaggerated. Women continue to have a psychic investment in maintaining high standards of housework. If husbands feel like they "can't get it right," this will encourage less participation on their part, and ultimately more work for their wives.

Allow your husband to handle the child care and household responsibilities in his own way. This will give him the opportunity to build confidence and become a well-rounded parent and contributing partner. Don't criticize his technique if he doesn't feed the baby the same way you do. In terms of housework, reduce your standards and refuse to view the cleanliness of your house as a reflection on you. If you take the "my way or the highway" approach, you'll be left handling everything.

These points can be made in reverse as well. Often men hover over their wives when they are experimenting with traditional male roles such as painting walls, hanging pictures, performing household repairs, or mowing the lawn. Men want to make sure their wives "get it right." Much can be said for both men and women stepping back from tasks associated with traditional gender roles, thus allowing their partners the opportunity to master these tasks in their own way.

TEAM APPROACHES TO DIVVYING UP HOUSEHOLD CHORES

There are several team approaches to consider in deciding how to divide the household responsibilities.

Split Chores According to Abilities and Interests

The best way to split chores is according to each partner's abilities and interests. What do each of you prefer to do? Jot down the tasks that each of you favors that the other doesn't. While men may prefer doing home repairs and yard work, and women may gravitate toward cooking and tidying up, the split of chores doesn't have to follow traditional gender roles.

Make another list of tasks considered neutral—that both of you could take or leave. Create a final list of the remaining tasks considered undesirable or undoable by both of you. Divvy up these lists evenly according to which of you does the tasks best, or take turns choosing. Anything that you both cannot or will not do, for whatever reason, should be delegated or farmed out (e.g., hire someone, exchange products or services with someone). Are there any chores you wish to delegate to your children that are appropriate for their age level? When you've finished negotiating, type up a list of the agreed-upon responsibilities, and put it in a visible place as a reminder for both of you.

Share and Exchange Roles

In our home, Bob and I share the majority of tasks. We alternate who cooks dinner and who cleans up. We take turns doing the grocery shopping and laundry. We're both fairly capable of handling what is considered traditional ''men's'' and ''women's'' work. The advantage of this approach is that you have the opportunity to learn and manage new tasks. It also breaks up the monotony of doing the same tasks day in and day out. If you like variety, rotate tasks with your partner every so often. Just make sure you're in agreement on who does what from week to week.

This approach has advantages for children as well. When children see their parents performing all types of household tasks, they are less apt to develop stereotyped views of women's and men's roles. Plus, if both parents handle child care, your children will grow up knowing both parents. Often, when one parent is the primary caretaker, children will naturally gravitate toward and favor that parent over the other.

Try a Team Power Cleaning

Chris, a magazine publisher, says that she and her husband split the housecleaning chores equally. They use an effective strategy whereby both team up to do a ''power cleaning'' on a weekend day. ''We'll take a Saturday when neither of us works, and we both just pitch in and do it,'' she says. ''It goes much faster that way.''

When agreed upon, this approach is very effective because partners can motivate each other if one is falling off the track. Much like committing to an exercise regimen at the gym with a friend, a dreaded task can be made palatable.

Give Each Other a Breather

All people like to have time to themselves, especially parents who are pushed in multiple directions. Regardless of what approach you take toward divvying up responsibilities, schedule in some relaxing time away from pressures for you and your partner. Greg and Kelly have a system whereby each gets one weeknight off to him or herself totally free of all responsibilities. Kelly can do as she pleases on her night while Greg takes over on the home front, and vice versa when it's Greg's turn.

They also give each other one Saturday a month off when each can have time to rejuvenate. This allows them the opportunity to catch up on a good book, take a class, or spend time with a friend. Greg, a cartoonist, loves his work and considers it to be his personal time. In fact, he often spends his "off time" putting in a little overtime.

INVOLVING YOUR CHILDREN IN HOUSEHOLD TASKS

It is not uncommon for children to help with household chores in a work-at-home arrangement. Homeworkers assign their children household responsibilities to varying degrees, depending on their ages.

Nancy, a math tutor and single mom, is proud that her kids, ages ten and eleven, set the table and help get dinner going each evening while she continues to work. Sue, a medical transcriptionist, says her fifteen-year-old son is a tremendous help around the house. She appreciates his efforts in preparing dinner and cleaning up with his dad each night while she finishes her work. (Come to think of it, Sue's son was doing the laundry during my interview with her.)

In a Homeworker Hint in the last chapter, Jenny, a secretarial service provider, introduced a method for gradually encouraging your children's participation in your work activities early on. The same approach will encourage their involvement in household tasks.

Get an Early Start

Children love to imitate their parents. You can buy inexpensive toy cleaning tools at garage and yard sales so they can do just that. By watching you, your children can learn how to use a broom and dustpan, push a vacuum, and iron clothes on their own toy sets.

Give Them Chores to Do

As your children develop, it's important for them to learn that everyone pitches in and does his or her assigned share around the house. If you instill the team approach early on, children are more likely to do their share without being asked repeatedly. In fact, children will want to help.

Assign chores that are appropriate for your children's age level so they can experience a sense of accomplishment. These positive experiences will lay the groundwork for later on when your children can really be a help. Pat, a newspaper publisher, explains that her husband does not support her work-at-home efforts, so she and her children split the household chores:

> I probably do 80 percent of the meal preparation. The housecleaning is pretty much fifty-fifty between the kids and me. My husband does the laundry and that's about it. Because I'm working a lot, the kids have responsibilities like putting things away, cleaning the kitchen, and doing the yard work.

Start small and expand responsibilities with age. Toddlers can do one-step tasks such as putting their toys away, and school-age kids can perform tasks that are under ten minutes, such as making their beds or picking up their rooms. As children get older they can handle large tasks such as cleaning their bedroom and bathroom, or complex tasks such as baby-sitting a younger sibling. Kids usually prefer chores that let them notice a benefit. Washing your dog Spot produces a visibly clean, fresh-smelling pet, whereas dusting doesn't produce such noticeable results. Assign chores according to ability and preference, and experiment to see what works best for your child.

Until about age eight, most children need supervision performing chores, and most kids under ten are likely to still need reminding to do their chores. Expanding on their level of involvement through the teenage years will prepare kids for when they leave the nest and are responsible for taking care of their own home.

Ben, a marketing consultant, describes how his kids, ages eight and ten, are responsible for taking care of themselves in the mornings, an effective strategy that allows him to immediately jump into his work. "The kids are programmed in the morning, and they're on their own," he says. "They get their own cereal, make their own lunches. They also clean their rooms and do certain chores around the house. We've got them very well organized."

Make It Fun

Find ways to make chores fun for your kids and they'll be more excited about giving you a hand. Some parents assign regular chores to their kids but keep a chore jar with tasks written down and folded on small pieces of paper. Your children can pick their surprise tasks from the jar blindfolded. This gives them a chance to add variety to their usual routine.

Pat, a newspaper publisher, finds that the best way to entice her four children is to make housecleaning a game in which everyone participates. Her "quick cleanup" strategy works like a charm:

> *I say, "Okay, you guys, we're going to take twenty minutes and straighten up the kitchen and the living room," and they think it's a game. It took us about fifteen minutes, and we had the whole upstairs straightened up yesterday. I think because I always put a time limit on it, they feel like, "Okay, we're not going to be working all day." They're excited to hurry up, get it done, and know that in fifteen minutes they can go out and play. It's effective, and it's the way I have to work with myself sometimes too.*

Pat's approach introduces another way to make house chores fun for children. They'll generally prefer doing chores with their parents rather than doing them alone. Work together and everyone will have fun. In fact, that's how children learn best. When they see you doing one of your assigned tasks, they'll often volunteer to help because it makes them feel grown-up when they can do adult tasks.

Don't Expect Perfection

Perhaps the worst thing you can do is take away your children's sense of accomplishment by redoing their work. A slightly imperfect chore completed is better than no chore at all. Remember what I said earlier about stepping back to allow your partner to learn new tasks in his or her own way? Well, the same holds true for kids whose self-images are developing.

Involving your children in domestic chores won't necessarily save time, especially if they're just learning, tend to complain, or have to be asked repeatedly. You may be tempted to do it yourself, especially if you're feeling tired and overworked. It's important to remember, however, that you're teaching your children that every family member is responsible for making a contribution toward maintaining the household. Your patience with their performance will go a long way toward building accountability.

Give Them Reminders

Kids have an easier time remembering their chores if they have reminders. One creative way to remind them is by making up a chart with words or pictures. If your children are old enough, let them use their artistic talents to make up their own chart. Even younger children can attach their own artwork to a chart you've made for them. This gives them the sense that it's their own personalized chart, complete with the tasks they're responsible for. You may have to remind them a bit in the beginning to check the chart daily, but once they're in the habit, it will become second nature.

Reward Them When Appropriate

There are many ways to reward children when they're doing a good job managing their chores. You might treat them to a favorite video or dessert, or an afternoon out at the movies. Probably the best way to reward them is to regularly express appreciation and recognition for their contributions.

It is not advisable to offer money as a reward unless the chore is not a part of your child's usual routine. Paul, an environmental product distributor, uses a cash-in ticket system with his seven- and nine-year-old kids when they do special chores. "They receive tickets for doing certain chores," Paul says. "So if they unload the dishwasher, they get two tickets, and that's worth fifty cents when they turn them in. It's been very effective."

One word of caution: It's not advisable to tie your child's allowance to the performance of household chores. In the real world people don't get paid to clean their own homes. You want to teach your child that each person has responsibilities around the house, and no one gets paid for doing his or her fair share.

Make It a Family Affair

As much as possible, make household chores a family affair. You can initiate this by scheduling a monthly meeting when you sit down as a family and ask your children what they would like to do. You may be surprised at what kids will volunteer for instead of being told what to do.

What if your children have no idea what they want to do? Pull out the lists of chores you created with your partner. If you decided that some of the chores on those lists could be delegated to your children, suggest those as possibilities, or write down the chores on little pieces of paper for them to select at random out of a jar. Rotating tasks on a weekly or monthly basis will break up the monotony for everyone and prevent boredom.

Another way to make housecleaning a family affair is to make up a family chore chart. You can purchase an erasable white board with imprinted black squares to serve as a monthly calendar at your local stationer. During your monthly meeting, fill in the days with each family member's agreed-upon chores. Some might stay permanent while you rotate others. Try anything creative to keep the team spirit alive. As parents, your efforts will help breed enthusiasm in your children when it comes time to decide who is responsible for what.

SAVING TIME ON THE HOME FRONT

If you feel like you currently waste time on housework, how will you feel when you're working at home and the undone chores are constantly in front of you? Following are strategies to help you optimize household efficiency.

Reduce Your Housecleaning Standards

This one will protect your sanity and in many cases your relationship, especially if you and your significant other disagree on what is considered "clean" or "tidy." Many homeworkers stress that lowering their housecleaning standards allows them to feel a greater sense of accomplishment in all areas of their lives. It also makes them feel more balanced.

"When you're a meticulous type of person, it's hard to leave some of the film on the table because you want it all perfect," says Chris, a magazine publisher. "You want everything organized, but you learn to let some things go." Would you rather have the cleanest house on the block, or more time to spend as you wish?

Creatively Integrate Housework

Many women, in particular, pride themselves on regularly integrating household tasks into their workday. Val, a travel agent, saves time by working her business and household chores around each other:

> I can run by the grocery store while I'm out, and it's not a major stress thing. When my work is more manageable, I can be making dinner while I'm working. I can throw in a load of clothes in between phone calls. It may only be one load of laundry, but on a slow day it's one less thing I have to do at night.

Would you be able to successfully integrate minor household tasks into your workday and get back on track? If so, you can benefit from one of the great advantages of working at home. You can accomplish a variety of chores during your workday, while those who work outside the home must use their time on nights and weekends to get caught up.

Simplify Grocery Shopping

Unless the grocery store is one of your favorite places to go and you look forward to your next visit, do what you can to simplify trips. Buy in large quantity so you can save money and trips. Since you work at home, you can shop during the low times. Many markets are open twenty-four hours. Ask the manager at the market you frequent when the least busiest shopping times are. If you can shop during the low times, you'll avoid playing bumper carts in a crowded store, and you won't have to wait in long checkout lines. I can accomplish twice as much in less time when I shop this way.

If you're anything like our family, you tend to buy a lot of the same groceries over and over. Rather than make up a new list for each visit to the store, we created a master grocery list on our word processor that has all the usual items we consume in about a one-month period, with a blank line next to each item for the quantity desired.

Do you usually do your grocery shopping at the same market most of the time? We have a favorite market, so our premade grocery list is arranged according to the location of the items in the store. Before I go to the store, I grab one of the lists and fill in the amounts for what we need. When I arrive at the store I can pick up the items in one circle, from produce on one side to meat and dairy in the rear, to the deli and bakery on the other side, and on to the checkout counter. It really takes a lot of the stress out of grocery shopping.

The other day I had the misfortune of going to a different market without one of my premade lists. I didn't know where anything was, so I ran from one end of the market to the other trying to find what I thought I remembered we needed. I couldn't even find an employee to ask for help. My "quick stop" for ten items lasted forty-five minutes. Oh, sure, I got plenty of exercise hauling my cart back and forth like a maniac, but I was amazed at how that episode threw my whole workday off.

Prepare Two Meals in One Shot

If you don't mind having two of the same meals in one week (or you can always freeze the second meal for another week), try two-in-one cooking. It's just as easy to make two casseroles when you have all the ingredients out. If you like to eat healthfully and appreciate fresh vegetables, do all your chopping for the week and store what you don't use in airtight containers. A lot of meal preparation involves getting things out (e.g., ingredients, utensils), cleaning up the mess, and putting everything away. If you can prepare all or parts of the meals for other nights in one session, you'll definitely save time.

Microwave While You Work

In our home, we have two microwaves that we often use simultaneously. You can cook, defrost, or heat up meals faster when you have two. With microwaves being so inexpensive, the time you save is well worth the extra cost.

Homeworkers primarily eat their meals at home rather than out. Some refer to themselves as the "micro" family because they rely so heavily on microwave cooking. "Stove-cooked meals are one of the things that had to go," says Val, a travel agent. "At least our microwave meals are healthy." Microwaves are a tremendous convenience. Don't work at home without one . . . or two.

Crock-Pots and Salads Are a Must

Crock-Pots, a favored wintertime cooking method, are tremendous time savers because the ingredients can be prepared the night before and put on to slow-cook for dinner the next evening. Chicken or rib dinners (with barbecue sauce) are terrific in the

Crock-Pot because the meat is so tender it falls off the bone. In her book *Smart Crockery Cooking* (Sterling Publishing Co.), Carol H. Munson offers variety and tips on how to do slow cooking safely and deliciously.

Favorite summertime dinners that are quick and easy are salads requiring a little attention here and a little attention there. Macaroni, potato, and taco salads are all great because you can cook the individual ingredients and let them cool while you concentrate on your work. For variety, try a big tossed chicken Caesar salad with a large baked potato and some hot bread. It's an easy meal to prepare and wonderfully satisfying.

Try a Picnic on Paper Plates

I know a family that only eats on paper plates. They never use dishes—except on holidays or to entertain important clients. Talk about a time saver. If this sounds a little drastic, how about an occasional family picnic on paper plates?

Laura, a freelance writer, describes a weekly ritual—"picnic night," when her family all take part in making (or taking out) an easy dinner that they can eat on paper plates. "The rule is, everything on the table is either plastic or paper," she says. "If it needs to be washed, it's out. Our cleanup that night consists of trash pickup."

Go for Low Maintenance

You can save a lot of time around the house by simply purchasing low-maintenance items. From clothes to household furnishings to children's activities, go for what is easiest to clean. If you buy clothes that are wrinkle-free when you pull them out of the dryer, it beats having to hand-wash, iron, or pick up clothes at the dry cleaners. (Just don't let clothes sit in the dryer, or they'll wrinkle and need touch-up ironing anyway.) When you work at home, one of the benefits is not having to purchase a high-maintenance wardrobe, so you save not only time, but money too.

Think low maintenance when you buy household furnishings.

You don't have to sacrifice taste, but consider how much time you'll have to invest in cleaning or maintenance. Even with children's activities and toys, look for easy cleanup. Also, try to confine messy projects to a particular area such as a favorite table that's "mess-proofed" with newspapers.

Clean as You Go

My mom taught me the "clean as you go" concept, and it's a definite time saver. She always kept the kitchen spotless while she cooked. She cleaned all pans and surfaces as she went along to avoid a huge mess on her hands at the end of a meal. As for dirty dishes, the rule in our house was that everything was rinsed and put right into the dishwasher. My mom ran the dishwasher every day so there was never a huge amount of dishes to unload. She also never walked through the house empty-handed. She would pick up something or do something along the way.

I used to think my mom's approach was going a bit far, until I went on my own and learned that it takes twice as long to clean up a big mess at the end—especially if any leftover food has permanently attached itself to the dishes. By not procrastinating and taking action immediately on your responsibilities, you can save time by getting a job done when it's easiest or before it gets out of hand.

Clean in Spurts

Turn on your favorite music (or use a headset radio if others in the house are trying to concentrate) and spend fifteen minutes each day maintaining your household. That way the chores won't pile up and seem so monumental. Fifteen minutes of housework can be fifteen minutes of fun if you challenge yourself to see how much you can get done knowing the end is right in sight. Jean, a computer research analyst, uses this approach to battle her share of the household chores and reduce her stress level:

> *I hate doing housework when I know I've got an hour or two worth of chores to do. I have a rule that I spend one*

*of my fifteen-minute breaks each day doing housework.
You'd be surprised at how much you can do in a concentrated effort. I can dust the living room and dining room,
and sweep the entryway. Another fifteen minutes is spent
vacuuming. I used to get really uptight because things always got out of hand, and the whole place would be a
pigsty. Now I stay on top of things a little at a time. This
"fifteen-minute rule" is great. I'm less stressed about
everything.*

You can use the fifteen-minute rule with your family too. Each
night after dinner, set the timer for fifteen minutes and have
everyone work on picking up that day's clutter. Similar to Pat's
quick cleanup strategy she uses occasionally with her kids, you
can take the daily "mess and stress" out of your life by ap-
proaching household chores with a team spirit.

Keep an Ongoing List

Don't you hate it when you make a trip to the store only to find
when you get home that you forgot something you can't do
without? How about forgetting to make a stop to do something
important when you were right in the area?

Keep an ongoing list that consists of things you need to pick
up at the store or errands you need to run. That way your trips
out won't be wasted because you forgot to pick up or drop off
that all-important item you had promised yourself to remember
to do.

Three-in-One Errands

You can also save time by knocking off two or three errands in
one trip. If you're going in a particular direction one day, handle
all the errands you can in close proximity. If you check your
errand list each time you head out the door, you may be able to
knock off a task in the direction you're headed. Save yourself
from having to make repeated trips unnecessarily.

Run Household Errands During Low-Traffic Times

Much like doing your grocery shopping during the low times, you'll save time running errands while the rest of the world isn't traveling to or from work. If you must go out during your workday, by all means don't do it when the "commuters" are out. It will take three times longer, and you'll have to do "therapy" just to deal with the stress you are no longer used to.

Keep a Big Calendar Handy

If you're like me and you tend to write down personal appointments on anything close to the phone that even remotely resembles paper, then get a big calendar you can post near the phone so you can jot down important dates. You'll have all your personal appointments in one place, and you won't have to transfer them from your pieces of paper to your calendar. You also won't risk losing the slips of paper you write them on, and forget the appointments altogether. Just make sure you block out your personal time on your business calendar so you don't double-book yourself.

Chat and Chores

Telephone headsets are a great invention and a must for all homeworkers. If you want company while you do housework, try talking to a friend or family member on your headset while your hands are free to make dinner or fold laundry. I get all my cooking (and folding) done this way, and it serves as a relaxing ritual to more or less wind down my workday. I never make work calls during this time because that would be too awkward (although Bob often negotiates real estate deals while he's preparing dinner).

If housecleaning is the last thing on your list of favorite things to do, try what my friend does. Holly, a work-at-home piano teacher, has a cordless headset she wears while she cleans. She and her friend Nancy (who also works at home as a math tutor for kids) do all their housecleaning together—on the phone.

When it comes time for a big household cleaning, Holly and Nancy spend three hours on the phone (wearing their cordless headsets, of course) getting the dirty deed done. They even do their vacuuming simultaneously.

WHAT ABOUT HIRING A HOUSECLEANER?

✍ Homeworker Hint

I had to let go of what has been stereotyped as *my* job duties in order to find what I needed to be the best woman I could be, the happiest wife and mother, and a good business professional as well. I knew that housecleaning was going to take some very important time away from my business—time that would allow me to make the money it costs to hire someone to come in and clean.

Sara, Fitness Trainer

Unless you clean houses for a living or just enjoy doing housework and find it to be a relaxing change of pace, those precious hours are better spent developing your home business, sharing quality time with loved ones, or spending time on YOU.

Most homeworkers use hired help on a regular basis for housecleaning. Ben, a marketing consultant, emphasizes the importance of this step in not only saving time but in alleviating pressure on his marriage:

Once I had someone come in and do the housecleaning, it was phenomenal how much time it freed up. It was the best investment we've made, and it keeps the divorce lawyers away. We don't have time—two kids with activities going full blast, she's working, I'm working. If we had enough money, the housecleaner would be doing everything.

Some homeworkers do not hire outside help because they don't want anyone in their home while they're working, as it's disruptive. Some say that housework serves as therapy for work. It gives them an opportunity to let their minds wander, and brainstorm new ways to get leads. A number of homeworkers in solo households used to have a housekeeper but decided that they can do the cleaning themselves since they're home more.

Whether you hire a housecleaner depends on numerous factors such as affordability, diminished privacy, desire to relinquish household responsibilities, finding someone you can trust and rely on, and whether you have good self-discipline. Will housework (much like unsupervised children) be a distraction, posing a constant invitation to not work? If so, you may be fighting a losing battle if you don't hire help.

The most important factor in the consideration of whether to hire help is the degree to which housework is treated as teamwork between you, your partner, and your children. The happiest homeworkers are those who either have a housecleaner to handle the majority of the load, or have families who value everyone doing their fair share.

Some frustrated women say that their husbands don't take their home business seriously, and actually expect them to do more housework than before they worked at home. These husbands are often unwilling to pitch in themselves or hire help to relieve the burden on their wives.

Dealing with an Unwilling Partner

We talked about the importance of communicating with your partner to negotiate a division of household labor that's perceived as fair and comfortable for both of you. What if your partner balks at the idea of sharing the load?

A few women I interviewed ran into such a dilemma when they started a business at home. They communicated to their husbands their desire to hire a housecleaner to allow them to put more energy into their work. The husbands were reluctant at first because they believed the home business was not producing enough income to justify the expense.

Rather than fight a no-win situation, these women took matters into their own hands in an effort to save their sanity—regardless of the cost. Guess what? Their husbands responded positively to their assertiveness. Sue, a medical transcriptionist, says it's important to be firm but fair:

I hired a housekeeper. My husband sometimes grumbles about it, and complains about the amount of money we spend. That is, he used to. I'd say, "Okay. Now it's time to clean the house." He'd say, "Okay." In about a half hour he'd say, "What was that girl's name?" "Oh, would you like to have her back?" "Yes!"

If your partner refuses to pitch in and do a fair share and you're feeling resentful and overwhelmed, look out for yourself. Reduce your stress and preserve your self-esteem. If all attempts to communicate with your partner end in stalemate, consider taking matters into your own hands. Every action causes a reaction.

IT'S UP TO YOU

It's up to you to decide whether you will hire a housecleaner, share the household load as a family, or do the work yourself. If you decide to do the work yourself, be aware that it's one thing to purposely integrate household tasks into your workday, and another to have undone housework in front of you posing a constant distraction from your work. Give yourself and your business every chance of succeeding. Take the time to create a plan for how you will manage household responsibilities before you make the transition to work at home.

CHAPTER SIX

Working at Home Can Enhance Your Relationship

📙 **Homeworker Hint**

Since I started working at home, my wife and I have more time together because I can be getting dinner ready while she's commuting from work. This arrangement has been a real boost for our marriage.

Mike, Screenwriter

If you share your life with someone special, working at home can enhance your relationship regardless of whether you're married, or living together or apart. You can create more opportunities for increased intimacy, as Mike's scenario reveals. This involves understanding and upholding the role that comes naturally in your relationship with your partner.

In other words, it's difficult to enjoy life or create balance when you maintain a role that's not an extension of what you feel inside. It doesn't matter what other people think. What matters is that you and your partner be yourselves, and work from there to create an arrangement that you both perceive as fair. It may take time to work out the kinks, but in the long run it will be well worth the effort you put forth.

In this chapter we will explore these issues by taking a look at what happens when women and men are freed from the constraints of organizations to go to work on their own. We'll address gender roles and relationship styles, and what makes a marriage happy or unhappy. We'll introduce strategies for helping you stay in tune with your partner, as well as useful tips for homeworking couples. We'll end off with conflict-resolution and goal-setting techniques.

ORGANIZATIONAL CONSTRAINTS
What Women and Men Are Up Against

If you work for a company, more often than not, you'll experience unfair treatment based on your gender and/or status as a parent or nonparent. Women with children are victims of the "mommy track"—a less demanding career track for women who are family-oriented. Women in general experience the "glass ceiling"—transparent but powerful artificial barriers based on organizational biases that keep them from advancing upward in their careers into management positions. In 1990 women held less than 5 percent of the top executive positions of the one thousand largest corporations in the United States. Furthermore, women held only 4.5 percent of the directorships and 2.6 percent of the officer positions in the Fortune 500 companies.

Although women have greater economic and legal equality with men than in the past, men still earn much more than women on average. In 1969 the median annual earnings of women were 59 percent of what men earned. By 1985 that ratio had risen to 63.3 percent, and by 1990 to 71 percent.

The same social roles that make it difficult for women to find equal opportunity in the workplace also place great constraints on men's options for combining work and family. There is some evidence that work-family benefits are more geared toward women than men, and that more women than men use existing work-family options.

Men's work-family accommodations tend to be less visible

than women's. Unfortunately, workplace culture can create expectations for male performance that exceed "official" obligations of the job. If a father leaves work at five or five-thirty, male co-workers may joke, "Are you working part-time now?" Fathers use a number of strategies to leave work on time without appearing uncommitted: for example, the "avoid the supervisor ploy" (not leaving work until after the supervisor leaves, or parking in the back lot to avoid being seen leaving by others), and the "another meeting ploy" (saying they have to break away from work for a "meeting").

As long as men continue to earn significantly more than women, it makes greater economic sense for women to take leave, a reduction in hours, or part-time work in order to ease the family situation. Furthermore, as long as men are perceived in the workplace as uncommitted to their jobs or unmasculine when they attempt to make work-family accommodations, organizations will continue to have the upper hand.

And what if you are child-free? You may have experienced the frustration of taking up the slack for a co-worker who frequently takes time off from work to tend to children. This could involve overtime or additional travel on your part, which places an unfair burden of work on you simply because you don't have kids. Unfortunately, most companies don't have policies in place that are sensitive to the varying situations and needs of all employees.

The good news? All of these constraints and inequities can vanish when you work at home. Poof! The beauty of a work-at-home lifestyle is that partners can control their individual levels of commitment to work and family based on their desires and values, rather than what is dictated by corporations. They are free to take part in either or both domains in a sharing fashion, in whatever way they decide is fair and logical (i.e., according to each partner's desires and talents). They have control over their time and how they spend it, as well as control over their career direction and opportunities for growth and advancement.

WHAT HAPPENS WHEN MEN AND WOMEN GO ON THEIR OWN?
Unlocking the Golden Handcuffs

What happens when men and women are freed from the constraints imposed by organizations on their lives and careers? What happens when they strike out on their own and start their own enterprise? A study by Andrews and Bailyn (1993) of successful M.B.A. graduates who eventually started a business of their own provides some insight. In the two scenarios that follow, consider which approach you would lean toward in a work-at-home arrangement.

Karen and Bill received M.B.A.s from the same school in 1979. The paths they pursued during the first several years after graduation were almost identical. Karen then launched a consulting company of her own, combining experience and expertise in biotech and computers, and Bill opened the doors of his own investment company. Along the way, each of them married and began a family.

Karen's decision to strike out on her own came as a result of a reevaluation of her aspirations and priorities. She no longer cared about the "fast track," and desired an interesting way to make money and stay flexible with her time. Karen saw her work as a complement to the rest of her interests. She was able to travel extensively for pleasure for five years, and take six months off to stay with her new baby.

Karen felt that her relationship with her husband, a software developer, facilitated her progress in her career. She believed that each of their respective careers allowed them the money and time to pursue their personal interests together. Karen named her husband as her primary source of emotional support, and said she had few problems with stress.

Bill, on the other hand, mentioned three reasons for becoming an entrepreneur: dissatisfaction with corporate life, the chance to take advantage of significant business opportunities, and the need to get wealthy. Bill worked long hours and traveled extensively. He characterized his relationships with his wife and two-year-old son as "constraints" on his progress at work. Bill identified his job as his primary source of stress, affecting both his performance at work and his personal life. He stated that he had "no real support," and that he spent "no time in nonwork-related activities" outside the home.

This study of M.B.A. graduates reflects that the majority of men applied a "segmented" approach to questions about work and family. A segmented approach represents a way of categorizing the world that keeps work and family spheres separate and distinct (also known as "compartmentalized"). Because Bill was used to his work and family roles being separate in prior work capacities, he viewed the two as "clashing" and had difficulty feeling positive if they overlapped whatsoever.

In contrast, the majority of women in the study applied a "synergistic" approach to questions posed about work and family. Karen viewed her work and family domains as enhancing each other, rather than taking away from one another. The synergistic approach represents a way that many women, and some men, link work and family in a complementary fashion.

What do the results of this study tell us about working at home? The synergistic approach would most likely promote a less stressful and more satisfying experience in a home-office arrangement because it allows work and family to come together in a complementary fashion, thus resulting in an enhanced situation.

The segmented approach, on the other hand, would most likely generate stress in a home-office arrangement, especially for individuals who constantly fight to keep their work and family roles separate. How can you completely separate the two and maintain your sanity when both domains are naturally blended together under one roof? It appears that the ability to mentally integrate them, to some degree, is imperative to mastering a satisfying work-at-home arrangement.

DETERMINING YOUR RELATIONSHIP STYLE

Entrepreneurship and (to some extent) telecommuting offer ways for both women and men to escape the dilemmas created by bureaucratic organizations. These work arrangements encourage personal and occupational freedom, as well as the ability to uphold flexible relationship styles.

Three types of relationship models reflect the extent to which couples exercise traditional gender-based roles. Read through the following descriptions and decide where your relationship fits. Keep in mind that these models are aimed at dual-career hetero-sexual couples. Even if you or your partner don't currently work, choose the model that most closely represents the characteristics of your relationship. It is also possible that you and your partner may represent a role reversal of the first two models, wherein the woman takes on more of the breadwinner role while the man takes on more of the homemaker role.

In the "traditional/conventional" relationship model, both partners are involved in careers, but the responsibility for house-work and parenting is retained by the woman, who adds her career role to her traditionally held family role. Typically both partners agree that work within the home is "women's work," and men "help out" as long as doing so doesn't interfere with their career pursuits. The men in these families tend to be more professionally ambitious than their partners and usually command much higher salaries. They're also apt to view the choice of whether to combine a career with family life as belonging to women.

Those who are "nontraditional" in their gender roles do not necessarily agree that men and women must uphold traditional behaviors. These individuals comprise the "modern/participant" relationship model wherein the parenting is shared by both part-ners, but the woman retains responsibility for housework. Most characteristic of this model is the man's motivation to be an active father. Although a man desires close relations with his children, he may still see other aspects of family work as his wife's responsibility.

Those who are "androgynous" in their gender-role identity inte-grate behavior typically associated with both sexes. Androgynous indi-viduals are best suited for the "role-sharing/egalitarian" relationship model. In this model both partners actively involve themselves in household work and family life as well as career pursuits. It is suggested that androgynous partners experience fewer tensions in their daily tasks. They may be equally comfortable mowing the lawn or ironing clothes, repairing the car or cleaning the house.

The role-sharing/egalitarian model best represents the pattern many couples strive for. It is also the model that researchers initially assumed described all dual-career couples. In reality, approximately one-third of heterosexual dual-career couples are egalitarian, one-third are modern/participant, and one-third are traditional/conventional.

Some researchers have concluded that partners' relative resources (income, job prestige) determine their role in the relationship. From this perspective, the division of labor in the home is a matter of relative power of the husband and wife. Other researchers have argued that attitudes and beliefs, particularly gender-role attitudes, are the factors that determine their role in the relationship.

WHAT MAKES A HAPPY MARRIAGE?

Do the happiest marriages result from one particular relationship model? Marital satisfaction does not necessarily differ among the three types of relationship models. Couples come to these arrangements based on personal and situational factors such as desired levels of work and family involvement, available resources, and work flexibility. Satisfaction with a particular chosen model depends on these factors, as well as on the degree of congruence between each partner's gender role attitudes and behaviors, the mutuality of support between partners, and each partner's perception of fairness about the arrangements they have worked out.

Avoiding Reverse Role Behavior

Men and women in contemporary Western culture may experience marital distress because they're susceptible to different forms of attitude/behavior incongruencies. The greatest marital dissatisfaction is apparent among partners who participate in reverse role behavior. This includes husbands who hold traditional attitudes but participate in egalitarian family roles, as well as wives who hold nontraditional attitudes but participate in traditional family roles.

Wives and husbands in the same marriage may therefore report very different levels of marital satisfaction, depending on the level of congruence between their gender-role attitudes and actual family role upheld. This is a critical aspect of any relationship. If you are engaging in a role that is opposite of what you feel inside, it can have long-term negative effects on your relationship with your partner. When you work at home, these "incongruences" are even more intensified, and it's critical that they be brought out into the open and resolved.

Mutual Support

Mutual support and affirmation are also vital to the success of the dual-career marriage. Competition is associated with less marital satisfaction. Competition may result when a man needs to be better than his partner, or when he feels inadequate or threatened. Studies have revealed that a wife's high earnings affect marital satisfaction negatively. It is not assumed that the wife's employment will negatively impact the marital satisfaction of either the husband or the wife. It is generally when couples subscribe to traditional gender expectations of the woman's role at home that the wife's employment is associated with a negative impact on the relationship.

Mutual support involves valuing and affirming your partner's abilities, goals, and accomplishments as well as providing emotional support, empathic listening, and the ability to nurture. This requires putting aside your immediate needs and doing for the other. Men have previously depended on women for support and affirmation. Their ability to give women the emotional support and encouragement women traditionally give them is especially crucial to partners' satisfaction.

Perceptions of Fairness

Satisfaction is also highest when each partner perceives the arrangement as fair, regardless of the particular division of labor in the household. We touched on this briefly in the last chapter. Equality of power is not the issue, but rather the perceptions of equity or proportional returns in the exchange of personal and economic resources. Wives who view themselves as "coproviders" rather than as "helping out" with the finances feel more entitled to participation from husbands, and feel dissatisfied if they perceive their husbands as not doing their fair share of family work.

Husbands usually involve themselves more in family work when wives make greater financial contributions, and when both partners attribute greater importance to the wife's work. I found this to be true among homeworkers. Some women admit that their husbands were not supportive of their home business initially. However, their attitudes miraculously changed when the amount of money the women earned from their business reached a significant level. "It was not an easy transition at first," says Val, a travel agent. "My husband looked at it as a 'quasi-mommy' business. Once he saw the real paychecks rolling in, he was a lot better about it. Now he's proud of it." The lack of support on the part of the husbands was partially the result of brewing resentment toward their wives for having to put so many hours into their businesses, and at the same time not produce what they believed was adequate income.

The lowest levels of stress occur in marriages in which both partners are employed, both want to be employed, and both share the housework and child care. The greatest distress for both partners is found in marriages in which the wife is reluctantly employed and takes full responsibility for family work. There is also a greater likelihood of divorce and lower marital satisfaction among career-committed women. This may relate to the greater ability of financially independent women to leave unsatisfying relationships or express negative attitudes.

CROSSOVER LEARNING

The ability of couples to function effectively as partners, parents, and wage earners relates to the flexibility of their gender-role identities. Some women are more familiar with nurturing and household roles, and some men are more familiar with activities such as working with tools or doing home repairs. Given the opportunity, however, women can learn to master more instrumental behaviors, and men can learn to parent effectively, resulting in a productive sharing of the various roles performed.

When men turn over some of their provider-role responsibilities and women turn over some of their household and nurturing-role responsibilities—*both behaviorally and psychologically*—an evening out of roles between men and women can result. The ability of couples to exchange roles is termed *crossover learning* and is essential to their effective functioning in career and family roles, especially in relationships wherein both partners work.

Ideally, decisions about who has prime responsibilities for various chores can be made according to interests, capabilities, and inclinations concerning who should do which tasks so both partners feel that home roles are shared equitably. Given this scenario, partners can be a tremendous support system to one another.

This mode of shared leadership is highly characteristic of entrepreneurial couples, and does not stress a hierarchy of greater and lesser authority, but rather a "give and take" style that's satisfying for both partners. Couples who strive for a relationship that allows both partners to grow in multiple areas represent healthy role models for their children. Boys and girls alike are brought up seeing and believing that they will have equal opportunity to develop their work and family lives as they become adults. Being a homeworking parent, you are in a prime position to set this kind of example for your children.

STAYING IN TUNE WITH YOUR PARTNER

Homeworker Hint

It's hard to stay sympathetic when he comes home grumbling and upset, especially with traffic and all that. I just have to keep in mind that he has a lot more things gnawing at him during the day. For me, I've had a peaceful, wonderful, productive day, and what's the problem here? So there's an imbalance.

Lynn, Bookkeeper

After working at home for a while, it's easy to forget the stresses of working outside the home, as Lynn's scenario suggests. Home-based and corporate work styles are *so* different that it's often difficult for partners in opposite positions to come together. Having little in common, they can easily go separate ways and gradually drift apart emotionally and physically. This poses a problem in terms of the ability of couples to relate and communicate.

Connecting with Each Other

"My husband and I see each other more now that I work at home because he works nights," says Beth, an accountant. "It's not like I'm a stay-at-home mom, though. I have to work while he watches the kids during the day, so sometimes it's a tease." While Beth is feeling somewhat deprived, too much togetherness can be a pitfall for partners who both work at home. Much like other issues we've discussed, finding a happy medium is an ongoing challenge.

Just because you work at home, it doesn't mean you automatically have built-in time with your partner, especially if you have a tendency to overwork. Take advantage of your flexible arrangements by planning days off while others are working. Bob and I will take a day during the week and go to Disneyland, Sea World, or Universal Studios. The crowds are minimal and it feels like we have the entire park to ourselves. It's great fun, and a wonderful chance to be together and break up our routine.

Even when you can't take time off, you have the advantage of being at home where you can let voice mail take your calls and squeeze in some alone time together. If your partner doesn't work at home but works close by, call on the spur of the moment and plan a lunch date. Here are a few ways that you can connect with your partner and keep the spark in your relationship. I also recommend *The Book of Love, Laughter and Romance: Wonderful Suggestions and Delightful Ideas for Couples Who Want to Stay Close, Have Fun, and Keep the Enchantment Alive* (Games Partnership Ltd.), by Barbara and Michael Jonas.

SCHEDULE A REGULAR DATE NIGHT
Most homeworkers schedule a regular date night with their partner in order to enjoy some alone time together. "Every Friday night we have date night and we go out by ourselves," says

Ron, a pet product distributor. "We have to be very intentional about that."

SHARE SPONTANEOUS SURPRISES

Nothing makes a person feel more special than a gesture that comes spontaneously from the heart. Flowers and cards are nice, but so are love notes, treasure hunts, long walks, romantic sunsets, and candlelight dinners. How about a nice bottle of wine or some hot chocolate by the fire? Let your imagination run wild and go with it. Don't wait for your partner to surprise you. Make the first move and get the ball rolling. While your former co-workers are on the road or in boring meetings, you have the time and freedom to indulge your relationship.

PLAN ROMANTIC GETAWAYS

A regular date night is one opportunity to get away and relax, but sometimes you need a bigger chunk of time to escape the routines of everyday life. Schedule in some periodic getaways. If you have kids, find someone to watch them. Perhaps you can create a reciprocal child-care arrangement with another home-working couple. If you can't get away for an entire weekend, try one night, or even one day. Take advantage of your ability to travel inexpensively during the low times.

TAKE TURNS DOING THE PLANNING

When you plan date nights, surprises, or periodic getaways, take turns doing the planning. If the responsibility for all of the planning is on one partner, it takes the fun and romance out of it, not to mention the element of surprise for the partner doing all the planning. Always remember to reciprocate.

SCHEDULE ALONE TIME TOGETHER

How about scheduling in daily alone time with your partner in the morning or the evening? Couples who work at home have the advantage of staying close this way. Even if for only a few minutes, it gives you a chance to get caught up on what is going on in each other's daily lives. Some homeworkers use this time with their partner as a morning or evening ritual to segue in and out of their workday.

TIPS FOR HOMEWORKING COUPLES

Partners who go their separate ways for the day don't usually have to worry about throwing each other off the track, or getting into a heated debate during work hours. Couples who work at home, on the other hand, are constantly confronted with this challenge. The ability to communicate effectively, resolve conflicts, and create boundaries is critical. Here are some tips to help you keep your relationship and business intact.

Communicate Constantly with Your Partner

If you plan to work at home with your partner, give it a lot of thought and talk it out extensively beforehand. Jan had mixed emotions before she started working with her husband in his property-management business. Fortunately, the outcome was positive—something she attributes to good ongoing communication between them:

> I talked with a lot of women who worked with their husbands, and I wouldn't say even one of them said it was a good thing to do. They said, "Do it for as little time as possible, then get out of it. It ruins your relationship." Because of that, I'm more aware of our relationship and how work affects it. We talked about it a lot before we started the business, and we continue to talk about it. I think working together has really made our marriage stronger.

Create Guidelines

Create guidelines concerning how you and your partner will work together. Make up a schedule you'll both stick to, and keep each other abreast of any changes that occur. Many husband-and-wife teams hold daily meetings to discuss the pertinent issues at hand and plan the next day. "We talk about what we each need to do the next day workwise and homewise," says Ted, a market researcher. "With both of us working at home, we're able to work most of our business needs around the kids."

Respect Each Other's Privacy and Space

Don't constantly interrupt each other while you're working. Give your partner the same courtesy you'd give a co-worker. If you maintain separate offices, you can always close the door when you don't want to be disturbed. If you don't mind frequent interruptions, that's fine too. Just make sure you're vocal about your needs, and respect each other's desires and differences.

If you share an office, you'll run the risk of getting in each other's way, especially if you don't maintain two sets of equipment. How will you time-share so each person has fair access? One solution is to start and end your workdays at different times.

Many couples who share an office also stagger their work schedules to have an opportunity to work alone or spend some personal time alone while their partner is working. Since you'll be together a lot, it's healthy for your relationship to schedule regular time apart. After all, absence does make the heart grow fonder.

Is one of you messy and the other neat? If so, what ground rules will you establish so you both perceive the situation as fair and comfortable? Mary, an insurance agent who works with her husband in the business, says his messiness took over the entire office they occupied together. "It was getting out of control," she groans. "His clutter was like one of those 'Creeping Charley' plants. When he started using my desk as additional storage for his mess, I moved my office into the dining room. I couldn't take it anymore."

Does one or both of you talk loudly on the phone, creating a tremendous distraction for the other? I remember when Bob and I shared a small work space for a brief period. He is great on the phone with clients, but is he ever *loud.* When I was on the phone next to him, the person on the other end of my conversation thought he was on our line. Needless to say, that arrangement didn't last. Just make sure you and your partner love each other's company and cute little quirks. Otherwise, you'll get on each other's nerves real quick.

Put Your Relationship First

It's not easy to share an office with anyone. If you decide to share with your partner and the situation isn't working, save your relationship and relocate one of your desks to another work space. If you're working together in the business (even in separate offices) and the situation isn't working out, period, terminate your work relationship before it destroys your personal relationship.

Always put your relationship first over the business. Realize that sharing your work and personal lives is a tremendous challenge—one that most couples wouldn't dream of taking on. It takes a strong, open, and caring relationship built on belief and trust in yourselves and each other in order to be happy and productive. Realize that the ups and downs of working together are normal and healthy realities that all couples face. It's when the downs related to your business relationship are far more prevalent than the ups that you should seriously consider ending your working relationship.

Don't Let Business Take over Your Personal Time

When you work at home together, be careful about how you spend your personal time. Don't fall into the trap of allowing your precious time together to serve as a business meeting unless you both agree to spend your evening alone that way.

Have Fun

Being able to work with your partner at home can be a wonderful experience. You have someone to share, brainstorm, and joke around with. Have fun and use your sense of humor with each other, just as you would in any office situation. Take advantage of the opportunity to spend time together and enjoy yourselves. Play hooky every once in a while and go to an afternoon matinee. The spontaneous escape from work will do wonders for your relationship.

Be Positive

Always strive to maintain a positive attitude around each other. When it's just the two of you, if one person is negative, it will drag the other down and create resentment. In an outside office you can escape negativity from co-workers a lot easier than when it's constantly in front of you in a home office. Be an inspiration to each other, not a hindrance.

Keep Work and Personal Affairs Separate

It's a good idea to establish boundaries concerning too much talk about business after work hours. This is one area that causes problems between partners who work at home. They have difficulty leaving work behind because not only is their office at home, so is their co-worker.

"A lot of times my husband will want to keep talking until ten at night about clients, and I'll change the subject because it's too much," explains Mary, an insurance agent. "I'm excited about our business too, but I want to incorporate our friends and family into the discussion so work doesn't become our total focus." Amy, a computer software distributor, has strict boundaries about work discussions after hours. "My husband would still be pumped to do it," she says. "I just say to him, 'I don't want to answer any more questions. It's after five P.M. and I won't.' "

Of course, the same is true in reverse. Don't allow your personal affairs to infiltrate your work environment. If you and your partner have a personal conflict, settle it outside of your home office during nonwork times. Your relationship and business will crumble if you don't establish clear boundaries and guidelines defining when and where it's safe to resolve work and personal conflicts independently of one another. The two don't mix. (For more information on strategies for homeworking partnerships, see Chapter 10.)

RESOLVING CONFLICTS

Conflict is a normal and healthy aspect of any close relationship, but it can be an increased threat to your level of happiness and productivity in a work-at-home arrangement. For homeworking couples in particular, it can be difficult (if not impossible) to work in the same household when you're at odds with each other.

When you work at home and have unresolved conflicts with your partner, it can have a negative impact on your work performance even if you don't work at home together. Let's say that I work at home and my husband, Bob, works somewhere else. One morning we have an argument that doesn't get resolved. Bob goes off to work where he occupies a different environment, surrounded by people and events that take his mind off of our morning tiff. He has people asking things of him. His day is cut out for him. He is swept away from the scene of our disagreement, both mentally and physically.

I, on the other hand, must face the day alone with my own thoughts. Wouldn't you know that on this particular day when I long for interruptions, nothing and no one distracts me? Not only that, I'm constantly reminded of our disagreement because I don't physically leave the scene of our spat. When you work at home, unresolved differences are magnified tenfold. Therefore, it's critical that you and your partner be able to work through differences quickly when they arise, otherwise you may find yourself "stewing" instead of "doing" your work.

How much conflict you have with your partner is not so much the issue, but rather how you handle it. Decide together how you will resolve conflicts when they arise. When an issue is so heated that a conversation easily escalates into an argument, you need to have ground rules describing how you and your partner will handle the situation before it spirals out of control.

Every couple is different, so it's important that you identify strategies that work for both of you. Ground rules for conflict resolution can include "check-ins" and "check-outs." Check-ins consist of "I" statements made by partners periodically to indicate where they are with respect to the conflict process. Take responsibility by always using "I" statements when a conflict arises. Don't blame your partner for what you feel because this will only encourage defensiveness and distance. You can only account for your own feelings.

When you or your partner realize that a conflict is stuck, destructive, or abusive, check out of the situation by calling a "time-out." Sometimes withdrawing from the conflict allows emotions to calm so you can discuss the issue in a more rational manner. If either of you calls a time-out, establish a time you will reconnect to resolve your disagreement as soon as possible. Don't think that time apart is all you need to heal the wounds.

Loving relationships tend to have sensitive issues that stir up emotions. To avoid hurt, it's often easier to ignore certain subjects. This approach puts a wedge between two people because anger and resentment grow in silence. Don't hide your feelings.

When things get heated, sometimes light humor helps. If you find that no matter what, you can't seem to carry on a civil discussion with your partner, then write your partner a letter describing your thoughts and feelings, but again, using only "I" statements. Offer a constructive next step you would like to take to resolve the issue. If writing doesn't appeal to you, try talking on tape to your partner. For more helpful strategies, read *Getting Past No: Negotiating Your Way from Confrontation to Cooperation* (Bantam), by William Ury.

Sometimes an issue is too sensitive to handle alone, and outside help is necessary. If all your efforts to resolve a particular conflict end in stalemate, consider finding a good therapist who specializes in conflict resolution for couples.

SETTING JOINT GOALS

When you can handle conflicts, it makes the task of setting goals much easier. Set joint goals that incorporate the desires of you and your partner. How much time together do you each desire? If you differ, how can you compromise? Take turns discussing your feelings about pertinent issues, and come to an agreement you're both satisfied with. You may want to put things in writing and make a copy for both of you to reread and update periodically.

Couples who maintain a close bond agree that their relationship comes first (over work) and act accordingly. They also have a high degree of intimate communication. They tend to complement each other's talents and attitudes, and constantly put their egos in check. When it comes to decision making, they use positive strategies such as turn taking when speaking and listening, and compromising while discussing various solutions.

Your work-at-home transition will be much smoother if you develop good communication skills with your partner from the beginning. This in turn will allow you to take advantage of the many ways that working at home can enhance your relationship.

CHAPTER SEVEN

Establishing Rules, Boundaries, and Schedules

✐ Homeworker Hint

There's no line of demarcation like there is when you leave and come home. Sometimes it's a struggle deciding what takes priority, the business or the family. If you're taking business calls at eight-thirty at night when you should be handling your daughter and her story time, then you're not in balance at all, and everything will suffer.

Sara, Fitness Trainer

It's common knowledge that working couples experience difficulties when their family life spills over into their work life and vice versa. The situation is aggravated by confusion over changing gender roles, particularly the issue of who is responsible for what between partners. Being pulled in multiple directions takes a toll on relationships, as the high divorce rate unfortunately reveals.

If couples working outside the home experience a spillover

effect, how must it be for homeworkers who continually have their work and family domains combined in one setting? How do they accomplish *anything* in either arena?

This chapter offers insight and strategies for maintaining your sanity in a home office environment. Since you won't be commuting to work each day, it is mandatory that you mark and protect your work time and space through the creation of rules, boundaries, and schedules that are tailored to your needs. Now is a good time to pull out your journal and review your writings from the early chapters. In this chapter you'll have the opportunity to implement what you learned so that you can lay the foundation for work-at-home satisfaction and success.

COMMUNICATING WITH CHILDREN

Homeworker Hint

Keep in constant communication with your kids. Let them know you really love them, that you're trying very hard to achieve something, and you'll be there as soon as you can. Talk about it before you get into it—the difficulties and the benefits.

Carol, Architectural Illustrator

Lisa, a medical transcriptionist, emphasizes the importance of considering the family in running a home business. "It has to be a group effort. It's not just you and your business, it's your whole family in a lot of ways."

Ideally a home business can be set up in a way that allows for maximum satisfaction for the entire family and maximum productivity for the homeworker. But what happens when children don't understand that their parent is home but not available? "Sometimes it's hard for them to understand that when dad gets to be with them in the afternoon, he has to make up for it at night," says John, a graphic designer. "They're frustrated when I'm home and not available. I get so focused on my business, it's hard to fit parenting into that."

It is imperative that you teach your kids to respect your work time and space. The best way to do this is to set limits and guidelines right from the start.

Setting Limits and Guidelines

Homeworker Hint

The kids need to see Mommy working. It makes them want to become independent. You have to set limits and guidelines. You have to tell them, "This is what it's going to be, this is how it's going to be," and you have to stick to it. Once they get used to it, you're pretty much set.

Wendy, Newspaper Editor

Depending on the ages and personalities of your children, what kind of rules of order can you realistically and fairly expect your kids to follow? You want to be able to achieve your daily work goals but at the same time allow for a family-friendly environment, especially if being closer to your family ranks high on your list of reasons for working at home. In your journal write down guidelines you wish to implement in your home during work hours. Here are a few examples of common guidelines homeworkers establish with their children:

- No TV or stereo allowed during work hours.
- Unless something is urgent, do not interrupt.
- Do not touch office equipment without asking.
- Do not answer the business phone.
- Dress and feed yourself in the mornings.
- Pack your lunch each day.
- Do your daily chores without prompting or complaining.
- Do your homework without prompting or complaining.
- Keep noise levels down during work hours.
- Control noisy pets.

Again, the rules you implement must be realistically tailored to the ages and temperament of your children. Most children have to be about four or five before they can comprehend that an open office door means "Come on in," and a closed office door means "Do not disturb." The preceding examples may give you something to strive for as your children develop. Much like delegating household chores, household rules can also be expanded with age.

Remember, kids will be kids, and you shouldn't be too disappointed when they challenge you or break the rules from time to time. Because the children of homeworking parents actually see their parents working, they may express more resentment (e.g., crying, whining, accusations, slamming doors, frequently interrupting your work) than kids whose parents work outside the home. When you are interrupted and must stop your work, write a note to yourself indicating where you left off and what remains to be done. This way you'll be able to pick right back up as soon as you return.

Help Your Children Understand

There are many effective ways to help your children understand and respect your work obligations. Depending on your child's age and personality, try one of the following strategies. Also, *The Gentle Art of Communicating With Kids* (John Wiley & Sons), by Suzette Elgin, is an excellent general resource on this topic.

FOSTER EMPATHY

Ron, a pet product distributor, had difficulty conveying to his six-year-old son that he needed undisturbed time to concentrate on his work. Ron decided to involve his son in finding the solution:

> *There were times when Jeff would be totally inappropriate. I'd be on the phone talking with a client, and he'd walk in and start jumping on me, happy to see Daddy. He didn't understand that this was my workroom. I was getting really mad, so I said to him, "What do you suggest? How can we solve this?" He came up with this little stop-light thing made out of cardboard. If it's a green light, it's okay to walk in and jump in my lap. If it's a yellow light, he'll know he needs to check first to see where Daddy's at, and if it's a red light, he turns around and goes the other way.*

*He knows that a red light means I'm seriously dealing with
something. It works, and it protects my work space.*

Ron fostered empathy in his son by encouraging him to relate
to his dilemma, and also sparked him to use his problem-solving
and negotiation abilities by asking for his advice. This made his
son feel important because his dad cared enough to ask his opin-
ion, rather than simply scold him or label him a "pest." While
Ron's approach may take time and effort, look at the valuable
skills you are teaching your children. You are involving them in
the solution and preventing hurt feelings or misunderstandings.

HAVE MUTUAL RESPECT

Be clear with your children about your needs and encourage them
to do the same. It is critical that you have mutual respect and
that you take each other seriously, but understand that it takes
time to develop because kids tend to forget rules when they're
excited. Even if your kids do interrupt, don't make the mistake
of taking out your work frustrations on them. This will only
create distance and stress between you. Instead, focus on the
positive. When you accomplish three hours of uninterrupted
work, spend a half hour of quality time with your children—
allowing them to create the agenda.

BRING IT TO THEIR LEVEL

Wendy, a newspaper editor and mother of two young boys, suggests that regardless of your child's age, you find ways to communicate on their level:

*The toddler stage is the hardest. That's when you've got to
start setting limits. It takes time, though. You need to tell
them, "Look, I'm busy, I can't read to you right now. You
have to respect that Mommy has to do this. If you want
these nice little toys, you have to leave Mommy alone so
she can make the money to buy these nice little toys." I
bring it down to their level so they understand.*

OFFER EXPLANATIONS

Don't just lay down the law, explain the rationale behind any
rules or guidelines you implement. You may have to do a lot of

explaining at first, but give them the gift of time and patience. They'll eventually come through without having to ask "Why?" As you initiate boundaries for yourself, you are acting as a role model for your children. They will learn that having boundaries and asking others to respect them is healthy behavior that preserves self-esteem and confidence.

REINFORCE GUIDELINES WHEN KIDS FORGET

Several homeworkers stress that setting up rules or boundaries to enable them to work when their children are present is a constant battle—one that takes tremendous time and patience. Ben, a marketing consultant, describes his struggle with his kids, who consistently forget the rules he's established:

> *The only problem is when I'm on the phone—noise levels, things like that. Sometimes when it's a screaming dogfight and I'm getting a phone call, we have to go back over the rules. Everybody interferes because I'm in my shorts, and not my suit and tie. Unfortunately, communication usually takes place after the damage is done.*

POST YOUR WORK SCHEDULE

Always let your children know your work schedule. Put it on paper, read it to your kids, and post it in a prominent place. If your children interrupt during your work hours, remind them of your schedule. Tell them you will be with them as soon as you take your next break or finish for the day.

WHEN DESPERATE, BRIBE

Mary, an insurance agent and mother of two young boys, admits that sometimes when she's on the phone and her son interrupts or gets noisy, she resorts to bribery:

> *They're just getting to the point where they'll keep quiet and wait until I'm off the phone. It's taken a while. I tell my four-year-old, "If you don't say a peep while Mommy's on the phone, I'll play a game with you on my break." Children are children, and they interrupt.*

CREATING PHYSICAL AND PSYCHOLOGICAL BOUNDARIES

✎ Homeworker Hint

Be sure to separate your work and family. Set aside time to spend with your family. Don't delve into your business eighteen hours a day, and just sleep the other six.

John, Graphic Designer

Homeworkers attempt to either separate work and family activities, or successfully intermingle them. This process takes a lot of trial and error in order to find what works best.

Choosing a Suitable Work Space

How do you envision your work space? Many factors come into play when making this decision. Look back at your journal notes from the first three chapters. Are you able to focus or are you easily distracted? Do you require privacy? The work spaces of homeworkers are generally designed to suit their personality and the household space available.

CAN YOU SWING A PRIVATE OFFICE?

Most homeworkers have a private office with a door they can close. A closed door will tell your family "Do not disturb" when work is in progress. It also represents a "Closed" sign to homeworkers when they leave the office and are done with work for the day. You might even want to hang an "Open/Closed" or "Do not disturb" sign on your office door to let your family know when you do not want to be interrupted:

We made a conscious decision when we bought this house, to make sure that we had a separate bedroom that could serve as an office. I think that's really important for me psychologically. You need some sort of separation to survive long term.

BE SURE TO LOCK IT UP AT NIGHT

A closed door discourages curious toddlers from entering the private office unsupervised. If you have older children, you'll probably need to lock the door. Jill, a desktop publisher, found this out the hard way:

> *I had a few disasters. My son renamed a hard drive one day, put a disk in backwards, and when that got stuck, he hit the wrong button on my terminal and zapped my hard drive, which I had to replace.*

Homeworkers with their own offices say that having the ability to close off the rest of the home is the most critical step they took toward separating their work and family lives. Many indicate that their eventual goal is to have an office that is entirely separate—with its own private entrance.

CONSIDERING A SHARED OR OPEN WORK SPACE

Many homeworkers have offices in a child's room, a den, or the dining area. Some home offices occupy a room in the house that's central and open to adjacent rooms. Most homeworkers who occupy a shared or open office eventually plan to set up their own office when they can add on or move to a larger home.

If a shortage of work space is an issue for you, please note that some of the most organized and functional home offices are not private. With the clever use of bookshelves, wall units, folding curtains, and plants, you can make even the most open of work spaces seem private. Also, by keeping excessive clutter to a minimum, you can make the most of an open or shared work space (or *any* work space, for that matter).

On the other hand, you may be like other homeworkers, such as Wendy, a newspaper editor, who are happy with a shared or open office because they like being in the mainstream of things:

> *I had a private office for a while. I found that I don't like being in enclosed places. I like having all this stuff going on around me. I think it's better that I've integrated it into the family room. If my kids are in here playing and I'm working, as long as they're playing independently without bothering me, that's fine. It's like a regular kindergarten*

here with paints, colors, you name it. There are plenty of things for them to do. I grew up in a family of four kids, so I learned to tune stuff out. My power of concentration is very strong.

Savvy Telephone Tricks

Homeworker Hint

Set boundaries with your family from the beginning. Get a voice mail/ pager system.

Ann, Personal Image Consultant

ONE PHONE LINE OR TWO?

Can you afford to install a second phone line in your home? Can you afford not to? We discussed business image in Chapter 3, and depending on whether you desire a strictly professional image or are comfortable with a more loosely run approach, you'll probably have your answer. Other considerations are how much you desire to separate your work and family roles, and the amount of client phone calls coming into your home.

Background noise can be a real threat to your business image. "I had a big client, and he gave no leeway for kids yelling in the background while he was trying to talk," says Jill, a desktop publisher. "It goes from bad to worse when the kids pick up the phone, and it's not cute. And then there are the dogs. They bark, and I can't get them to shut up without yelling at them . . . a real problem when clients call."

To maintain their professionalism, most homeworkers have at least two phone lines in the house, with one devoted to business calls and one devoted to personal calls. Candace, a small-business consultant, has six phone lines dedicated to business: two lines for incoming and outgoing calls, a fax line, a line for modem use, a line for client use, and a mobile cellular line. "All my phones are ringing constantly," she says. "If I tied up my two business lines with all the faxing and modem activities I do, my business would fold up quickly."

Homeworkers rely heavily on a voice-mail system or answering machine. "That's a big psychological thing, getting the appropriate equipment,'' says Phil, an attorney. ''You've got to have something that allows you the freedom to walk away.''

Val and her partner work three days a week opposite of each other. When one partner has the day off, the business phone is forwarded to the other partner who is working that day, so that the partner who has the day off is entirely free of business responsibilities. ''We forward the phones back and forth between offices, depending on who's on for the day,'' says Val. ''That way when each of us has a day off, we're really off.''

You may decide you can't afford a second line, and depending on the kind of work you do, you may be able to pull it off. Some homeworkers have so few clients they don't feel the need for a second line.

Homeworkers with one phone line tend to answer their phone with their business name, and have a message reflecting their business on a tape machine when they're not available to take calls. ''There's just a business line, no home line,'' says Pat, a newspaper publisher. ''The kids are usually really polite about answering the phone with the business name and saying, 'One moment please.' '' If young children will be answering your business phone, be sure to rehearse with them what to say. Toddlers, however, will find it hard to distinguish between business and personal acquaintances.

Some homeworkers can't afford to miss business calls and generally take them at all hours, any day of the week. ''I'll take business calls at any hour,'' says Sue, a medical transcriptionist. ''If people want my attention, I still put the business first. I feel a sense of obligation to do that.''

The type of business you have and the number of incoming client calls you envision will help you decide whether to have one or two phone lines, and whether to take business calls during off hours. Also, consider the kind of business image you wish to portray when deciding to go with one phone line or two.

USING VOICE MAIL TO PRESERVE FAMILY TIME

Do you want to be able to clearly separate your work and family roles? Most homeworkers do not take business calls when they want to tend to their families or need concentrated time to focus on their work. The use of a voice-mail system allows them to return calls at their discretion, thus establishing a boundary with clients. "Basically, what I do when my son is awake during the day is leave the phones forwarded to my voice mail," reveals Beth, an accountant. "When he's down taking a nap, I unforward the phone and clients can talk to me."

TURN THE RINGER OFF OR UNPLUG THE PHONE

This method may sound a little drastic, but it works for some homeworkers who are desperate to get work done and preserve their concentration. Jean, a computer research analyst, claims she cannot concentrate when her personal phone rings during work time. "I just can't let the machine take calls," says Jean. "I either want to listen in or pick up the phone. It was interfering with my work productivity until I finally turned the ringer off so I wouldn't hear the calls. I now have established times that I check personal messages and return those calls. Fortunately, that has allowed me to focus 100 percent of my efforts on my work."

Val, a travel agent, has absolutely no problem keeping the ringer off while she's working, and she does it regularly. "When I'm at work, I'm at work," she says. "If it's a dire emergency and I'm waiting for a call from the pediatrician, I'll turn the ringer on. Otherwise, the ringer on my personal line stays off. If I don't have those boundaries, my business dies and I no longer have a job. It's called survival."

Laura, a freelance writer, unplugs her personal phone when she's on deadline and needs to concentrate. However, if you decide to regularly unplug or turn off the ringer on your phone, carry a pager so your loved ones can reach you in case of an emergency.

KEEP A RECORDING OF A RINGING PHONE HANDY

Kevin, a real estate agent who does a lot of cold-calling for business, devised a clever strategy that allows him to gracefully end long-winded phone conversations with acquaintances or "go nowhere" prospects who are wasting his precious work time. "I tape-recorded the sound of a phone ringing," says Kevin. "Whenever I need to get off the phone in a hurry, I just put my little recorder up to the mouthpiece, hit play, and say, 'Oops! There's my other line, and I'm expecting a call. It's been nice talking with you.' "

USE A SPEAKER PHONE OR HEADSET

In Chapter 5 I recommended using a telephone headset to carry on personal conversations while you handle domestic responsibilities such as food preparation. If your work requires a lot of telephone work, try using a headset or a speaker phone so you can keep your hands free to accomplish mindless, routine tasks such as preparing mailers or cleaning your desk. This will relieve strain on your neck from endless hours of cradling a phone on your shoulder. Chris, a magazine publisher, was grateful for her speaker phone when she had to nurse her newborn daughter during a conference call with a client. "This guy was really cool," she says. "He knew I was calling from home and he said, 'What are you doing right now?' and I said, 'I don't think you want to know.' I still laugh about that to this day."

Preventing "Drop-in" Client Visits

Homeworkers suggest establishing firm boundaries with clients about "drop-in" visits, in an effort to eliminate surprises that catch you off guard. "I've designated days I have an open-door policy for my customers," says Ann, a personal image consultant. "That has helped tremendously in cutting down on unplanned drop-in visits."

Jill, a desktop publisher, recommends being firm about your workdays and hours with clients:

> I told my friends who are also clients, "I work Monday, Wednesday, and Friday. Tuesday and Thursday, I'm a mom and you'll get a kid when you call. I don't do business on those days." To other people who are not my friends but are clients, what I say is, "I work in the studio Monday, Wednesday, and Friday during business hours. On Tuesday and Thursday, those are my days to do all my pickups and deliveries. I'm not in the office during those hours. You can't reach me, except by voice mail."

In Southern California there are organizations that offer another solution for frequent client visits. For a minimal fee they provide a mailing address in an elegant office complex that's centrally located, along with the use of their private conference facilities for meetings with clients. Do some checking to see if similar resources exist in your area.

A WORD ABOUT PETS

A chapter on boundaries wouldn't be complete without a word about pets in a work-at-home situation. Pets are wonderful sources of friendship and companionship, but as many home-workers know, they can also be a tremendous distraction. Dogs barking and cats jumping on computer monitors can surely wreak havoc in your home office.

I recently lost my eighteen-year-old canine companion. She slept by my chair constantly while I worked. I cherished her company. She required very little to be happy in exchange for tons of unconditional love. Six months after she died, Bob and I broke down and bought a ten-week-old puppy. Wow! Did our work production decline. Since we both work at home, we take turns caring for Katie, tiring her out (so we can work) and training her so she gets housebroken as soon as possible. Because we work at home, it's especially critical that Katie behaves. We're enrolling her in "puppy kindergarten" so she learns good manners from the start.

If you have pets with bad habits that interfere with your work, consider professional training that focuses on behavior modification. If you're working full-time and running a household, you probably won't have the time, energy, or patience to deal with it yourself.

Distractions and interruptions from pets can be a real detriment to your work, not to mention a turnoff to clients who call or pay a visit to your home office. You don't want loud barking dogs or pets that jump all over your clients during an important meeting when you're about to make a deal.

Do what you can to keep your animals in line. Since everyone isn't an animal lover, you may want to keep them outside or in a separate area when clients are around. Like kids, pets need discipline and boundaries. They also need lots of love and attention—or they'll let you know about it at the *worst* possible moments. Take responsibility and see to it that your pets are well trained and respectful of your work space and clients. In the long run you'll all be happier for it.

IMPLEMENTING PERSONAL RULES OF CONDUCT

Kids and pets aren't the only ones who need to know what is expected of them. When you work at home it's critical that you know what you expect of yourself. Homeworkers implement a variety of personal rules on a regular basis to help them feel more satisfied and accomplished in their work and personal lives. In fact, some take things one step further and put their personal rules in writing.

The following are examples of the most common rules homeworkers implement. Consider your own position on each, writing down in your journal any rules you wish to follow in your home office arrangement.

Handling Personal Phone Calls

There are a variety of ways to handle personal phone calls while you work, and it's best to establish a rule concerning this from the start. Otherwise, you may find your work hours dwindling away as you talk on the phone with family and friends. About half of the homeworkers I spoke with have a firm rule that they don't answer their personal phone while working. "When I'm on the phone with a client, the client gets my full attention," says Paul, an environmental product distributor. "I don't take personal phone calls. I just keep working."

IF YOU TAKE PERSONAL CALLS, BE FRIENDLY BUT FIRM

Another rule for handling phone calls is to take personal calls while working and keep them brief, offering to call back later. People eventually understand that their friend or loved one is working and not available during certain times of the day. This understanding alleviates hard feelings.

Most homeworkers emphasize honesty up front. "I've learned to just tell them, 'Ya know, I'm on deadline right now. Let me take your number and I'll call you back after six P.M.,' " says Jim, a fund-raising consultant. "All my friends have gotten used to it by now. It's not a problem and they don't feel put off by it." Sara was very direct in her approach. "It was up to me to communicate to my friends not only what they meant to me, but that there was no quality time while they were here during my work time unless we set that up separately. They finally got that."

No Housework

We talked earlier about managing your time by integrating housework into your workday. Most women make a habit of doing this quite effectively. On the other hand, many women and most of the men I interviewed have a rule about not doing housework during working hours. "I have set times I work," says Mary, an insurance agent. "I don't empty dishwashers, I don't wipe off counters. These things allow for creative avoidance. It's much easier to empty dishwashers than make phone calls. If I were in an office, I wouldn't be watering plants or doing laundry, so why should I do it here?"

No Breaks

Depending on your schedule and what works best for you, you may not wish to take breaks during your workday if you need to make the most of the quiet time you have. Many homeworkers don't take breaks while they work in order to make the best use of their time, especially when kids are not present. "I don't take breaks," says Bob, a financial adviser. "I can get more out of five hours than most people get out of eight. Prime time for me is between eight-thirty and two-thirty when the kids are gone and it's totally quiet. I can put in a good concentrated effort."

Take a Break

If, on the other hand, you're working long hours, it's probably best to establish a rule of taking breaks during your low-energy periods. This is a good time to take a walk around the block, check your mail, or catch up on a little personal reading. Making a habit of giving yourself well-deserved breaks throughout the day will rejuvenate you so that you don't sit in a stupor wasting time at your desk.

Learn your energy cycles and know when you need to walk away for a designated break time. If necessary, set a clock (or timer) and time your breaks so you don't overindulge in household distractions that can keep you off track.

Kevin, a real estate agent, takes a regular three-hour "siesta break" during his workday. He works a split shift from 8:00 A.M. to noon and from 3:00 to 7:00 P.M. During his three-hour break from noon to 3:00 P.M., he spends time with his three-year-old son. They make lunch together and go to the playground or an afternoon matinee—often with ice cream afterward. Although Kevin doesn't normally nap during his siesta break, this daily three-hour time slot allows him to spend quality time with his son during the low-traffic times. "It works out great," says Kevin. "Bobby and I can goof off together during the day while everyone else is working the eight-to-five grind."

No Personal Computer Activities

Many homeworkers have strict rules about personal computer use during work hours. Laura, a freelance writer, admits that once she got E-mail on her system, she became obsessed with checking and answering her messages all day while she was supposed to be working. "I know it was a way for me to avoid work," confesses Laura. "But it's also the nature of my work. Being an author, the isolation was getting to me, but I've since taken care of that. Now I have set times in the evening when I handle my personal messages or do frivolous on-line work. I wasn't accomplishing a thing until I put restrictions on myself."

No TV

If you're a "TV junkie," another popular rule that proves to be effective among homeworkers is "No access to TV during work hours." "I don't allow myself to go upstairs where the TV is during my work time," says Jenny, a secretarial service provider. "That part of the house is off limits because it's too tempting to turn on my favorite talk shows."

Carol, an architectural illustrator, attributes her strong self-discipline to the fact that she hates TV. At nights while her husband and son are glued to the set downstairs, she's productive at work in her private office upstairs. If you have favorite TV shows that are on during the day, you can always tape them and watch them during your off hours. It's much more time-effective to watch "Oprah" in forty minutes (without commercials) instead of an hour. Plus, it will give you something to look forward to, and a chance to wind down your workday.

Work During Peak Energy Periods

This rule goes hand in hand with the "take a break" rule because it allows you to maximize your work performance when you're at your best. If you know your peak energy periods are in the afternoons, don't make a habit of slipping off to the afternoon bargain matinee to catch the latest flick. Productive homeworkers make it a rule to work when their energy levels are highest. "There are certain times of the day when I'm more productive, when I have more energy," says Jim, a fund-raising consultant. "By 3:00 P.M. I start to fade, and then I get a second wind at night. I sometimes work until 3:00 A.M.; however, I try to do less demanding, less creative work as the night wears on."

Dress for Success

How do you feel about having a dress code for yourself? After all, isn't one of the greatest advantages of working at home the ability to work in your shorts and T-shirt, or even your bathing suit (after a quick dip in your neighbors' pool while they're at work)? Most homeworkers dress up for work when they have an important meeting with clients, and that's it. A minority, however, have a strict rule about always dressing up for work, regardless of whether they're meeting clients. "Ninety-nine percent of the time I get dressed up,'' says Sara, a fitness trainer. ''It affects how I communicate over the phone because I come across as more confident. I'm used to dressing up and I work better when I do. It puts me in the right mind-set for work.''

No Work During Vacations

Some homeworkers don't handle work matters while on vacation. They have someone cover for them while they're gone. Those who do conduct business during vacations primarily return phone calls, keeping their business activities to a minimum. Depending on whether you'll be working for yourself or for someone else, if you can implement the ''no work during vacation'' rule, you'll relieve much stress from your life. Everyone needs a chance to take an extended break away from work every now and then. So if you can swing it, by all means find a way to do it, for you and your family.

MANAGING YOUR SCHEDULE WISELY

 Homeworker Hint

I think that people need to create a ritual or a set schedule that allows them enough cornerstones to be anchored. When you work at home, you don't want to be completely flexible at first because you'll find that you sometimes shirk the responsibilities because you love the freedoms. I think you just have to understand that you need to do certain things each day. Once you do that, you become accustomed to it.

Ted, Market Researcher

Successful homeworkers are master schedulers. They find creative ways to juggle their work, household, and family activities by effectively integrating or compartmentalizing them. The importance of considering their family in this juggling act is vital to the process of establishing boundaries and gaining the respect of others. Of course, you must consider yourself first and foremost in this process. Under what kind of schedule do you work best? Do you like to jump into your workday or ease your way in with a slow and smooth transition? The main goal of this section is to help you decide the best schedule for you.

Regardless of the schedule you choose, most homeworkers have a morning and evening ritual to start and end their workday. These rituals replace the "commute" between home and work, often cited as a useful interlude among people working outside the home. Rituals not only spark motivation but they also serve as ways to relax or manage stress, topics we'll touch on further in the next chapter.

Use Rituals to Ease in and out of Your Workday

Homeworkers don't have the forced rituals of shaving, showering, and dressing that millions of commuting office workers experience between 6:00 and 7:00 A.M. daily. Therefore, self-created rituals represent a similar line crossed—an experience unique to the individual—marking the end of one role and the beginning of another.

Most homeworkers have a regular ritual they perform prior to starting, or just before ending, their workday. The rituals can be as simple as having a cup of coffee and reading the newspaper prior to starting work, or turning off the computer, clearing the desk, and closing the office door at the end of a workday. A few homeworkers pray in the morning before starting work. Bob says, "I'll read a devotional or I'll pray about the day in the morning." Some take a walk at the end of their workday. Others use exercise, dressing and grooming, journaling, or tidying the house as their morning or evening rituals.

"When I pick the mail up, that's when I start my day," says Ron, a pet product distributor. "When I drop off my product for shipping at UPS, that's when I'm done." Other rituals are quite unique. Remember Sara, the fitness trainer who regularly dresses up for work? She performs an evening ritual that clearly marks the end of her work role, similar to those working outside the home. "At the end of my workday, I peel off my bra, I go upstairs and put on the most yucky, ripped-up T-shirt, and sit around looking like the biggest slob in the world, but I feel like I'm done," Sara says.

What type of rituals would work for you as you begin or end your workday? Some people don't use rituals because they can't spare the time. Homeworkers with very young children, for instance, often prefer to jump in and out of work when the opportunity strikes. Rituals don't have to be time-consuming, however, and they can serve a very positive purpose.

Lisa, a medical transcriptionist, and Phil, an attorney, both feel that not having a ritual is to their detriment, but for opposite reasons. "Not having a morning ritual is my biggest problem because I have nothing to get me going," says Lisa. "I haven't figured out what my trigger is. I really don't know what motivates me, other than if I don't work, I won't make any money." On the other hand, Phil never feels finished because he does nothing to symbolize the end of his workday. "I don't have an end-of-the-day ritual," he reveals. "So that's why my day drifts into the evening."

Choose a Suitable Work Schedule

 Homeworker Hint

Set up a routine! The hardest thing is getting a work routine set up. It's hard for the family to see you in a home situation and not have them as your main focus.

Beth, Accountant

What type of schedule would work best for you? The following are homeworkers' descriptions of five different types of work schedules, ranging from no routine, to a flexible schedule spread out over various days and nights (including evenings and weekends), to a traditional eight-to-five schedule with evenings and weekends off. See what homeworkers have to say. Then decide on the schedule that suits you best, given your work style and your personal needs.

FLEX SCHEDULE

Most homeworkers with kids at home fall into the *flex schedule* category. Generally, these individuals start work at a specific time each day, and then tailor their work schedules around their children's activities or needs. Work and family activities are intertwined, with the schedule and needs of the children taking precedence during the day so that parents can work at night while their kids are asleep or being watched by their partner. "I work around his naps," explains Kevin, a real estate agent. "I'm like a sprinter for one or two hours. I keep a long list of things to accomplish during that time, and sometimes I get more done than I do in an entire day."

Homeworkers in the flex-schedule group tend to not make business phone calls when their children are present. All but a few in this category work on the weekends. "With a toddler, flexibility is the key," says Carol, an architectural illustrator. "I think I've become much more efficient. I had all this time before and never utilized it." A recurring pattern among this group is that light housework is incorporated into their workday, whether serving as a time-management strategy or a distraction to "creatively avoid" work.

Chris, a magazine publisher whose work style is a good representation of the flex category, describes how her workday evolves around the needs of her two-year-old daughter:

> *I'll get up at 6:00 A.M. and work for a couple hours before my daughter gets up, and I'll work for two or three hours at night after dinner. You have to find those hidden hours. It's all planned around my daughter, so every day is different. Last week she was sick and that killed the whole day. At two and a half they can be diverted for short periods of time, fifteen or twenty minutes, but then you have to sit down and play with them. I work sometimes when I can do routine tasks like mailing brochures or putting stamps on, things I can do while she's playing here. I don't even attempt to do phone calls while she's around.*

A common strategy among the flex-schedule group involves taking time away from work to fulfill personal or familial needs, and making up the time later. "My day is scattered. I can pick and choose and work whenever I want," says Ron, a pet product distributor. "During the day I may take an hour and go get some exercise, but if I do that, I need to reallocate that hour somewhere else, and that will usually be in the evening."

CONSOLIDATED WORK WEEK

Another typical schedule used by many homeworkers is the *consolidated work week*. This schedule consists of consolidating a five-day work week into fewer days. Most homeworkers who take advantage of this type of schedule work during "power shifts" when their children are being supervised. "You learn quick to be real productive in the time you've got," says Sue, a medical transcriptionist. "I work twelve hours a day, two days a week, and then I work weekends. A lot of times, I pump all weekend while my husband takes our daughter. I don't work when she's here and nobody's home. It just doesn't work."

TRADITIONAL EIGHT-TO-FIVE

A minority of homeworkers fall into the *traditional eight-to-five* work schedule, with evenings and weekends off (unless they have to handle an emergency situation). Homeworkers in this group tend to have only one child who is being cared for by someone while they're working.

Parents visit their child during breaks and at lunchtime. Also characteristic of this group is the incorporation of the "no housework during work hours" rule. Ted, a market researcher who has an in-home sitter, is representative of the homeworkers who have a compartmentalized workday:

> *I basically work from eight to five, Monday through Friday. It works out nice because my wife works part-time with me, and we can take breaks and see our daughter. When I'm working, I'm working, and I don't handle anything personal or domestic during my work time.*

ALTERNATING FLEX/TRADITIONAL

If you want to have the best of both worlds, try the *alternating flex/traditional* schedule. Amy, a computer software distributor (who works with her husband in the business), created a hybrid of the flex and traditional work styles by incorporating both into her week. She works an eight-to-five schedule two days, and a flex schedule three days, integrating household activities on those days. She also takes evenings and weekends off.

We have someone come into the house two days a week for our son, so those are my solid workdays. It's really nice. The sitter feeds him, bathes him, and changes all his diapers. All we do is come out and be like grandparents and play with him and then go back into the office. During my solid workdays I ignore the house. On the days I don't work straight through, if he's napping, I go in and finish up work things I didn't do the day before, mostly little things. I also manage our home on those days. That leaves the weekends free, which is a lifesaver. When I didn't have specific days when I could totally focus on work, it was too easy to get distracted.

NO ROUTINE—WHENEVER THE MOOD STRIKES

If you hate schedules and choose to work at home on your own for that very reason, you may fall into the *no routine* category like a minority of homeworkers do. Basically, you work when you feel like it, or perhaps when your energy levels are highest. Most homeworkers who fall in this category find that their hours vary from day to day. "I don't work a set schedule," says Liz, a computer programmer. "It puts a lot of stress on, and you might as well go to work. I'm more of a night person, but it takes its own natural progression as we go along. Either your family fits into the business, or your business fits into the family."

Lisa, a medical transcriptionist, has an approach that represents the no-routine work style. Basically, she performs no rituals to start or end her workday. She works when she wants to, and doesn't work when she doesn't want to.

I like not having a routine. I haven't used an alarm clock in three years, and that's really wonderful. I enjoy the flexibility. Some days I get up early and work. Other days I work in the evenings. We're very unstructured, which is probably not the norm. I think most people need some sort of routine to work well.

Whatever schedule you choose, communicate and coordinate it with your family. "Sunday night my wife and I review our schedules to make sure we're on the same page," says Ron, a pet product distributor. You'll most likely gain the support of your family if you make efforts to stay in close touch.

ACHIEVING YOUR ULTIMATE BALANCE

What rules, boundaries, and schedule appeal to you? What strategies can you implement to satisfy your goals and personality? Through trial and error you'll find a balance that makes you happy. Be patient with yourself and your family, and be prepared for some setbacks. If you approach the challenges of working at home with an open mind, you'll discover creative solutions.

CHAPTER EIGHT

Dealing with the Big Three Psychological Challenges (ISOLATION, MOTIVATION, STRESS)

Homeworker Hint

When you aren't working productively, check out. Go to bed, go to the beach, go with your kids. Whatever you need to do to rejuvenate, do it, so you can be a thousand percent when you're at work. Otherwise, you'll constantly fight yourself and create never-ending stress.

Amy, Computer Software Distributor

Isolation is the number one challenge homeworkers face. Chronic loneliness can create intense feelings of disconnectedness, making it difficult to establish a routine or make contact with people. Isolation can take you on an emotional roller coaster that zaps your motivation, leaving you feeling preoccupied with problems and overwhelmed by trivial issues. Such a scenario leads to increased stress, and the vicious circle repeats until you finally take control and do something to break the pattern.

The main goal of this chapter is to introduce strategies for dealing with the big three psychological challenges—isolation, motivation, and stress—so that you can develop positive habits right from the start, and prevent this negative spiral from occurring.

CONQUERING ISOLATION

Homeworker Hint

If you're a totally career-focused person, you'll face a huge adjustment when you come home to stay with your kids. All of a sudden you have no network of friends or associates. It's just you and the children. All my self-esteem was tied up with work, and it's not easy. What's missing is not having people to bounce ideas off of.

Chris, Magazine Publisher

When you work from a home office, it's easy to withdraw and drop out of the mainstream. Isolation can take its toll in several ways. "At first I felt really alone," recalls Mary, an insurance agent. "I missed the office lunches. I was constantly surrounded by people in my job." Bob, a financial adviser, misses being in a position that enables him to use his management skills. Many miss having others available to delegate administrative functions to, such as answering the phones, which sometimes results in a loss of business. Unfortunately, when clients need something in a hurry, they may not leave a message. Instead, a client might call the next person on the list in search of someone who can do the job immediately.

Sue, a medical transcriptionist, finds it difficult having a partner who works outside the home, who wants to come home and stay home, while she feels "cooped up" and anxious to get out of the house. "Working in the home, you find that you must change your surroundings," says Sue. "I get desperate for it on the weekends. It's hard for my husband because he has worked all week long, and wants to be at home and relax. We struggle with that quite a bit."

Men and women tend to differ on what provokes feelings of isolation in a work-at-home setting. Men focus on the inability to use their management skills. Women, on the other hand, focus on the connections with other women they miss.

● **Isolation**

Which of the following ways of feeling connected will you miss when you work at home?

_____ Peer support/camaraderie

_____ Adult stimulation

_____ Office gossip

_____ Office lunches

_____ Praise/recognition

_____ Feedback from others

_____ Bouncing ideas off of others

_____ Decision making/problem solving with others

_____ Expertise available in areas unfamiliar to you

_____ Administrative help or support

_____ Managing others (being a boss)

● _____ Having a boss

Getting Connected

Many of the new activities started by homeworkers are ways of dealing with isolation, and are aimed at establishing a feeling of connectedness to the outside world. One woman started bicycling in her neighborhood because working at home "was getting claustrophobic."

Schedules and routines that incorporate outside contact with people in the community are excellent strategies for warding off feelings of isolation. Joining business or personal networking groups is an effective way to connect with other people. "I belong to seven different groups," says Carol, an architectural illustrator. "I can network for business, but mainly it gets me out and interacting with other people." Going on-line and networking on the digital superhighway can also provide expertise and human interaction worth tapping into.

A by-product of isolation that several homeworkers speak of is a reduction in their grooming standards. "I've let my physical appearance slide because I don't have to stay current," says Wendy, a newspaper editor. "That's an easy one to let go of when you work at home. I don't dress up for work anymore. I don't put makeup on. A bad hair day is like, 'So what!'"

If dressing up makes you feel better about yourself, join a professional group that meets regularly. This will encourage you to get dressed up on occasion, and it will break up your routine by getting you out of the house. (It will also encourage you to promote your business.)

Forging professional connections can also aid in the business decision-making process. This is a critical requirement for home business owners who don't have colleagues in the office to bounce ideas off of. Brainstorming ideas with others brings synergy to the decision-making process, thus eliminating the narrower perspective inherent in working alone. Val, a travel agent, has an outside partner she relies on for frequent interaction and exchanging of ideas. "I run ideas by my partner, which helps," says Val. "I don't think I could be doing what I'm doing if I were a solo act. There'd be too much stress."

Fortunately, telecommuters have built-in connections with their co-workers at the office. If you're a telecommuter, it's worth going the extra mile to keep those relationships alive through frequent communication, in-person meetings, and attendance at social gatherings.

How about creating a "mastermind" group of selected people you can meet with on a regular basis to share stories, brainstorm ideas, and resolve business problems? Find a few people who are on a similar track, who are willing to commit to meeting every other week for coffee at a convenient location. You can find other homeworkers through local home business association meetings. Check the resource list in Chapter 13 for national associations you can call to get information on groups in your area, or check with your local chamber of commerce.

Some homeworkers talk on the phone frequently to feel more

connected. Others visit with friends or family regularly. "I feel isolated sometimes, but I try to keep it in perspective," says Jan, a property manager. "I do have the opportunity to go out with girlfriends if I choose to, or take a half day off and spend it with my son. Why should I feel sorry for myself when I can do something about it?"

The gym is another popular way to break up your day, get some exercise, and be around people. Also, short trips in the car or a walk around the block can get you out of the house. "I go out and do my mail runs," says Ted, a market researcher.

Jenny, a secretarial service provider, calls the office where she used to work when she feels isolated. "Once in a while I call the office where I used to work just to get the gossip," she says. "I miss the coffee and the chatter."

Isolation is one obstacle you can beat because you have the ability to control your schedule and spend time with the people you choose. Even if you have loner tendencies, it will most likely give you a boost to occasionally share with others. Set aside time each day to do something that puts you in contact with people. This will keep you from feeling isolated, and help rejuvenate you for the rest of your workday.

What are some of the ways that you can combat isolation? Following is a list of ideas worth considering:

● **Isolation Busters**
  - Join a personal or professional networking group.
  - Create a mastermind group that meets regularly.
  - Phone a friend.
  - Meet a friend for lunch.
  - Run errands.
  - Partner with someone.
  - Team up on a work project with another telecommuter or entrepreneur.
  - Connect with your former co-workers.
  - If you telecommute, keep in frequent touch with the office and participate in office social events.
  - Go to the library to do some research for your business.
  - Volunteer.

- Join a local gym. (This is a good way to meet other homeworkers if you work out during the low times.)
- Make contacts on-line through the Internet.
- Attend a class or a seminar.
- Form ties with neighborhood homeworkers.
- Do some of your work at a local coffeehouse.
- Frequent the same places to do business and get to know the employees who wait on you.
- Give talks to professional organizations to promote your business.
- Conduct a workshop that provides your expertise in an area that may or may not be business-related.
- Get a pet that will provide company. (A dog will appreciate regular walks around the neighborhood and so will you.)
- Go to an occasional afternoon matinee.

HANDLING INTERNAL AND EXTERNAL CYCLES

The flexibility of a work-at-home lifestyle can lead to problems for people who work best in a structured environment. Without outside stimulation or support, it's easy to lose motivation. Working at home takes an incredible amount of self-discipline to avoid falling into bad habits such as procrastinating or overworking.

We established in Chapter 7 that keeping regular business hours with morning and evening transition rituals will help create boundaries around your work schedule. It's also critical that you're aware of the cycles inherent in a home office arrangement and learn how to deal with them. The cycles can be internal (a lack of motivation), or they can be external (economic highs and lows).

Understanding Your Internal Cycles

Most homeworkers don't work when their internal drive is low. A loss of motivation can be triggered by a variety of events such as a work-related problem, working too much and being tired, or feeling burned out. Ben, a marketing consultant, says there's a tendency to go with the low feeling until it passes.

Losing a job to somebody else or failures of one kind or another tend to throw you into a funk. I have a tendency to walk away for a bit. I'll shut it down and go do something. I learned that sometimes you need to recharge your batteries, and then you discharge your batteries, and go through cycles. I'm not so worried about being ineffective for a month because I realize my enthusiasm will come back, and it does.

There is a small minority of "diehard" homeworkers who continue to plug away at work no matter how low their motivation gets—*procrastination* is not a word in their vocabulary. "I think that when you're self-employed, you have built-in self-motivation because you know that if you don't work, you're not going to get paid," says Ted, a market researcher.

The threat of not getting paid doesn't do the trick for many. To spark their motivation, most homeworkers turn to a variety of relaxing activities that include: playing with their kids, taking a short trip in the car, taking a nap, creating new dreams, playing computer games, housecleaning, working on creative projects, getting organized, exercising, reading, visiting friends, learning something new, or shopping. "Most of the time, I'll go out and sit on the patio and read something that takes my mind completely off of work," says Liz, a computer programmer. "Then I get over that little hump and I'm okay." Some rely heavily on their partner when their motivation gets low. "My wife is my shoulder to cry on, my coach," says Ron, a pet product distributor. If you have someone you can trust and confide in when you're feeling down about your work, it helps.

When I lack motivation, I use "Sandy's Law of Perpetual Motion." I keep moving, in *any* direction. I get my mind off of my work troubles by diverting my attention to something else. I might turn to creative projects I've had on the back burner, or as a last resort, clean out my files. Amazingly, that little break away makes all the difference in my attitude.

We spoke in Chapter 1 about visualizing an ideal work-at-home scenario that comforts you and validates your reasons for working at home. Jenny, a secretarial service provider, relies on her image for a motivational boost:

> *Before I opened my doors to the business, my husband asked, "Would you rather be walking out the door, trying to shuffle your kids off to day care and get yourself to the office, or sit at home with a cup of tea working in your home business?" That hit home. That's what I wanted to do! And even though I've never actually sat down and had a cup of tea since I opened, that image keeps me going through the difficult times.*

An occasional loss of motivation is a normal part of life, but it's more enhanced when you're working at home alone, with no one to turn to but yourself. When you have difficulty staying motivated in your work, step back and do a quick "check-in." What's hindering your performance? Are you tired? Burned-out? Upset? Bored? Frustrated? Once you are aware of what you're feeling, you can take steps to remedy the situation. Following are some motivation boosters to help you get back on track.

● **Motivation Boosters**

- Eliminate distractions. (See Chapter 7 for strategies on creating boundaries.)
- Set clearly defined, achievable business goals.
- Visualize and write down your reasons for working besides making money (i.e., clarify your personal goals and dreams, including your reasons for working at home; update your "ideal" work-at-home fantasy from Chapter 1).
- Stay away from negative people who don't support your efforts. (See Chapters 5 and 7 for dealing with a lack of support from family members.)
- Realize that rejection is a part of life and welcome it, knowing that you're one step closer to success. Find someone to share your war stories with and quickly move on.
- When faced with an undesirable or overwhelming challenge, break down the project into small tasks of a half hour each and create an arbitrary deadline for yourself. Complete the first half-hour task and give yourself a break to celebrate. Promise yourself a reward such as dinner out or an afternoon off when the project is completed on time.

- Avoid overwork by creating a schedule with set hours, taking short breaks, planning regular vacations, postponing less important tasks, and delegating as much as you can. Allow yourself to experience the luxury of having no commute by using the additional time to enhance your personal life.
- If you're tired, take a nap or get some fresh air and exercise.
- If you don't feel like working, don't. Take a break and do something you enjoy. Allow yourself to rejuvenate.
- Vary your activities when you're bored with your work.
- Don't deal with personal problems during work hours. Set aside specific times for taking care of personal issues that are upsetting you.

Reacting to External Cycles

When business is slow, most homeworkers try to drum up new business or get caught up on current business. "I get nervous when business is slow," says Sara, a fitness trainer. "Instead of reacting passively, I jump right into action. I start the fire back up." Some relax and enjoy the slow periods. "After five years we look forward to that point because it gives us a chance to relax," says Beth, an accountant. "The other times of the year are so busy, we can't take any time off."

Some do an evaluation of themselves or their marketing strategies when business is slow. "I start doing an evaluation of what's going on in the marketplace to see if my personal life is affecting what I'm doing," says John, a graphic designer. "I want to know what's causing the down cycle."

It's important that you recognize and prepare for the cycles of your home business in order to avoid undue stress. "If I do what I'm supposed to do, even though there are ups and downs, it will all come out in the wash," says Ron, a pet product distributor. "I keep my eye on the end result. If I hit my monthly goals, I'll hit my year-end goal."

How you react to bouts of slow business is dependent on your nature and understanding of the cycles characteristic of your particular business. After you've been in business for a while, you'll know what to expect. If you have typical slow times of the year, you can plan time off accordingly. "We do have slow times, and we're learning those,'' says Amy, a computer software distributor. ''We take those times and we go away.''

The majority of homeworkers respond to internal and external down cycles in opposite fashions. Most withdraw their efforts in their work when they experience feelings of low motivation, and step up the pace when business is slow. They tend to be in tune with themselves and trusting of their feelings. Pushing themselves when their bodies or minds are not up for it only worsens the situation—adding stress upon stress. So confident are these individuals, on the other hand, that when their business slows down externally, they again trust that their energies will jump-start the business back into action.

In this situation, homeworkers are subject to external forces. For the most part, these individuals left the corporate world to ''be their own boss'' and determine their own destiny. Their immediate action in response to the presence of external forces that threaten their business reflects their discomfort with being controlled.

MANAGING STRESS

Homeworker Hint

You experience a different type of stress when you work at home. It's a *self-imposed* stress. Whereas before you always had somebody telling you what to do and what your deadlines are, now you're setting those deadlines for yourself. I think you probably tend to be harder on yourself, but it's easier to take because you have control.

Beth, Accountant

Many of the activities that ward off feelings of isolation and boost motivation will also reduce stress. In order to keep your stress level down, be a good boss and take care of yourself physically and emotionally.

Diet and Weight Control

''I'm thirty pounds overweight, all of which I gained since I started working at home,'' says Mary, an insurance agent. ''I tend to eat more because I'm so close to food, and I exercise less because I get overly engrossed in my work and the time slips away." Some people gain weight while working at home because food is close at hand, and it serves as a source of comfort (especially during a stressful start-up period). By knowing this up front, you can take precautionary measures.

Make sure you eat properly and drink plenty of water. Don't stock the refrigerator with junk food that will lure you away from your work. Have on hand ready-made nutritious snacks and lunches that keep you energized throughout your workday. A healthy sandwich and carrot sticks may not be as exciting as a bag of chips and candy bar, but it will satisfy you longer.

Diet can also affect your energy levels and moods, which will have a definite impact on your work performance. A good resource on this topic is *Food and Mood: The Complete Guide to Eating Well and Feeling Your Best* (Henry Holt & Co.), by Elizabeth Somer.

Exercise

Exercise is an excellent form of stress release. "I try to go to the gym four days a week," says Paul, an environmental product distributor. "I think my workouts really help with stress." Don't get so caught up in your work that you neglect this wonderful outlet that offers numerous health benefits and can add years to your life. Whether it's jogs, walks, or trips to the local pool or gym, you can't afford not to do it. After all, working at home allows you the flexibility to exercise while others are working, so take advantage by plugging it in as a mandatory part of your work week. Your mind and body will thank you, and undoubtedly pay you back tenfold in terms of work productivity.

Sleep

"When I haven't had enough sleep, the next day I'm fuzzy-minded, crabby, and hungry all day," says Lynn, a bookkeeper. It's hard to be enthusiastic or productive when you're lacking sleep. Make sure you get plenty of rest. If you have difficulty sleeping at night, take brief afternoon naps to give yourself a boost (and you don't have to tell a soul).

If you have a tendency to lie awake worrying at night, write down all your worries on a "worry log" before you go to bed. Then you can relax and count sheep, knowing that everything is accounted for. If you consistently have insomnia, do more exercise during the day to tire yourself out. Also, eat an adequate meal each night for dinner, and allow at least two hours before you go to bed. If your insomnia persists, see a doctor.

Physical Comfort

Even if you decide against scheduling regular breaks into your workday in an effort to save on time, don't sacrifice your health. Take brief time-outs from repetitive tasks by standing and stretching, and walking around the room at least once an hour. If you're tense, take some deep breaths and roll your head from side to side with your eyes closed. Ask your partner or one of your children for a quick shoulder and neck massage.

Reduce your stress by taking care of your wrists, neck, and back. If your wrists or fingers feel sore, take short breaks and wiggle your fingers. Choose furniture and equipment that's ergonomically correct, which will provide physical and psychological comfort tailored to your needs. You can use padded wrist rests, a footstool, and pillows for additional relief and comfort. An excellent book on relieving pain and tension quickly is *60-Second Shiatzu: The Natural Way to Energize, Ease Pain, and Conquer Tension in One Minute* (Henry Holt & Co.), by Eva Shaw. We'll discuss physical comfort in more depth in the next chapter when we touch on office furniture selection.

Take Time out for Yourself

Be sure to carve out some personal time for you. Involve yourself in creative projects for relaxation such as gardening, cooking, writing, or various crafts. Treat yourself to something relaxing such as a massage, a bath, or a good book. "I like to read while I take a bath," says Pat, a newspaper publisher. "I probably take one a week when I make everybody leave me alone for an hour. Of course, the kids always want to take a bath with me, and I have to fight them off." This is your opportunity to spoil yourself and take advantage of your flexible lifestyle.

Jim, a fund-raising consultant, says sex is his favorite form of stress release. If sex doesn't work for you, try playing a musical instrument, singing, listening to music, working in the yard, going to the beach, going to church, sewing, or watching a video. Try the Internet. "I'll get on the Internet and read my E-mail for a while," says Liz, a computer programmer. "That relieves my stress."

Spend Time with Your Family

We discussed the importance of spending alone time with your partner in Chapter 6. Also make a habit of spending one-on-one time with your children. When you work at home you have golden opportunities to plug this into your day. Take a break and have a tea party, dance to the music, or play a computer game together. "My stress release is my daughter," says Val, a travel agent. "She comes and hugs me, and says, 'Mommy, I love you,' and the stress is all gone."

For various reasons, starting a home business may initially put a damper on long vacations. You can overcome this obstacle by planning mini family vacations on a regular basis. "We don't take traditional vacations," says Sue, a medical transcriptionist. "We sneak in a three- or four-day weekend here or there." Mary, an insurance agent, goes camping at least once a month with her family. "We take off and get away from the phones," she says. "We're 100 percent there. I don't know anybody among our peers who goes as often as we do."

Many homeworkers treat their families to a trip, the purchase of a big item, or a special dinner out when business goes well. "We've got ourselves on a little incentive program," says Beth, an accountant. "If we meet our goal this year, we'll go on a Caribbean cruise in December."

Use Humor and Optimism to Lighten Things Up

Research suggests that those who use humor regularly suffer less fatigue, tension, anger, depression, and confusion in response to stress. Whenever a stressful event occurs, try using humor and optimism to ease the tension. When Kevin, a real estate agent, gets yelled at by someone he cold-calls, he hangs up the phone, laughs, and moves on to the next prospect. Jan, a property manager, was able to laugh at her situation during the early months of her pregnancy:

> When I was pregnant with my son, I had a really hard first trimester . . . morning-sick, afternoon-sick. I remember these business calls. I'd be lying on my office floor with the speaker phone and mute button on, deep breathing. No one ever knew. I would laugh to myself. If people only saw how terrible I looked—I was gray and green. And yet, it was business as usual for them.

Develop a Stress-Hardy Attitude

Stress-hardy characteristics—challenge, control, and commitment—are associated with a decreased incidence of illness. To develop a stress-hardy attitude, learn to view stress as a challenge rather than a threat, take control of your life, and commit to your work and personal lives. Stress-hardy people approach life with enthusiasm, get involved, and thrive on learning new things. Their zest makes them feel vital and up for the challenge, rather than overwhelmed.

Learn to Say No

Defining your physical and psychological boundaries and sticking to them in an assertive fashion will help minimize stress. Establish your priorities and learn to say no to requests that take away from what matters to you. Time is your most valuable resource, and everyone will waste yours if you let them.

Talk About Stressful Events

Before you reach a breaking point, talk about your upsets and frustrations with a friend or loved one. Crying can also help release pent-up feelings. If you need additional help, consult a mental health professional.

Explore Relaxation Techniques

Relaxation techniques and self-hypnosis can do wonders for relieving tension and feelings of anxiety. Some people have a natural ability to concentrate deeply and place themselves in a relaxed state of consciousness (something you can regularly do while working at home). You can learn these techniques by attending a class or reading a book on the subject. *The Big Book of Relaxation: Simple Techniques to Control the Excess Stress in Your Life* (Relaxation Co.), by Shakti Gawain, is one good resource.

Eliminate Negative Self-Talk

The majority of our stress and emotional suffering comes from how we perceive a situation. The thoughts that cause us stress are usually negative, unrealistic, and distorted. Unfortunately, our bodies don't realize the difference between what we imagine and what we actually experience.

Pay attention to your automatic thoughts. Learn to recognize negative self-talk or irrational beliefs. Notice how your thoughts affect your moods, behaviors, and physical condition. This is vital when you work at home. Since you're alone with your thoughts most of the time, how you talk to yourself will have a direct impact on your work performance.

Journal Your Thoughts and Feelings

Keep a journal and write down your thoughts and feelings. This is a healthy way to get things off your chest on a daily basis.

Journaling can also serve as a wonderful morning or evening ritual to segue in or out of your work role.

You can use it as an opportunity to write down your automatic negative thoughts as you become aware of them. At the same time, jot down a positive replacement thought. You can create new mental habits by consciously substituting negative thoughts with positive thoughts. If you work at it, your positive thoughts will eventually become automatic.

Associate with Positive People

If you want to be a positive, upbeat, forward-thinking person, it's important that you eliminate the people in your life who drag you down and deplete your energy. Seek out the people who want to support your efforts. Lillian Glass has written two excellent books in this area: *Toxic People: Ten Ways of Dealing with People Who Make Your Life Miserable* (Simon & Schuster) and *Attracting Terrific People: How to Find, and Keep, the People Who Bring Your Life Joy* (St. Martin's Press).

Spirituality

Call on your belief system in times of stress. This is an excellent strategy for coping with daily hassles or crises. Ann, a personal image consultant, starts her workday praying on the phone with a friend. "My friend Barbara also works at home," she says. "Every morning we pray together. It's become a ritual that we rely on and look forward to."

The Four-Step Approach to Reducing Stress

In *The Wellness Book* (Simon & Shuster), Herbert Benson, M.D., and Eileen M. Stuart, R.N., introduce a four-step approach to reducing stress, which is also effective in breaking the habit of automatic negative self-talk.

1. **STOP.** Each time you encounter a stressful event, say "STOP!" to yourself before your thoughts begin to escalate into the worst possible scenarios.
2. **BREATHE.** After you stop, BREATHE deeply to release physical tension and break the negative stress cycle.
3. **REFLECT.** Once you have stopped the automatic cycle of negative thoughts and taken a deep breath, you can REFLECT on the cause of your stress.
4. **CHOOSE.** After you have stopped the process of responding automatically, taken a deep breath, and reflected on the cause of your stress, take a moment to CHOOSE how to deal with the stress.

HOMEWORKER ATTITUDES TOWARD STRESS

Homeworker Hint

There are two different types of stress. Working for someone else, you get pressures put on you from negative individuals who really don't influence you into being your best. You rely on people who aren't skilled at running your life. My stress is action-oriented—get the job done, call somebody up and say, "How can I handle this?"—and that stress is "yummy." It's a yummy stress I can enjoy, being on my own.

Chris, Magazine Publisher

Although homeworkers refer to their stress as "self-imposed," they like having the ability to control it. One way they accomplish this is to lower their expectations because many are so achievement-oriented and, to a large degree, compulsive about their work. "Don't beat yourself up," says Lynn, a bookkeeper. "Figure out what you can accomplish and do the best you can. Be happy with it."

Although most homeworkers indicate that their lives are not perfectly balanced, working at home allows them to strike a happy medium better than any other work arrangement. "I think it's an ideal situation," says Nancy, a math tutor for kids. "No matter whether you work at home or for a company, it's hard being a working mom, period. But this, I think, is the best of both. I'm surprised that everyone isn't doing it.''

CHOOSING THREE-IN-ONE ACTIVITIES

Homeworkers use a variety of strategies for handling low motivation, isolation, and stress. Because the methods for alleviating these three problem areas are somewhat similar, you can save time by regularly performing activities that satisfy multiple areas at once. If you frequently feel isolated and stressed-out, rather than do a solitary activity such as reading a book to alleviate your stress, try taking a walk with a friend or visiting the gym to relieve stress *and* feelings of isolation (or low motivation). The exercise will also aid in weight and health management.

If you regularly choose strategies that satisfy as many needs as possible simultaneously, you'll conserve time and be less apt to experience burnout. In the long run you'll be more productive. Mike, a screenplay writer, swims in the pool with his family at the end of his workday. This daily event serves as an evening ritual that allows him to make the transition from his work role into his family role, but it also provides a great form of exercise and stress relief.

When I worked in real estate I did a tremendous amount of telemarketing. I devised a way to get some exercise and relaxation while making those *dreaded* calls. I set up a phone station next to my stationary bike, and rode the bike while prospecting for business. In between calls (waiting for someone to answer the phone), I'd read a motivational book. I was never more successful in obtaining leads. Use your creativity and experiment until you find what works for you.

CHAPTER NINE

Organizing Your Time and Work Space

📎 **Homeworker Hint**

I found that I could create systems in my home and in my business that
would allow me to be free when I'm with my family and friends, and
they appreciate that. I've got Monday systems and Friday systems, and
they're entirely different from my Tuesday, Wednesday, and Thursday
systems. You have to create systems. There's too much coming at you.

Sara, Fitness Instructor

While good time and space management are important in any
work situation, they're an absolute necessity in a home office.
Because you're subject to constant distractions and your space is
limited, you need to establish good habits from the beginning.
This chapter offers strategies to help you conserve time, and
design and organize your work space.

SAVING TIME ON THE WORK FRONT

I find that I can accomplish in four hours working at home what
it might take eight hours to accomplish working for someone in

an office setting. Let's discuss the ways you can make the most of the time you invest in your work so you can operate at maximum productivity.

Handle It Once

As much as possible, try to handle things once. If you have a place for everything right at your fingertips, there's no need to transfer information from place to place. If someone gives you a phone number, don't just scribble it on the nearest piece of scratch paper (and likely lose it), record it in your Rolodex, address book, business-card file, or computer database. Get into the habit of taking care of things immediately.

When working on a project, clean up and file it before getting started on the next. Don't put off paperwork, handling mail, or boring tasks that are a required part of your work routine. It's easier and more confidence-building to stay on top of things than to experience that sinking feeling when you're constantly trying to play catch-up.

Clear Your Desk Daily

If you get accustomed to handling things once, you'll find that your desk stays neater. It will be so much easier to find things—especially if you have "a place for everything and everything in its place." There's no need to be a perfectionist, but when you're working at home under space and time constraints, the only way to keep from being buried under your desk is to keep it cleared off daily.

Homeworkers claim that clearing off their desk at the end of their workday gives them a feeling of being done for the day. It also allows them to start the next day feeling organized and on top of things.

I will not allow myself to start my workday with a messy desk. Like many people, I am most productive in the mornings—when my energy level is at its highest. I can't afford to waste precious morning time cleaning my desk. The same holds true if you're an evening person and tend to be most productive in your work later in the day. Clearing off your desk at the end of your workday also provides a way to wind down and make the transition out of your work role.

Use Templates Whenever Possible

When you find yourself writing down the same thing repeatedly, whether it's a letter, a memo, or a list, store a copy of it in your word processor as a template. If, for instance, you send out the same letter over and over, store a standard letter that you can access to make minor changes.

If you perform the same steps to complete a task repeatedly, generate a master checkoff list that you can make copies of to ensure that all steps get completed. When I worked as a real estate agent, I made checkoff lists for all the steps necessary to take a listing and successfully close an escrow (with a blank for the date of completion for each step). This saved time and served as a memory aid so nothing slipped through the cracks.

There's no need to reinvent the wheel each time you perform duplicate tasks. Constantly be looking for shortcuts in managing your projects and paperwork. But by all means, don't compromise on quality.

Create Daily To-Do Lists

Successful homeworkers make up daily "to do" lists for what they plan to accomplish the following day. They also prioritize their lists so they get the most pressing tasks done immediately. "I'm the queen of lists," says Jenny, a secretarial service provider. "I don't even try to remember anything anymore, I just write it down and prioritize with an *A, B,* or *C.* I'm neurotic about my lists."

Many homeworkers plan their entire work week ahead of time. "The last thing I do at the end of the week is plan the next week," says Ron, a pet product distributor. A "to do" list helps you stay on track because you don't waste time thinking about what you need to do next.

Plus, it's rewarding to see your list with the majority or all of the tasks marked off at the end of the day. "The more planning I do the night before, the more effective I am the next day," says Paul, an environmental product distributor. "It gives me a great sense of accomplishment to cross things off my list."

Just don't keep transferring undone tasks for too long. Evaluate the importance of the task, and if it doesn't merit being on the list of immediate-action items for the day, then don't waste time writing it down day after day. You might want to create a "future projects" file where you keep ideas or unfinished tasks that would be nice to accomplish when you get some downtime in your business. As philosopher William James said, "There's nothing so fatiguing as the eternal hanging on of an uncompleted task." Do it, or cross it off your list and put it in your future projects file.

Keep a Calendar/Planner

Even if your work doesn't require you to set appointments, it's a good idea to keep a calendar or planner. You can write down important calls to make, meetings to attend, or deadlines for work projects. "I have my Bible—my Daytimer," says Carol, an architectural illustrator. "I have everything scheduled in it, and usually within that I've got 'stickies' posted all over. It's kind of disorganized organization." Find out what works and create a system of your own. Just be sure to write down and track your business affairs in one place.

Physically Prepare the Night Before

Can you physically prepare for your workday the night before? "Every evening I spend time getting ready for the next day," says Candace, a small-business consultant. "I get everything in the car the night before that I need in order to drop my daughter off at the baby-sitter the next morning. The biggest challenge is getting out of the house. Two-year-olds are easily sidetracked, so you have to save time wherever you can."

If you like to dress up for work, have your outfit pressed and ready to wear the night before. Set out cereal, bowls, and utensils for breakfast. Is there a way you can prepare lunches the night before? We do all the grocery shopping early Monday morning and plan the week's meals. Instead of wasting precious work time in the kitchen staring into the refrigerator to see what jumps out for lunch, we have everything all decided and, if need be, prepared ahead of time. Think of things you can do to prepare the night before your workday, so that you can devote 100 percent of your energies to your work during the hours you have scheduled for it.

Reduce Your Work Standards

We talked about reducing your housecleaning standards in Chapter 5. This bit of advice holds true for work as well. Good time managers are able to channel their efforts in multiple directions with the goal of creating balance. If your work standards are too high, you're setting yourself up for frustration and overwork.

If you drain all your energies trying to reach unrealistic, self-imposed standards, there will be nothing left over for you or your loved ones. Ann, a personal image consultant, learned this lesson early on in her home business. She says it saved her marriage and her sanity:

> *I came to grips with what my goals could be instead of being continually unrealistic. Based on the fact that I only have so many hours a week to work, I'm happy with the success I'm getting. I would love to be number one at what I do, but I'm not willing to sacrifice my personal life. I love my work, but it's not my everything.*

Look for Windows of Opportunity

Find time for yourself and your family during the hours you're least effective, or when it's not possible to conduct business. Pat, a newspaper publisher, plans short excursions with her four kids when her clients are at lunch and she can't conduct much business anyway. "It's real common for me to take a one- or two-hour break in the middle of the day to go do something fun—

take the kids to the park, the library, or the beach,'' she says. ''Between noon and 2:00 P.M. nobody is in their office. It's a good lag time for me to spend with the kids, run errands, or catch up on my reading.''

Delegate

 Homeworker Hint

Stop trying to master every single aspect of your business. Don't try to be a "do-it-yourself" accountant or attorney. You need to have boundaries and hire professionals who will make your business look good. The biggest lesson I learned is that I don't have the answer for everything.

Jan, Property Manager

When it comes to working at home, maybe you can handle all the responsibilities yourself, but is it time- and cost-effective? If you aren't getting back more than you're investing, the law of diminishing returns has set in and you're wasting precious time. Eighty percent of homeworkers delegate or subcontract business or household responsibilities to varying degrees and for a variety of reasons. The reasons all boil down to saving time and maximizing profits.

WHY DO HOMEWORKERS DELEGATE?

- I've never subcontracted work when there's too much work. I only subcontract when there's a particular job I don't know how to do. (John, Graphic Designer)
- I have a phenomenal assistant. That has freed me to go out and do what I'm good at, which is interacting with people and getting business. The assistant handles the running of the business. (Sara, Fitness Trainer)
- When I get overwhelmed I hate to say no to anything, so I'll sub it out. (Jill, Desktop Publisher)
- I do all the thinking work and subcontract the rest. Every question is, ''Is this value-add or not?'' If it's not value-add, it goes, or it gets subcontracted out. Same with the house. The

health department isn't going to shut it down if it doesn't get done. (Val, Travel Agent)

Reallocate Personal/Family Time with Caution

Past research suggests that homeworkers have a habit of reallocating their personal time in order to get more work done, rather than delegating tasks to others. Personal time reallocation strategies commonly include the reduction of time spent with family and friends, time spent on volunteer activities, and time spent sleeping. It also includes a reduction of time spent on housecleaning and preparing home-cooked meals.

Be careful how you reallocate personal time. The feeling of being spread too thin is a common problem among one-person businesses. Don't fall into the trap of allowing the demands of your work-at-home lifestyle to deplete your personal time or health. Recognize when it's time to delegate and do it. In Chapter 11 we'll discuss ways to delegate wisely.

DESIGNING YOUR HOME OFFICE

Since I had the opportunity to conduct interviews in the homes of my research participants, I was able to observe their work environments. With few exceptions, their work spaces were very organized, ranging from a small area along the stairway in the dining area that makes the most efficient use of every bit of space, to a large private office with a view of the hills and a highly functional, custom-designed U-shaped work area with lots of storage space for files and office supplies.

"You need more space to run your business than you'd think," emphasizes Jim, a fund-raising consultant. "Besides my office, I had to take over part of the garage." Most offices are moderate in terms of space and office design, with an emphasis on functionality. "I think you need to create a comfortable place," says Jack, a copywriter. "Everything I need is at my fingertips."

The most important considerations in setting up your home office are budget, space availability and location, comfort, functionality, expansion, and equipment needs. Since you are in control of your environment, you can design a work space that facilitates your ability to work happily and productively.

Budget

How much can you afford to spend on your home office? Try to remain flexible in the beginning. Even if you can afford to build your own work surfaces or have someone do it to your specifications, it may be best to hold out for a while to learn your likes and dislikes. Experiment first with non-built-in furniture that's versatile and adjustable. If you keep a list of "pet peeves"—those drawbacks and inconveniences that really annoy you—you'll then be able to invest in customized furnishings with self-knowledge and experience behind you.

Space Availability

How much available space do you have for your home office? Most homeworkers agree that the more space you have, the better, because it allows for room to grow. (Now, that's a positive thought.) Home-office space is a lot like money—the more you have, the more you use. How much room will you need? This is largely dependent on your work habits, the type of work you'll be doing, the equipment you'll be using, whether you'll be meeting with clients in your home, and whether you plan to hire employees. Will you need a second work station for yourself or someone else? Find a space that will accommodate your needs.

Consider your work style when scouting out an ideal place to set up shop. Do you prefer a private, quiet office or do you work better in a setting that's closer to Grand Central Station? If space is in short supply in your home and there isn't room for a private office, look for ways to create boundaries—both physical and psychological. Consider using wall units, bookshelves, or folding curtains to section off a portion of a room. Establish some type of barrier to mark off the limits of your office, even if it's with tables, rugs, or plants. This is the time to set your creativity in motion.

Be sure to set up rules and guidelines for yourself and family members so you can concentrate during work hours (see Chapter 7). At the same time, respect the space and schedules of others in your household. If you'll be setting up your office in your twelve-year-old son's room because that's the only space available, talk with him first to gain his support, and decide on a work schedule that satisfies both of your needs for privacy.

A Comfortable Location

Comfort is one of the key factors in deciding on a suitable work space. Choose a location that has adequate lighting and sufficient electrical outlets and telephone jacks. You'll need a space that's not too damp and has a temperature that doesn't get too extreme, or at least can be controlled. "I set up my office in our spare bedroom but had to relocate because the heat was unbearable in the midmornings," explains Bob, a financial adviser.

If you have small children at home, be sure to **childproof your office.** Look for anything dangerous at your child's level such as loose cords, wires, unprotected outlets, sharp corners, small objects, and accessibility to drawers or storage containing sharp or small objects. Many parents put a security lock on their office door so their children can't enter when the office is closed. Protect your children and your hard work and equipment.

When you choose your office space, consider noise levels and traffic patterns in the household, and whether your work will disturb other family members (especially if you intend to work while others are sleeping). If you live close to your neighbors, how much noise readily comes from their direction? You don't want to set up your office in a bedroom next to dogs barking or kids playing outside—especially if you keep your windows open during the hot months.

If you work odd hours, choose an office space that's easily accessible. This would be critical if your office is detached from your house and one hundred feet away when there's six feet of snow on the ground. Consider the temperature and weather conditions for all seasons of the year when choosing a work space. Last but not least, a bathroom in close proximity to your office may be important if you make frequent trips throughout your workday.

Functionality and Health

A key factor in setting up your office is making it functional and convenient. If you access certain manuals, files, or supplies frequently, don't put them across the room. As much as possible, have everything you need on a daily basis within reach.

You can do this by creating a list of personal priorities that you wish to transfer to your work space to make it functional. What will you need to have easy access to? Where do you want things positioned so they're accessible but not in the way? At what height? How big a work surface will you need? As you design your office in your head or preferably on paper (in your journal), keep thinking as you go along, "How can I economize on space and maximize on efficiency without sacrificing comfort?"

Where possible, think of building up rather than out, with shelves or stacked bookcases, for instance. Don't put things in places that will jeopardize your health. Set things up in an ergonomically correct fashion—according to your height and arm length in order to prevent back, neck, and wrist problems or eye strain. The *Consumer Reports Home Office Guide* offers these tips:

- **Chair:** Ideally your feet should be flat on the floor, with your elbows and knees forming right angles. If need be, use a footrest or prop yourself up on a cushion to get into position. The back of the chair—or a strategically placed pillow—should give you support in the lumbar region where your back naturally curves. You should be able to adjust the chair's arms so you can rest your forearms without slumping or hunching your shoulders.
- **Desk:** The top of your computer desk should be deep enough to place your monitor at a comfortable viewing distance—arm's length, more or less. Allow at least sixteen inches for a fourteen- or fifteen-inch monitor, or twenty inches for a seventeen-inch one, plus three to six inches for wires. Unless you're fairly tall, you'll need a lower tray that is wide enough for your keyboard and mouse. Standard desks are generally too high for a keyboard.
- **Lights:** Make sure that no light sources will bounce off your computer monitor, causing glare that contributes to eyestrain

and headaches. Place your monitor at a ninety-degree angle to a window or other bright light.

- **Keyboard and Mouse:** Position them together on a surface in front of you, low enough so that you can type and move the mouse while holding your forearms comfortably at a right angle. The goal is to neither slump nor lift your shoulders.
- **Monitor:** Position the top of the screen at eye level or slightly below so you don't have to tilt your head back or forward. If you have to look at the keys when you type, position the monitor and keyboard to minimize the movement of looking up and down. Place the monitor as far from your face as you can, keeping the screen easy to read. Keep the monitor clean and use a glare screen to improve contrast if necessary. If you look at documents while you type, attach a document holder to the side of the monitor.

Fortunately, computer equipment, like office furniture, is increasingly being designed with user comfort in mind. Workstations, tables, and chairs are equipped with knobs you can adjust to find just the right height or angle for maximum comfort. You can buy a keyboard that has wrist rests built in, and a nest for your mouse that supports your wrists. *How to Survive Your Computer Workstation,* by Julia Lacey, offers information on office ergonomics. It also includes information on how to reverse carpal tunnel syndrome without surgery, and prevent headaches from eyestrain. To order a copy, call (800) 256-4379.

Personalizing Your Office

Creating a home office that's functional doesn't mean you have to strip it of personality. Some homeworkers like to personalize their work spaces with family pictures, mementoes, inspirational pieces, or various other decorator items. Others don't because of a lack of space, or because such items can be a distraction.

Find a place for personal touches that's not in your way. You don't need the frustration of picking up the picture of your dog Spot off the floor every time the telephone cord knocks it off your desk when you reach over to grab a file from the filing cabinet. What matters is that you create an atmosphere conducive to working comfortably and efficiently.

ORGANIZING YOUR HOME OFFICE

Your best ticket to good time management is getting and staying organized right from the start. Janet Taylor, president and owner of Totally Organized, a professional organizing service in Philadelphia that helps clients save time and money, offers some quick pointers to help you set up an efficient and smooth-running office. For more detailed information, *Organizing Your Home Office for Success* (Plume), by Lisa Kanarek, is one of several books available on this topic.

Desk

Put only the necessary items on your desk, such as a calendar, pens and pencils, and a clock. Do, however, keep the supplies you need at easy access in your work area, so you don't have to run all over the house looking for a pair of scissors. Use trays to organize papers and projects, but don't overload them, and always clear them out daily.

Filing System

For the sake of conserving space, vertical files are usually more desirable than horizontal files. Create a filing system that meets your individual needs by categorizing your paperwork. Title your files by name, category, or subject. If you expect to have a large filing system, you may want to consider color-coding to distinguish files (e.g., clients, vendors, suppliers).

Always arrange your files alphabetically. To ensure that your files stay alphabetized, insert manila folders inside the hanging folders. Each time you need to pull a folder, its respective hanging folder will always stay in place. Eighty percent of everything that goes into file folders never gets used, so make it a habit every three months or so to go through your files and toss what you don't need. This is the best way to prevent paper pileup.

Magazines

If you must keep the magazines you purchase, then store them on shelves or in bookcases. Your best bet is to use a reading basket to hold your current magazines and some scissors. You can take it with you on the run so that in your spare time you can clip the articles you wish to keep and toss the rest. If nothing interests you, consider donating the magazines to a hospital, nursing home, or library. Create a file for the articles you wish to keep and categorize them by topic.

Business Cards

After each meeting or networking event, take some time to enter your business cards into a database so you can access a number easily—by type of business, for instance—if you forget someone's name. Then you can store the cards in a card file box or Rolodex, or better yet, save space and throw them away.

Mail

Sort your mail into a file box divided into categories you create such as: Payment Requested, Reply Requested, Order Requested, and To Be Read. Prioritize your mail categories so that when you set aside the time to handle your mail, you deal with the most urgent items first.

The Portable Office

A portable file box comes in handy when you need access to pertinent files on the road. You can keep separate files for clients, marketing materials, catalogs, handouts, you name it. This is a real convenience when you travel to client meetings, speaking engagements, exhibits, conventions, or trade shows.

STAYING ON TOP OF IT ALL

Implementing strategies to save time and stay organized requires a great deal of effort on your part, especially in the beginning. You'll be setting up files, records, equipment, and arranging (and rearranging) your office to your liking. Keep in mind that the strategies introduced in this chapter will work if you do. Once you've established chosen systems, stay on top of things on a daily basis. The ongoing effort you put forth will help keep your business running smoothly and efficiently.

PART III

SAVVY
BUSINESS
STRATEGIES

CHAPTER TEN

Making the Transition to a Work-at-Home Lifestyle

📎 **Homeworker Hint**

Do a lot of thinking beforehand. Be as clear as you can on what you want to accomplish and take steps to prepare yourself. You need to have a real sense of purpose and direction when you make the decision to work at home, and very important—a plan.

Liz, Computer Programmer

Before we delve into making the transition to a work-at-home lifestyle, let's take a quick time-out to see how far you've progressed. Think about the effort you've put forth as you've read each chapter in this book. You did a lot of introspective work to determine whether you feel suited to a work-at-home arrangement. You pondered and defined the line of work you're interested in, and whether you choose to work for yourself or someone else. You identified your true reasons for desiring to work at home, and potential pitfalls you may encounter along the way. You've contemplated strategies to help you stay balanced and on track.

You deserve a quiet moment of praise for your hard work. Congratulations! All this preliminary work is laying a solid foundation of awareness for your satisfaction and success. You are preparing yourself and your loved ones to succeed—both financially and emotionally. What more can you possibly hope for? The answer? A plan.

CREATING A REALISTIC PLAN FOR MAKING THE LEAP

It is vital that you establish a well thought out plan for addressing all issues relevant to making the leap to work at home. In the sections that follow we will address important considerations relevant to launching your home business. We'll touch briefly on issues of a personal nature since that has been our main focus thus far. The primary goal in this chapter is creating a plan to assist you in the technical aspects of getting your business up and running.

If you're a telecommuter, some of these issues may or may not apply to you. However, you might want to address them anyway if you have any thought of ever working on your own— as an independent contractor for your company, for instance. A section at the end of this chapter is devoted to special tips for telecommuters that you'll also want to review closely.

In this planning exercise you'll be making up a big "to do" list that consists of the steps you need to take in your personal and work lives to create a successful work-at-home arrangement based on your needs. I will be probing you along the way to help you target the tasks you need to complete to get established. Since homeworkers are big on "to do" lists, now is the time to start good habits.

At the top of an empty page in your journal write "Preparing for My Work-at-Home Transition." Create one large column on the left with the header "Things to Do," and one small column on the right with the header "To Be Completed By . . ." so that you can jot down the date you intend to have each task on your list accomplished. As I introduce and discuss the following tasks, write down those that apply to your situation in the "Things to Do" column and your planned date of completion in the "To Be Completed By . . ." column. If an issue doesn't apply to your personal situation or business, skim it and read on.

TARGETING YOUR START-UP DATE

It will be difficult to identify dates of completion for the tasks on your "to do" list if you don't have an estimated time frame for making the transition to work at home. Therefore, the first item on your list should be your planned start-up date—the date you plan to be up and running in your home office.

How do you plan to make the move? Do you desire to create a proposal for your employer that describes the benefits to both parties if you telecommute a few days each week? Or do you wish to moonlight part-time in a home business while maintaining outside employment until you have enough clients to make the move to full-time? Perhaps you're ready to jump right into a home business full-time and give it all you've got.

Most homeworkers make a slow transition into their home business. They build their business on a part-time basis while continuing to work for someone. "If you're working full-time, don't quit that job yet because it's going to take a while to really get up and going," advises Jack, a copywriter. "Do as much as you can to develop your home business in your spare time while working to help with cash flow."

Candace, who quit her job cold turkey to start her home-based consulting business, learned this lesson the hard way. "Even if you have a couple of clients, it's better than nothing," she says. "I had no clients and had to spend all my time cold-calling to get something going."

Wendy is in the process of building her home-based freelance writing business while working full-time as a newspaper editor:

Working full-time for someone while working part-time in my writing business is my way of paying my dues without cutting my income. I'm getting ready to make the transition. It's a slow but sure process that works for me. Why should my income be cut in half just because I want to do something different?

Not everyone has the desire or circumstances to carry on a full-time job while moonlighting part-time in a home business. If your company was downsized, you may be out of a job, or you may have family responsibilities that preclude you from working two jobs. Whatever the case, sometimes the "go for it" approach makes the most sense. If this is the case, try to secure a client or two before leaving your job. Also, you'll need to have adequate financial backing or support to allow enough time to get up and running. We'll cover finances in the planning process shortly.

Jill, a desktop publisher, explains that it took her about a year to get her business going from scratch. "There's not enough time to get clients, keep clients, do the work, and make any money at first," she says. "So you better not be relying entirely on your income. If I were a single mom, I never in a million years would have started a business from scratch without financial backing. There's absolutely no guarantee."

PREPARING YOURSELF AND YOUR LOVED ONES

In previous chapters I asked you to note in your journal the strategies you'll use to manage your personal and work lives when you join the two in one setting. Go back and review the strategies you chose, and itemize action steps you need to take in order to implement them when you begin working at home. Write the steps on your "to do" list along with the date you plan to accomplish them by.

Here is a sample list of steps Michelle plans to take in her personal life so she can make a smooth transition into her home-based desktop-publishing business. Michelle realizes she needs the support of her family and friends, so she created specific action steps as reminders to set aside time to ask for their support.

Use Michelle's list as a model to help generate the action steps you need to take to set up yourself and your loved ones for a successful and satisfying home-office experience. The more detailed you make your "to do" list, the better. Jot down little notes to yourself and be specific. This will act as a reminder when the time comes to complete each task. Also, don't forget to write down your targeted dates of completion.

● **Preparing for My Work-at-Home Transition**

Michelle's "To Do" List

1. Hold a family meeting to discuss the pros and cons of my home business. Ask for support from Jeff and the kids.
2. Hold a family meeting to discuss boundaries, rules, and schedules. Discuss the creation of complementary schedules that work together. Discuss work hours, days off, and vacations. Talk about planning regular family time together.
3. Hold a family meeting focused on dividing household chores.
4. Meet with Jeff to discuss our relationship and scheduling alone time together. Talk about having regular date nights.
5. Call the child-care resource referral service and ask friends for recommendations on in-home child-care providers.
6. Ask Jeff's mom if she can pick Katie up two days a week after school and watch her until I'm done working.
7. Interview potential in-home child-care providers with Jeff.
8. Talk to my friends Bev and Cathy about my home business plans and ask for their support. Explain that I'll be busy getting my business going and won't have much time, so it will be necessary to schedule time together. Tell them about my "no socializing while working" rule that I'll be implementing until I confidently have my business up and running.
9. Ask friends about low-cost housecleaner referrals.
10. Look into professional organizations and publications for desktop publishers.
11. Visit a local home-business professional organization to get my feet wet with networking.
12. Establish a board of directors, coaches, or mentors—a few people I can trust and confide in about my business—who will regularly advise me on how to improve my business and overcome specific obstacles to success (and vice versa).

13. Set a free appointment with a SCORE [Service Corps of Retired Executives, sponsored by the Small Business Administration] counselor to discuss my business idea. Investigate their resources.
14. Join a local gym for outside contact, stress reduction, weight control, and a way to get energized when I'm feeling low motivation.
15. Talk to ex-co-workers about meeting periodically for lunch.

Notice how most of the steps on Michelle's list involve the establishment of support systems. She realizes that even though she'll be on her own, she can't possibly do everything herself. She's asking for support and accountability up front from her family. She's preventing potential misunderstandings and hurt feelings by talking to her friends ahead of time. She's getting systems in place for managing child care and household chores. She has also targeted a number of strategies for managing isolation, motivation, and stress.

LAUNCHING YOUR HOME BUSINESS

In this section we'll address the steps necessary to launch your home business. Write down each step that applies to you, along with any personal notes (ideas, points of contact you can turn to for additional help or information, further research required, estimated costs), and jot down the date you plan to accomplish the step by. By putting these steps in writing, you're making a contract with yourself. You're mapping out your future, and will be that much closer to realizing your dream.

Financial Planning

 Homeworker Hint

When I left my job, we tried living off of one income for a year. When you go from two paychecks to one, you learn how to budget. Then you can start the business already used to that way of living, instead of plunging in without making that financial adjustment first.

Chris, Magazine Publisher

Don't let money, or the lack thereof, stop you from starting a home business. But do create a plan for how you will raise start-up capital and handle sporadic cash-flow cycles. Eight out of ten businesses fail because they are undercapitalized.

The best way to prevent being another statistic is to plan ahead. If you want your business to be successful, it will take some degree of financial investment up front to get things off the ground. "Have twice as much money in savings as you'll ever imagine using, because you'll blow through it—quick," advises Kevin, a real estate agent. The type of business you start, your budget, and the image you wish to project will determine how much you need to get going.

As you progress through each section that follows, keep track of the approximate costs to implement each task. When you do your research, write down the costs in your journal so that you have accurate estimates. You'll be able to do many of the tasks yourself, while you'll want to hire out others. If money is an issue, see if you can barter for services or get by with the office supplies and equipment you have on hand.

You shouldn't expect a profit from your business for the first eight to ten months, so give yourself enough cushion. Determine how much you need to get the business up and running, as well as how much cash you need each month to cover living and business expenses for at least eight months to one year. If you're not relying on your income immediately, then estimate what your monthly overhead expenses will be in the business for eight months to one year in addition to your start-up costs. When creating a financial plan, it's best to inflate your estimates a bit so you don't wind up short.

If you can get your business started without maxing out credit cards or taking on a second mortgage, do it. "I don't recommend taking out big loans," suggests Wendy, a newspaper editor. "I think you really get yourself in a hole that way. The less up-front costs you have, the better off you'll be."

Look at all your financial options. What cash do you have available to launch your home business? Some homeworkers have steady retirement checks coming in from previous employment. Others rely on their partner's income to get their business going. "This wasn't a situation where I had to have income coming in right away," says Paul, an environmental product distributor who was laid off from his corporate job. "My wife makes enough money to cover our living expenses, with a little left over to cover my minimal business expenses until I really get things going. Things are tight now, but we see the potential, and we both appreciate the fact that I no longer have to travel like crazy and commute two hours every day."

Several homeworkers rely on their investments or retirement funds as sources of capital for starting their business. Jenny, a secretarial service provider, used her life insurance policy. "To get started we took a loan out on our life insurance," she says. "If I don't repay it, I don't have to worry, as long as I'm alive. It just hurts my husband if I go first."

Other homeworkers didn't borrow any money to start their business. Ann, a personal image consultant, wishes she had. "If I could go back and do it all again differently, I would take out a business loan," she says. "I would have bought all the business equipment up front instead of working until I needed something, and paying a little for it and charging the rest."

If you don't have adequate resources on hand to meet your start-up costs, you may have to turn to higher-risk sources of funds such as personal loans from family or friends, borrowing on your home, or funds from credit cards or signature loans. Small-business loans are difficult (but not impossible) to get from banks unless you have an established relationship and can secure the loan with some form of collateral.

Bank Loan Requirements for Home Businesses

To be considered for a loan, banks tend to look at the following factors:

1. Your business plan
2. Profit and ability to repay the loan
3. Past payment history
4. Character and attitude of borrower(s)
5. Professionalism
6. Previous experience related to the home business
7. Sufficient space to grow the home business during the life of the loan
8. Exclusive office space in the home devoted to business
9. Sufficient collateral

Your best bet is to contact the local U.S. Small Business Administration (SBA) office. This agency makes two types of loans, with one primarily made through banks but guaranteed by the SBA for the majority of the value of the loan. For more information call the SBA at (800) 8-ASK-SBA.

Besides generating start-up capital, you need a strategy for handling cyclical cash flow. Homeworkers who live high on the hog during the prosperous months find themselves scraping to get by during the low times. Prevent this inevitable stress from the beginning by creating a plan for handling the financial highs and lows. "After five years we finally got a line of credit," says Val, a travel agent. "We want to pay ourselves, feast or famine, and this helps the cash flow during the cycles." Some months will be fat while others are lean, so budget yourself accordingly.

FINANCING ALTERNATIVES FOR YOUR HOME BUSINESS
- Personal savings
- Sale of personal assets
- Personal borrowing (e.g., life insurance, credit cards)
- Financing from friends, relatives, and acquaintances
- Bank loans
- Finance companies
- SBA-guaranteed loans
- Other government financial programs
- Business partners
- Individual investors
- Small Business Investment Companies (SBIC)
- Venture capital
- Starting small and reinvesting all the profits

Training and Educational Needs

What type of training or education will you need to successfully launch your home business? This may involve taking classes to learn a new field or become more knowledgeable about business in general. It also entails doing your own research. "Evaluate the business you're getting into twice as carefully as you think you need to," stresses John, a graphic designer. You can never be too knowledgeable or too prepared when it comes to launching a pleasurable and profitable home business.

Consider setting a free appointment to talk to a SCORE counselor at the SBA in your area. Call the 800 number in the previous section for the office nearest you. These volunteers offer workshops on how to select a legal entity, create a winning business plan, secure funding, and various other aspects of starting a business. You can also take advantage of seminars and workshops offered through adult learning centers or community colleges on starting a home business.

Remember the informational interviews we talked about in Chapter 3 that involved talking to people in career fields that interest you? The object was to ask insightful questions to see if a particular field coincides with your interests and values. Homeworkers rely heavily on informational interviews to gain an understanding of the ins and outs of operating a home business before getting started. "I talked to other people who had home businesses," says Val, a travel agent. "At the time there was no class I knew of that would tell me how to get started. My approach was informal and seat-of-the-pants."

If you're starting a business at home, many of the steps that follow will require research on your part to identify the course of action you'll need to take to accomplish each goal. Each situation is different, as is each community. If I want to set up a home-based counseling service in San Diego, the zoning regulations will likely be different than for someone setting up the same business in New York. In many instances you'll need to seek specific information from the city or county where you plan to do business.

Choosing a Mentor/Coach

Homeworker Hint

Create a board of directors for your company right from the start— advisers and mentors who will support you for free, or a small fee, or barter for services. You don't have to re-create what has already been created.

Ron, Pet Product Distributor

Successful homeworkers have a mentor or a coach—a trustworthy person they can call or meet with periodically to confide in, express concerns to, and bounce ideas off of. Ideally a coach is someone who knows the ropes of your business, or is at least familiar with the many aspects of business (e.g., marketing, finances, customer service). The more knowledge and experience your coach brings to the relationship, the better.

A good coach will assist you in setting realistic goals and help you stay on track. This is effectively done through careful probing and listening, and helping you work through obstacles that hold you back. Once problems are brought to the surface, your coach can help you brainstorm solutions. Because you confide in your coach, it's necessary to establish a relationship built on trust and confidentiality.

Besides being your trusted confidant, a coach is someone you learn from. He or she can be a relative, friend, or successful mentor in the business you wish to enter. Paul, an environmental product distributor, appreciates the time his wife takes each week to act as his coach:

> *My wife is an excellent salesperson. Each week we have a meeting, and besides teaching me something new about selling, she allows me to vent my frustrations with the business. She always offers logical advice that I don't think of because I'm so caught up in things. I can't believe how much our weekly meetings do for my motivation and, most important, my bottom line.*

As Ron pointed out in the beginning of this section, you can choose mentors who will support you for free, for a small fee, or you can exchange services. In some instances the relationship can be a reciprocal one wherein you act as a coach to each other. If you use this approach, make sure you are able to be objective in the relationship, and that you have each other's best interests at heart.

Set up ground rules ahead of time to keep the relationship fair. Establish time limits for individual coaching sessions, so each person has equal opportunity to talk about his or her business. Disallow negative attitudes, destructive criticism, or judgments that hurt the other person. Strive for open, positive, supportive behavior, and unconditional acceptance. You might even want to create a mission statement for your coaching goals, such as "Our mission as coaches is to facilitate growth and help each other overcome obstacles to success."

Selecting a Business Structure

Do you plan to structure your business as a sole proprietorship, a partnership, or a corporation? Most home businesses in this country are **sole proprietorships.** The advantages of this type of structure are that it is the easiest and least expensive form of business to start, it's subject to less government regulations than a corporation, and the tax rates are generally lower than corporate rates since income is taxed at a personal level. The disadvantage of a sole proprietorship is that it provides no shield for your personal assets in the event of business-related lawsuits. It's also difficult to raise capital or obtain business loans as a sole proprietor. And when the owner dies, the business dies, which may leave the business assets subject to inheritance taxes.

Partnerships consist of two or more people going into business together in an agreed-upon arrangement. The advantages of a partnership are the synergy and sharing that take place between two or more individuals. In a home business this can be a tremendous benefit in terms of warding off isolation. Having a partner gives you the opportunity to bounce ideas around and share in the decision-making process.

Having a partner can make it easier for owners to schedule vacations and deal with personal emergencies. In a sense it's like "job sharing." There is less downtime because you can cover for each other. Also, each partner brings a different set of resources and talents to the arrangement so there are more assets to draw upon. With more assets, you can attract more business, bid on larger projects, share expenses, and increase your revenues.

Most homeworkers who work with their spouse or a partner reflect how their counterpart has opposite personal qualities or talents that allow them to complement each other and work well together as a team. "My business partner handles all the sales and marketing, and I handle all the technical aspects of the business,'' says Beth, an accountant who specializes in retirement planning. "I'm more analytical and he's more creative. He's also more of a risk taker than I am, so we tend to balance each other out.''

Pat has a goal in her publishing business—to create a unique family business partnership that will allow her children to use their complementary talents:

> *My long-term goal is to have a very profitable family business that the kids can step into if they want. The reason I'm in publishing is that I have an artistic child, a business-minded child, and one who is very good in math. In this business they can use their talents and all work together.*

Setting up a partnership is relatively simple, and like a sole proprietorship, income is taxed at a personal level. Partnerships may find it easier than sole proprietors when it comes to getting loans because lenders tend to view the arrangement as less risky since more than one individual is committed to the venture. Government regulations are also less stringent for partnerships than for corporations.

A downside of partnerships is that partners are legally and financially liable for each other's actions in the business. Unless otherwise stated in writing, the business ends upon the death or retirement of one partner. To be on the safe side, it's generally best to have an attorney draw up a written partnership agreement. If you draw up your own agreement, strongly consider having an attorney review it.

Other potential disadvantages of partnerships include incompatibility, disagreement on long-range plans, disputes about who is responsible for what, and the potential for dishonest dealings (e.g., client stealing, embezzling, misrepresentation of the business). Business partnerships also have a high rate of breakup, even higher than that of marriages. Often this is because inequities in the relationship that are not brought to the surface become increasingly difficult to approach and resolve.

Before you jump into a partnership arrangement, try working on several low-risk, short-term projects together. Take small steps to see how well you work together, and gradually move to larger endeavors to build trust and confidence in one another. What if your personalities clash? You'll want to identify potential problems before you commit.

As in any relationship, open and honest communication is the key to a healthy and happy long-term arrangement. Establishing and following agreed-upon procedures for problem solving and conflict resolution from the outset can prevent misunderstandings and inequities from building. Chapter 6 introduced strategies aimed at conflict resolution and maintaining a healthy home-working partnership between husbands and wives. These strategies can be applied to all types of business partnerships and family businesses as well.

If you view your home business as the start of a much larger enterprise down the road, you may want to consider the **corporate** business structure. While establishing a corporation can be complicated and expensive, it's even more so when you wait and do it later on in the game. The advantages of incorporating are the strength and status it offers when it comes time to raising capital. A corporation extends beyond the life of its owners, and the ownership is transferable. There is also limited personal liability in reference to lawsuits and debts. It is generally easier to obtain insurance benefits and deduct them for income tax purposes.

The downside of incorporating is that it's expensive and time-consuming to form and maintain. Corporations are heavily regulated by the government, requiring extensive and complicated paperwork. Corporations are also subject to higher taxes, and in some instances risk paying double income tax.

The majority of homeworkers are sole proprietors. A small minority establish corporations from the beginning in order to protect their personal assets and be able to raise capital when needed. They also see their business as eventually expanding to a much larger enterprise. Val and her partner in the travel agency business established a corporation for these reasons. They also offer a company-contributed retirement account, three weeks paid vacation, and eight weeks paid maternity leave for each partner.

When in doubt, do your research. Talk to friends and acquaintances who have home businesses similar to yours. Approach this issue during informational interviews to see what type of structure other homeworkers choose.

If you don't draw up a partnership agreement or articles of incorporation, you will basically be a sole proprietor, which is where most home business owners in the United States start out and where most end up. Don't pick a complicated path in the beginning unless you know exactly what you're getting into, and can clearly see that given your situation, the advantages outweigh the disadvantages. Remember, if need be, you can always change your business structure down the road, even if it is more expensive.

Generating a Business Plan and Goals

Some homeworkers operate their business without a written business plan. They keep their business plan in their heads, referring to it as a gut feeling that guides them. The reason for this is that a business plan is normally a requirement for getting a loan. So if you don't need a loan, why write a business plan?

Most homeworkers stress the strength, clarity, and commitment they feel in simply writing things down. "I have goal boards," reveals Jan, a property manager. "Visualizing the achievement of my goals works wonders. Also, I believe a mission statement is a must for every business. If you don't know your purpose and exactly what you intend to offer clients, how can you possibly set goals or make decisions?"

Even if you don't need a business plan because you won't be applying for loans, take the extra step to put things in writing. You can create a basic plan with a minimal investment of time. For more detailed information, *How to Write a Business Plan,* by Mike McKeever (Nolo Press), is one of many books available on this subject.

Your plan will consist of your mission statement and a brief description of your business, including your business structure and time frames for getting started. It also includes a management plan, service and product plan, marketing plan, and financial plan.

The **management plan** explains qualifications and responsibilities for yourself, your employees, and people you intend to delegate to. The **service and product plan** describes in detail the services and products you plan to sell and the pricing you'll offer. The **marketing plan** describes who your clients or customers will be. Ask yourself, "Who fits my client profile? How large is my target market? What problems can I solve for my clients? What goals can I help them achieve?" The marketing plan also conveys your intentions for marketing and selling to the targeted population, as well as an assessment of the competition that includes the outlook for the future.

The **financial plan** is especially critical if you're applying for a loan. You may want to hire an accountant to assist with this section. Here you'll include a balance sheet reflecting your business's assets and liabilities, a projected income statement reflecting the anticipated monthly sales and expense figures for the first year, and a cash-flow projection showing whether you have enough cash on hand to meet expenses, and how cash will be acquired and used in the first year of business.

With a little planning, you'll find that you can avoid most financial difficulties. Here is what the SBA suggests:

Start-Up Costs: To estimate your start-up costs, include all initial expenses such as fees, licenses, permits, telephone deposit, tools, office equipment, and promotional expenses.

Projecting Operating Expenses: Include salaries, utilities, office supplies, loan payments, taxes, legal services, and insurance premiums. Don't forget to include your normal living expenses.

Projecting Income: It is essential that you know how to estimate your sales on a daily and monthly basis. From the sales estimates you can develop projected income statements, break-even points, and cash-flow statements. Use your marketing research to estimate initial sales volume.

Cash Flow: Working capital—not profits—pays your bills. Even though your assets may look great on the balance sheet, if your cash is tied up in receivables or equipment, your business is technically insolvent—in other words, you're broke.

Make a list of all anticipated expenses and projected income for each week and month. If you see a cash-flow crisis developing, cut back on everything but the necessities.

Naming Your Home Business

One of the most fun and creative parts of starting your home business is choosing an appropriate name. You can work under your own name, but generally it's best if the name of your business suggests what you do, such as Sally's Secretarial Service or Bill Robert's Plumbing. A good business name can be your most valuable marketing tool if it hooks potential clients with a descriptive ring.

Some home business owners add terms such as "Enterprises" or "Center" to their name to suggest a larger, more solid organization, as in Birch Financial Enterprises or The Center For Child Development. You can be creative and clever with your business name, but also consider the nature of your business and the image you wish to project. If the name is too cute, it may turn off potential customers. Brainstorm and have fun with it until you arrive at a name that feels right.

Employee Identification Number

Unless you structure your business as a sole proprietor without employees or independent contractors, you'll need to obtain an Employee Identification Number (EIN) from the IRS. Clients will use this number to report payments they make to you. While sole proprietors without employees can use their Social Security number for tax-reporting purposes, some find it beneficial to have an EIN when opening a bank account or applying for a resale certificate. Contact your local IRS office to obtain an EIN or call the IRS at (800) 829-1040.

Fictitious Name Statement

If you are a sole proprietor doing business under anything other than your own name, you'll need to file a fictitious name statement with the county clerk's office, and pay a nominal filing fee. This statement is also known as a DBA (doing business as). It allows you to do a search to verify whether your name is in use, and prevents the competition from using your name. It's usually necessary in order to obtain a business license or open a bank account in the name of your business. You must also publish your fictitious name in a general-circulation newspaper. Check the newspapers in your area to find one that publishes fictitious names. Some keep DBA forms on hand and will assist you with the necessary paperwork.

Trademarks and Patents

If you wish to prevent others from using your business name, logo, or the name of a specific product or service you are marketing, consider obtaining a trademark or service mark from the U.S. Patent and Trademark Office (PTO) in Washington, D.C. The process is costly (at least $275 if you do it yourself) and fairly lengthy.

In order to protect the design of your product, it may be necessary to apply for a patent. This process takes an average of eighteen months and can run as much as $3,500, but much less if you do most of the work yourself. For more information on trademarks and patents, contact the PTO at (800) 786-9199.

Zoning Regulations

Many communities prohibit residents from telecommuting or operating home businesses, while others allow it with restrictions. Despite these prohibitions, home businesses are popping up everywhere. Check with the planning department in your city to see what's allowed in your community. Also, if you belong to a homeowners association, there may be limitations and restrictions within your own housing development.

Since it's usually difficult to determine who works at home and who doesn't, most homeworkers keep quiet about their arrangement. Home businesses that are shut down for violating zoning restrictions are an exception, and usually occur because a neighbor reports a problem resulting from the home business.

There will likely be restrictions on the number of people coming to and from your home, parking, noise, pollution, unsightly debris, and so forth. Check out possible zoning restrictions carefully. Above all, be courteous to your neighbors by not overstepping your bounds in the preceding areas. Ask for their support in your home-office venture and you'll establish cooperative and respectful relationships. Addressing issues up front with the individuals who are affected will prevent potential hassles and expense down the road.

Fortunately, the issue of home-business zoning regulations is gaining national attention. The laws are being brought up-to-date in an effort to accommodate the increasing number of people working at home. These are people who pay taxes, vote, and contribute to their communities. There is no reason to penalize them for working at home. As updated guidelines are set in place, it is hoped that within the next five to seven years, zoning battles will no longer exist.

Business Licenses and Permits

Home businesses are usually required to get a local business license to operate in a specific city or county. Generally this involves filling out a form and paying an annual fee based on the volume of business you expect to do. The license is usually renewable each year by mail. Some areas require permits for individuals running home businesses as well. Contact the Business License office of the Tax Collector in the city or county office where you plan to do business. Find out about the requirements at both the state and local level.

Resale Permit

Most states and some local governments impose sales tax. If your state charges sales tax on the products or services you intend to sell, you'll be required to collect the tax and turn it over to the state periodically. The benefit of the permit is that you can purchase materials for resale and avoid paying sales tax, as long as your resale permit is on file with your vendors. Similarly, if clients buy products from you with the intention of reselling them, it is necessary for you to keep their resale numbers on file so they can purchase tax free. Check to see if your state or local government requires a resale permit, and find out what regulations apply to the products or services you plan to offer.

Marketing Materials

Home business owners agree that one place not to cut corners is in the creation of marketing materials to spread the word about your business. "Prepare written materials that are all your own," suggests Sara, a fitness trainer. "If you don't have a great brochure, flyer, business card, or something that really reflects your business, you'll be cutting yourself at the knees." Sara prides herself on the eye-catching logo she uses on her business cards, brochures, and letterhead stationery.

If you're artistic by nature and have access to desktop publishing software, create your own unique materials. Most home business owners, however, prefer to hire a professional to do the job. If you're trying to keep costs down, provide definite direction on the design, layout, and style. If you leave these decisions up to the professional, it will certainly cost you.

Another way to save is to barter with a local home-based desktop publisher who is in need of your products or services. Or do you have a friend or loved one who is adept at this type of work? Just don't take shortcuts or cut costs if it means sacrificing the quality of the end product. "How people perceive you is everything," emphasizes Amy, a computer software distributor. "You have to look professional." Your business card or brochure is your opportunity to make a good first impression. Make it a lasting one with good-quality, descriptive, eye-catching materials.

Pricing Your Service or Product

Many experts agree that there is a psychology of setting a price for your service or product. If your prices are too low, people may think that what you are selling is cheap or lacks quality. On the other hand, you don't want to price yourself out of the market either. Do some research to see what your competitors are charging for something comparable to what you are offering.

Jenny, a secretarial service provider, called all her competitors before she got established. "I got out the Yellow Pages and started calling all the secretarial services in my area," she says. "I pretended to be a potential customer and gave each one the same job to bid. That information was what I relied upon most heavily to decide my pricing structure.''

If you're offering a service, you'll have to decide whether to charge per hour, per day, or per project. The hourly approach is most common; however, many clients prefer a flat fee per project because they like knowing the costs in advance. Charging per day or half day is common for on-site work such as consulting. When you bid on jobs, always include some buffer time to allow room for error. If you charge by the hour, let clients know that there will be a pro rata charge for any fifteen-minute period above a daily hourly total.

One formula for determining your hourly rate is to take the hourly rate earned in a comparable job where you worked for someone else, double it, and increase that figure by 25 percent. If you worked as a computer programmer for someone and your hourly wage was $20, and you left to start your own business, you would charge $50 per hour using this formula.

"Have an hourly fee that covers your overhead—in my case, my health insurance," stresses Jack, a copywriter. Plug in all your overhead costs when determining your fee or price. This includes the costs to keep your business up and running such as furniture and equipment, software, utilities, on-line services, supplies, child care, taxes, marketing, travel, shipping and postage, insurance, wages paid to employees, fees paid to professionals (e.g., attorney, accountant), business-related books, periodicals, professional memberships, and bank account and loan charges.

Make sure you not only cover your overhead expenses but that you make a desirable profit without being priced too low or too high. If you're setting a price for a product, include the total cost of raw and finished materials used, manufacturing costs, overhead costs, your profit margin, and a retail margin.

Acquiring Credit Card Merchant Status

For the most part, banks are reluctant to grant merchant status to home businesses, allowing them to accept credit cards for purchases. Much like the requirements involved in applying for a loan, when you apply for merchant status, banks look for proof that your home business is professional, profitable, and sustainable. *How to Achieve Credit Card Merchant Status* (Todd Publications), by Paul Madjenovic, provides in-depth information on this topic. You can purchase a copy by calling (800) 747–1056.

Evaluating Your Furniture and Technology Needs

In the last chapter you selected a space for your home office. Let's talk more about your furniture and equipment needs. If finances are tight, there are many ways to cut corners when you're first starting out. Take an inventory of what you have on hand. Check out garage and yard sales for furniture and equipment. Look for ads in the local papers. Scope out used-office-equipment stores and thrift stores such as the Salvation Army or Goodwill. Ask friends or loved ones if they know anyone who might be moving from a home office back to the corporate world (highly doubtful) who has office furniture or equipment for sale.

Write down each item you need to furnish and equip your office, along with an estimated cost if you don't currently have the item on hand. What will you need in the way of office furniture—filing cabinets, tables, bookshelves, etc.

I mentioned that you can cut corners by purchasing used equipment, but don't sacrifice comfort. Buy a chair that has good lower-back support and a backrest that tilts. Make sure it adjusts up and down. If you'll be at the computer keyboard frequently, it may be best to use a chair that has armrests so you can position your arms parallel to the floor while you type.

Most homeworkers can't get by without investing in technology. "We keep everything on the computer," says Mary, an insurance agent. "We have our client database, record keeping, and we do our budget every year on the computer." Make a list of all the equipment and resources you'll need, including a computer, printer, scanner, software, modem, Internet access, additional phone lines, mobile phone, cordless phone, headset/speaker phone (especially if you do a lot of telemarketing or phone work), voice mail (or answering machine), fax machine, pager, and copy machine. There's a variety of affordable, space-conscious office equipment, including fax-copy machine combinations, desktop copiers, and laptop computers.

For information on how to choose technological equipment based on your needs, as well as desirable warranties and maintenance agreements, talk to other homeworkers. Read the latest computer magazines such as *Home Office Computing, PC Magazine, Computer Shopper,* and *Mobile Office.* Know what you can afford, and remember, flexibility is the key when first starting out.

Covering Yourself

Most homeowners' and renters' insurance policies do not fully cover home-office equipment. Another consideration when it comes to insurance is liability. If you are a sole proprietor without liability insurance, you may be personally liable if a client gets injured on your premises, or if you are sued by a dissatisfied client. If you are a telecommuter, consult with your employer, because you'll most likely be responsible for personal injury, damage, or loss that occurs in your home office. Fortunately, many insurance companies are starting to offer "homework" insurance that can be attached to an existing homeowner's policy. Call your state insurance office or the National Insurance Consumer Helpline at (800) 942-4242 to see if this is an option for you.

Health insurance is another necessity if you or your spouse will not be covered by an employer. This can be a major expense depending on your age, health, health habits, number of dependents, and the deductible and amount of coverage you choose. In the San Diego area, a healthy family of four can expect to pay about $5,000 per year for an HMO plan that requires a $15 copay per doctor visit. In the New York area, the same plan would run closer to $7,000.

Verify that the company you're considering has a license and has been in business for a while. To receive a free printout of health insurance options based on your requirements, call Quotesmith at (800) 556-9393. Also, Support Services Alliance provides group dental, health, and life insurance to small-business owners. For information, call (800) 322-3920.

You'll also want to look into carrying extended car insurance if you transport expensive products, or frequently travel with clients or employees in the car. Other types of insurance to consider carrying when you begin working at home are product liability insurance, malpractice insurance (for service-oriented businesses), life insurance, workers' compensation (a requirement in most states if you have employees), and disability insurance.

Homeworkers generally don't carry a disability insurance policy. "We had disability insurance for a while, but I dropped it because we were too insurance-rich," says Mike, a screenplay writer. Sue, a medical transcriptionist, feels differently. "I have a friend who relies on her work as a transcriptionist to pay the bills," she says. "She hurt her wrist and now she can't type. She has no disability insurance. Even if you're being covered by somebody else's medical, you really ought to get a disability policy of your own in a home business."

Investigate your existing policies, and talk to your agent to verify that you're adequately covered in the appropriate areas if you aren't already. If you don't have an insurance agent, ask other home business owners for recommendations. This is probably the best way to find a good broker who is committed to helping you meet your insurance needs. Check with the State Insurance Department to ensure that any agents you interview are properly licensed and don't have complaints against them.

Retirement Planning

If you or your spouse don't have retirement plans when you begin your work-at-home career, make it a goal to research options for investing in your future. Since you won't have an automatic retirement deduction, it is best to start now and take a proactive stance.

Sit down with a highly recommended financial planner and ask about pension plans for small business owners that allow for tax-deductible contributions. Investigate stocks, mutual funds, bonds, and real estate. Can you continue adding to a pension plan you are already in, or roll it over into an individual retirement account (IRA)? Check out your options. A retirement plan is a critical step toward ensuring the comfortable lifestyle you deserve and have worked hard to achieve.

SPECIAL TIPS FOR TELECOMMUTERS

If you're pondering the decision to telecommute in your current job and are wondering how to go about it, here are some suggestions to help you get started.

The Upside and Downside of Telecommuting

We discussed the pros and cons of working at home in Chapters 1 and 2. If you wish to telecommute, however, there are also upsides and downsides you can stress to your employer. The first thing your employer will want to know is the impact on the company, and it's critical that you've examined it from all angles and are able to overcome any objections.

Many companies are offering telecommuting to selected employees. Small businesses, which can be greatly affected by the loss of even one worker, are leading the trend. In her informative book *Telecommute!* (John Wiley & Sons, Inc.), Lisa Shaw stresses the upside and downside to the employer of having employees who telecommute:

UPSIDE OF TELECOMMUTING
- Decreases office expenses, including rent, utilities, and equipment
- Increases productivity
- Decreases employee turnover
- Increases ability to self-manage, thus relieving management of total supervision responsibility
- Ability to meet Clean Air Act requirements
- Sets up an automatic disaster-recovery program (after a fire, earthquake, flood, etc.)
- Fosters a more content work force
- Creates jobs and equipment to meet the needs of telecommuters
- Ability to be more competitive in the marketplace
- Shows workers the employer cares about them
- Teaches supervisors to exercise a more flexible management style

- Communication with colleagues and managers occurs in a more focused, concise way
- Enhances computer literacy

DOWNSIDE OF TELECOMMUTING

- Some managers don't trust employees they can't see, and are used to basing performance on attendance rather than output or results
- Telecommuters are less able to meet customer needs
- Work teams deteriorate when members are scattered
- Telecommuting appears to favor some employees over others
- Meetings must be coordinated in advance
- Future promotions may be affected; however, the effect of telecommuting can be positive (if work performance goes up) or negative (if management overlooks you because you are not physically present in the office)
- Managers must adapt to using different methods of supervision

Is Your Job Right for Telecommuting?

Do you currently work in a job that lends itself to telecommuting? Service-oriented work such as computer programming, bookkeeping, or writing is ideal for telecommuting. The work that's best suited for home is that which requires independent actions and large blocks of concentration: reading, writing, planning, budgeting, and so forth. These activities will take up varying percentages of time for different employees. It all depends on your job. A lawyer would be able to use at least one day at home to conduct research and write law briefs. For some positions it would be difficult to justify telecommuting. These might include upper-level managers, retail sales positions, customer-service workers, manufacturing employees, and health-care professionals.

To determine if your job is appropriate for telecommuting, write down your regular and irregular job responsibilities. From that list, estimate what percentage of the work can be done just as easily from home as in your office. If you work a five-day work week and at least 25 percent of your work can be done at home, then you could probably justify telecommuting one day each week. This exercise will help you reflect a breakdown of the duties you will perform on the day(s) you work at home in your proposal to your employer.

Writing Your Telecommuting Proposal

If you're interested in creating a telecommuting arrangement in your current job, don't just bounce it off of your manager casually. Put together a detailed, well thought out proposal that shows not only that you've done your homework, but that you mean business. Lisa Shaw offers some basic points you should cover in a one- or two-page succinct proposal to your manager or supervisor:

1. Why do you wish to telecommute?
2. How many days a week do you want to work at home? Will this remain the same each week or vary according to your workload?
3. What changes need to be addressed (yours or other employees' responsibilities, performance evaluations)?
4. What equipment will you need?
5. Which tasks are you going to perform from home?
6. Will you require a separate phone line?
7. Are you planning to use this as a temporary or permanent work arrangement?
8. How will you stay connected with the office?
9. Who can cover for you at the office?
10. Why will this arrangement help the company?
11. How much money will the company save?
12. Other issues: child care, work space, and the question of who is responsible for equipment.

Include your company's mission statement somewhere near the top of the proposal. Make it clear that you're a team player whose primary interest is in working to achieve the company's goals. Also, do as much research as possible before you present your proposal. Be prepared to overcome any and all objections from management.

One hint: Investigate whether your state requires companies to abide by stricter Clean Air Act regulations. Some states are required by law to reduce emissions by a certain percent by mandating that corporations implement flexible work schedules (including telecommuting) that keep cars off the road. If your state must meet such a requirement, this bit of information will certainly encourage acceptance of your proposal.

Establishing Your Telecommuting Agreement

Once you have the approval to telecommute from your manager, prepare a written agreement that details all the terms of your telecommuting arrangement. In the agreement spell out who will pay for what in terms of phone-line installation, phone bills, and necessary supplies and equipment. Itemize the tasks you will complete when working from home. Also, state what measures you'll take to secure all materials (especially those of a confidential nature). If you will be working at home on certain days or for a certain number of hours each week, put it in the agreement.

Specify how you will keep in touch with the office (E-mail, phone, fax, memo) and when, as well as how you'll participate in meetings or conferences held in the office during your absence. Also reflect how your performance will be evaluated. Be as detailed as possible so you can prevent misunderstandings by having guidelines to fall back on should anyone ever question your telecommuting arrangement.

Setting Goals and Monitoring Your Progress

Setting goals is crucial to your success as a telecommuter. Involve your manager by sharing your work goals and making sure that your goals are on track with the goals of your team and company. Your manager can be your mentor if you have a good working relationship. If your manager is relatively positive about your telecommuting arrangement, don't hesitate to discuss difficulties you are having so you can brainstorm potential solutions together.

Talk with your manager about how your work progress will be monitored or evaluated. Usually the work of telecommuters is measured by results in terms of what they produce. This could relate to the number of sales made or the completion of certain tasks or projects. Spell this out clearly in your telecommuting agreement (see the preceding section).

Maintaining Contact and Accessibility

It's important that you maintain visibility with your manager and co-workers at the office. You can do this by phone and E-mail or by scheduling specific times to meet. In your telecommuting agreement you will most likely designate the chosen method and frequency of communication with your manager. Go out of your way to stick to the agreement so your manager can feel your presence even when you're working from afar.

Make a point of keeping in touch with the office regularly to avoid isolation, stay in the loop, and keep current on what's happening. Encourage co-workers to call you at home so they don't worry about interrupting you. You are still a part of the team. When you talk on the phone, get into the habit of keeping conversations brief.

Last, make yourself easily accessible to clients. If you rely on voice mail to take client calls, check it frequently throughout the day. Clients won't suspect you are telecommuting if you stay on top of calls, and tell the receptionist at your office to convey that you're working at another site for the day.

Dealing with Co-Worker Resentment

Be aware that resentment from co-workers who aren't given the option to telecommute might surface. Some may try to sabotage your arrangement by scheduling meetings behind your back or not passing along crucial information.

You can prevent resentment toward your telecommuting arrangement by ensuring that none of your co-workers is taking on some of your workload as a result of your absence. You'll also circumvent resentment by continuing to keep in touch with co-workers and share information and stories. Tell them about the realities of telecommuting. Those who are in such a position may be considering it themselves.

Preplanning Your Telecommuting Days

You'll do yourself a big favor if you plan in advance for what you will need (files, supplies, equipment) to work at home. Keep a file or a list of tasks you will work on at home along with a breakdown of everything you'll need from the office to complete the tasks (including special supplies). You don't want to get stuck on a project because you forgot some important notes you left in a file back at the office. By planning ahead, you won't have to interrupt your co-workers to ask them to fax the notes to you.

If possible, don't take original files from the office that your co-workers might need access to. Instead, make the necessary copies or jot down the information you'll need. Also, plan for what can go wrong when working on a project at home. If for some reason you must halt your work on a particular task, have something else on hand that you can work on as a backup.

Who Will Cover for You?

Find someone you can trust to cover for you at the office in your absence. This could be an assistant or a fellow telecommuter who can receive or deliver mail and faxes for you. Remind your manager and co-workers of your telecommuting days and hours. You may want to post your schedule at your desk or with the receptionist. Also, keep a bin handy for your incoming mail, memos, and magazines to prevent desk pileup and ensure that important items don't get lost or misplaced.

Handling Safety Concerns

Most companies have basic guidelines for safety standards applicable to your home office, including the need for a fire extinguisher, smoke detector, evacuation plan, and a first-aid kit. Some have requirements with regard to the type and placement of furniture and equipment you'll be using. Before you start telecommuting (and anytime thereafter), your employer may want to inspect your home office to verify that it complies with designated safety standards. Be aware of what those standards entail so you can be prepared.

Managing Security

Before you begin telecommuting, discuss with your manager how you will handle proprietary materials you need to access when working from home. Usually you'll be required to maintain a level of security equal to what exists in the office. Also, determine how you will store information and materials in case of fire or theft. Consider what rules you will follow, and the measures you'll take to keep all information secure.

APPROACHING YOUR PLAN ONE STEP AT A TIME

You now have a detailed plan for making the transition to a work-at-home lifestyle that includes time frames for completing the necessary tasks to get started. Approach the plan as a series of action items rather than an overwhelming agenda. Take things one step at a time, and before you know it, your work-at-home fantasy will become a reality.

CHAPTER ELEVEN

Managing and Growing Your Home Business

 Homeworker Hint

The hardest thing to realize when you start a home business is that you don't know it all. Thinking that you do is why businesses fail.

Ben, Marketing Consultant

Now that you've made the transition to working at home, it's time to talk about strategies for managing and growing your business. In this chapter we'll discuss pertinent issues such as marketing, goal setting, conserving cash, expanding your business, keeping records, and handling taxes.

FINE-TUNING YOUR MARKETING TECHNIQUES

In Chapters 2 and 3 I asked what you're comfortable with in terms of marketing your home business. Given your personality and level of drive and commitment, which of the following strategies appeal to you?

Active and Passive Techniques

Homeworkers use a variety of active and passive marketing techniques to build their business. Many rely solely on passive techniques such as advertising, the Yellow Pages, direct mailings, trade shows, free publicity, writing industry-related articles for publication, and their own circle of influence. Others rely primarily on active techniques—cold-calling in particular—to build their business. Some use a combination of active and passive strategies.

WORD OF MOUTH

Most homeworkers say that once their business was launched from initial marketing efforts, it continued to grow from referrals. "Now my main marketing weapon is word of mouth," says Jack, a copywriter. "I haven't had to compete for a lot of business."

CREATIVE STRATEGIES

Homeworkers offer creative strategies for marketing their products and services—techniques that emphasize their own ideals and values. Jenny, who has a new secretarial service, markets her services as *always available*. "Clients sometimes want you to work on the weekends," she says. "I'll work anytime they want to get things going. When I get to a point where I'm too busy, then I can afford to be selective."

Jill, a desktop publisher, reduced her prices below the competition to attract clients in the beginning. "At first I kept the rate fairly low," she explains. "When I started getting more work than I could handle, I raised my prices." While it is generally not advisable to offer cut-rate prices if you are new to the business, Jill found this strategy to be effective.

Carol, an architectural illustrator, researched the marketing materials of others. "Before I write my marketing materials, I go through the competition's and pick theirs apart," she says. "I look for what I do that's different and highlight that."

Amy, a computer software distributor, offers a strategy that boosts her business. "I spend two hours on the phone every day calling customers who haven't ordered recently just to check in and see how things are going," she reveals. "That has sparked a lot of business." Some call it "follow-up" while others call it the "sale after the sale." Remind your clients of your past service to them with tools such as newsletters, Rolodex cards, periodic mailings, and phone calls.

Homeworkers use strategies that emphasize good customer service and going the extra mile to treat clients, suppliers, and employees well. "I write a thank-you card or call everybody who makes an inquiry or a purchase," says Paul, an environmental product distributor. "I've had people call and say, 'I can't believe you thanked me for inquiring about your product.' They're not used to getting that kind of personal contact."

NETWORKING GROUPS

Homeworker Hint

If you can take the selling process out of what you're doing, and you know you're offering the clients valuable gifts, you'll suddenly become the biggest *influencer* in the room instead of the biggest salesperson.

Sara, Fitness Trainer

Most homeworkers belong to at least one professional organization or networking group that's business-related. Mary, an insurance agent, belongs to six professional organizations that she joined to market her services. "I go to meetings with plenty of cards and brochures," she says. "I pass a card out to everyone new I talk to. I keep my services fresh in everyone's mind and constantly ask for referrals. I'm amazed at how much my business has grown as a result of opening my mouth at those events."

MARKETING ON THE INTERNET

Many homeworkers access the Internet for business purposes—primarily to scope out the competition or do research. "I've tried to invest in my business by being technologically superior to my competition, as long as it makes economic sense," says Ben, a marketing consultant. "It's almost like Desert Storm—if you have the right weapons or tools, then you have an unfair advantage over others."

Many home business owners view the Internet as a way to market their products and services. O'Reilly and Associates, a California publisher of computer books and software, conducted a recent poll concluding that approximately 9.7 million people have direct access to the Internet or an on-line service such as America Online, CompuServe, or Prodigy, and this number is rapidly increasing. It was also found that these users have a median household income between $50,000 and $75,000. Obviously there's money to be made in cyberspace, but how can you reach your target market?

There are many low-cost ways to market your business on-line. The least expensive way to make your on-line presence known is by using forums, which are electronic bulletin boards users subscribe to for free to ask questions, give advice, or state opinions. Thousands of users access these bulletin boards daily, so it's a great way to capture a large audience. Just visit the forums that relate to your business and look for user questions that allow you to offer your expert advice. If appropriate, make mention of a useful product or service you know of (that just happens to be yours) and the Web site to access (if you have one). No overt selling is allowed, so be helpful, respectful, and discreet.

You can hire a professional to design a Web page that advertises your business on the Internet for as little as $100, or purchase the necessary software to create your own. It's an inexpensive way to get the word out about your products and services. E-mail can be used to directly contact customers or send information about what you do (similar to direct mail) at a minimal cost. You can even start a store on the World Wide Web and use E-mail to invite customers to shop. The Internet may be a powerful marketing tool for your business. Check out the resources mentioned in Chapter 13 to see how your business can benefit further from creating an on-line presence.

FEW CLIENTS VERSUS MANY

Depending on the type of home business you run, you may have the option of maintaining a few large accounts that give repeat business, or numerous small accounts that do business more infrequently. There are advantages to either option. Jill, a desktop publisher, doesn't like having a lot of clients who need her services infrequently. "It's much more efficient to have three big clients with repeat business so I don't have to keep reinventing client contact,'' she explains. ''I look for clients who are already up and running—for years and years—that know how to hand off work and are organized themselves.''

Sue, a medical transcriptionist, feels it's much more secure to maintain a large base of clients. ''I have learned the hard way that I need to keep multiple accounts rather than throw all my eggs in one basket,'' she asserts. ''It's a disaster when you lose that one.''

Whatever marketing strategies you choose, be sure you have the capital and the personal drive to follow through. Any kind of marketing effort takes time to see results. It is critical that you create a marketing plan, continually analyze your return from ongoing marketing efforts, and update the plan accordingly. If your ads or direct mailers aren't pulling calls, do a reevaluation of your materials. Ask for feedback from a trusted coach or mentor who understands your business. Don't bounce from one thing to another unless you've exhausted your chosen approach. Much like line hopping in the supermarket, you'll generally come out ahead if you keep your nose in a magazine and stay where you are.

Try to stick with two or three marketing strategies that are comfortable for you, both personally and financially. Remember to be patient and implement good follow-up with a smile. To ensure this, keep a small mirror by the phone when you make your calls. It will serve as a constant reminder to keep smiling.

UPDATING YOUR BUSINESS PLAN AND GOALS

Many homeworkers use their business plan as a working document to help them stay on track. ''I keep all my short-term and long-term goals for my business right in my business plan,'' says Kevin, a real estate agent. ''Each year I evaluate and update the entire plan, putting a major emphasis on my goals.''

For the first couple of years in business, it's a good idea to update your business plan every six months, and then annually thereafter. Regardless of whether you maintain a business plan, establish short- and long-range goals for your business, write them down, and reevaluate them each year.

HANGING ON TO YOUR MONEY

Once you're up and running in your home business, you'll want to take steps to conserve and hang on to your cash, and most important, ensure you get paid for your hard-earned work. Take heed of any of the following that apply to you or your business.

Get a Retainer Fee

When you do work for a client, ask for a portion of the amount owed up front. If your client cancels the order after you've done most of the work or doesn't have sufficient funds to pay you upon completion of the work, at least you will have minimized your losses.

If you're working on a long, involved project, consider having your client make graduated payments as the work progresses. You might ask for 50 percent up front, another 25 percent when the project is 75 percent complete, and the remaining 25 percent when the work is finished. It's good practice to secure a deposit before doing any work. Clients who are serious about doing business with you won't object.

Put It in Writing

Protect yourself and your business by putting everything in writing. Anytime you take an order from a client, make sure you both sign and date a contract that specifies exactly what service or product you're providing, when it will be delivered, and the method and schedule of payment. This will prevent misunderstandings between you and your clients down the road. Some consultants recommend that you include a clause indicating that you or your client can terminate a contract on thirty days notice so that if any ethical, personality, or other problems arise, you can make an exit. Consider having an attorney help you develop a contract you are comfortable with.

Cut Your Losses

One positive aspect of working on your own is that you can pick and choose whom you wish to do business with. Trust your instincts. Don't let negative, nonpaying, impossible-to-please clients drain your energies. Instead, take that energy and channel it toward finding people who will appreciate and gladly pay for the gifts and talents you offer.

Don't Underestimate Your Worth

If you're always willing to cut your fees to make a sale, people won't see the value in what you offer because you don't. If you allow yourself to fall into this trap, you may wind up working for *free*. Some may suspect you're desperate and try to take advantage. This is most apparent when you provide a service, because the focus is entirely on your performance. The commodity you're selling is your time. Don't sell yourself short. Put a value on what you offer, and know your worth.

Persist in Collections

What can you do when clients don't pay their bills? Stay on top of outstanding (unpaid) invoices by following up with an overdue notice (along with a copy of the original contract highlighting the payment schedule) and a phone call. Some people don't pay until you remind them. Be persistently polite but never rude. Before you do business with slow-paying clients again, however, go over the payment schedule of their contract verbally.

Never do business with clients who have questionable credit, unless they pay you up front with cash. If possible, check their credit in the beginning by asking for three recent credit references, or have them screened through a credit service for a fee.

Unfortunately, home business owners are often victims of bad-check writers. Jill, a desktop publisher, asks her husband to come to her aid in collecting on bounced checks:

> *Not getting paid by a client is a big hassle. I had a client bounce a huge check on me. This client was in deep financial trouble and it took a year to collect on their bill. Owning a home business, you sometimes have to do collections. My husband poses as "J&B Collections." Let me tell you, when he calls,* they respond.

Ask for identification when you accept a check from a client to verify that the check isn't stolen. Don't accept a check from anyone you feel uncomfortable with. Instead, request another form of payment.

● **Check Acceptance Guidelines**
- Require a valid driver's license and record the number on the check.
- Verify the photo and physical description on the driver's license to ensure they match the person writing the check.
- Make sure the numerical and word amounts on the check match.
- Accept checks written with only the current date.
- Accept checks only for the purchase amount.
- Ask for a daytime and evening telephone number and address.
- Don't accept checks that were previously signed.
- Don't accept checks written on new accounts.

In the San Diego area, the district attorney's office now offers help to home business owners who receive a bad check. At no cost, their Bad Check Enforcement Program can locate bad-check writers, return the money to the victims, and prevent future offenses through a diversion program and possible criminal prosecution. Check with your county district attorney's office to see if help is available in your area.

Take Advantage of Discounts

Always ask for a business discount when you make purchases from stores that serve the general public, such as supply and stationery stores. Generally, if you pay your vendors on time, you automatically get a discount. These discounts offer a tremendous savings when you regularly take advantage of them.

Establish Business Credit

It's always a good idea to establish business credit with your major vendors. This will give you the ability to even out your cash flow when need be. You'll also build a good credit history for possible future credit needs.

Try Leasing

A popular way to conserve cash is by leasing rather than buying assets. A lease allows you to budget for and defer expenditures by spreading payments out over time (three to five years), instead of requiring a large outlay of cash up front.

Don't Overstock

Don't let the materials you use to produce your product or service get too low, but don't overstock either. Bargains or "stock-up" sales are tempting, but before you indulge, ask yourself if you can afford to tie up your cash and space. If you can't, you are better off making the purchase when it's really necessary.

EXPANDING YOUR HOME BUSINESS

How quickly do you want your home business to grow? How will you accommodate that growth? "With electronics and office equipment I can make up for one or two people, which is fine for now," says Ben, a marketing consultant. "But beyond that I'll need to move out of my home into an office for space purposes, to hire employees and all."

Gradual Growth

Some homeworkers prefer to grow their home business gradually because of their children. Many have a spouse who makes enough money to cover the bills (just barely for some). "If they can afford it, I would advise work-at-home parents to keep their business real small at first, especially if their kids are little and they want to work without child care," suggests Jill, a desktop publisher. "You can't expect much at first because little ones take so much out of you."

Liz, a computer programmer, has a similar approach. "When I first got started, there weren't that many hours involved," she says. "So it was a gradual buildup, increasing the hours worked as the children got older." Other homeworkers who are not relying on their income to pay the bills start small and conservatively, and continually put all of their earnings back into their business to keep it growing (also known as "bootstrapping"). They don't pay themselves a salary. "Reinvesting the income back into the business is the only way I can create what I need to create," says Sara, a fitness trainer.

Delegating

As mentioned in Chapter 9, most homeworkers delegate tasks that will free them to focus on what they do best. Are you willing to delegate to allow your business to grow, or are you more comfortable being a one-person operation? A small minority of homeworkers don't delegate or subcontract work to others because they're reluctant to become managers, and want to maintain a firm grip on quality control (reasons they decided to go on their own in the first place). "I never subcontract work to others, perhaps from greed or from a sense of obligation—these are *my* accounts, and I know that I will do the best job possible," says Sue, a medical transcriptionist.

Most homeworkers do wind up delegating certain tasks in order to allow their business to grow. At the very least, they hire someone to help with child care and household chores. Remember, as the number of hours devoted to child care and household chores increase, the number of hours devoted to your home business decrease, and so does your income.

Author Jay Levinson says that people who are reluctant to delegate should realize that they can accomplish their objectives while someone else is accomplishing others, thus creating a ninety-minute hour. He stresses that squeezing extra minutes out of every hour requires the ability to identify work that can and should be delegated, and finding and checking out the people who are capable of doing the work. In *The Ninety-Minute Hour* (E.P. Dutton), he offers tips for delegating wisely:

- Don't delegate to someone who won't do the work as well as you can do it.
- Recognize that every time you delegate successfully, you double your effectiveness.
- Don't delegate tasks to someone if you're not willing to train that person to do them excellently. And let that person set the terms, timetables, and objectives so he or she can measure how the work is going.
- Don't always tell the person to whom you are delegating how to achieve the results, just talk about the results themselves and encourage initiative.
- Don't limit the concept of delegating to work chores; consider it also for the multitude of home chores.
- Don't do it if you can delegate it. Just recognize that you are delegating not only work but responsibility for results.
- When delegating, provide as much information about the task as possible.
- When you delegate, be sure you delegate the authority to make important decisions.
- Tell the truth to the person to whom you delegate. If it is drudgery, don't say the task is glamorous.
- If you don't know how to trust, you'll have problems delegating. So be sure you learn how to trust, how to give up some territory and power.

If you're uncomfortable with the idea of delegating, take things one step at a time by delegating small tasks to begin with. As your confidence grows and you find people you can rely on, you can increase the amount and type of work you delegate. If your needs in certain areas of the business are irregular, you can hire independent contractors to work on an as-needed basis. If you find you need help on a regular basis, you may want to consider hiring employees. Before you hire full-time help, however, make sure your income warrants the expense.

Hiring Employees

When it comes to hiring employees, you may be tempted to recruit from your family and friends. This is fine as long as your family member or friend understands what's required and has the needed skills and experience for the job. It's critical that you set boundaries for how your relationship will be conducted during work hours. Communicate your expectations in advance and create a job description.

If you hire family members or friends in an effort to save money, their resentment will build, their work performance will suffer, and you'll wind up regretting it. If you want to develop a fair relationship, be willing to pay what you would pay someone on the outside at the same skill and experience level.

When hiring employees outside of your circle of influence, consider a variety of methods for finding them. Running a classified ad is the most obvious way, but often the least effective. Usually you can find well-qualified people by networking among your business and personal associations, including professional organizations, church, neighbors, and friends. Check the Internet for résumés of qualified people, or consider posting a job opening. Also look into local trade or vocational schools and colleges. They usually have placement services. Employment agencies are another source, and they can assist with applicant screening.

When you hire employees it's necessary to comply with minimum wage and employee health and safety laws. Develop job descriptions and a company policy for handling vacation, sick leave, and other personnel issues. Putting these items in writing will avoid misunderstandings and prevent legal issues from arising.

Moving Out

You will know when it's time to move your business out of the home. Any unused space will be taken over by your business. You'll reach a point when you refuse to step on one of your employees to answer the phone hiding under a pile, or you can no longer find past client files because you've moved them into storage in the garage—your neighbor's garage, that is. You'll know because you and your business will start to suffer.

When that happens, start making a list of what you need to do to move out, rent or buy an office space, and make it known to all. Consider your needs, possible resources, what you can afford, and the current costs. Then make a plan for how and when you'll make the move, and go for it. It's a risk, to be sure, but it's likely to be more of a hindrance and risk if you don't move out so that your business can continue to grow.

RECORD KEEPING

Establish a good record-keeping system that tracks your expenses, sales, inventory, and payroll. Also keep a chart of accounts, a cash-flow statement, and a monthly profit-and-loss statement. These tools will allow you to keep organized books as well as monitor your ongoing progress in relation to competitors. When you spot a dip in performance, you'll be able to take immediate action to improve your operating efficiency.

There are many software programs available to manage your records. The best way to find suitable programs for your business needs is to (you guessed it) ask other home business owners in a similar line of work. The best recommendations come from those who know from experience. Also, *Keeping the Books* (Dearborn Financial Publishing), by Linda Pinson and Jerry Jinnett, is one of many excellent resources available on managing and tracking the financial performance of your business.

Keep a separate bank account for your business, and write

checks for business expenses from that account. Some banks offer on-line services allowing you to download statements, check your account balance, and verify whether checks have cleared any time of the day or night.

Take the time up front to set up files for all your tax deductions. When receipts come in and checks clear, enter them into your record-keeping program and put them in their respective file. At the end of the year, when you clear out your files, you won't have to do a lot of sorting before you turn the package over to your accountant. You'll save yourself a lot of headaches and hassles if you establish an efficient record-keeping system from the beginning.

TAXING MATTERS

A number of expenses are deductible when you work at home, and one of the biggest is the home-office deduction. Talk with your accountant to see whether you qualify, because this deduction is heavily scrutinized by the IRS. Other deductible expenses include a percentage of health-care costs, travel and entertainment, child care, retirement plans, and of course, business expenses. Always keep detailed data on your expenses at the time of expenditure. For tax information on working at home, order Publication 587 from the IRS at (800) 829-3676.

Since you won't have an employer withholding your taxes, you'll be responsible for making advance quarterly payments of your estimated federal and state income taxes. These payments must also include your self-employment taxes, which are the employer's and employee's portions of your estimated Social Security tax. The payments are due on April 15, June 15, September 15, and January 15 of the following year. You can be penalized if you're late or don't make a payment. If you overpay, you'll receive a refund at the end of the year.

It's a good idea to establish a separate bank account for taxes so you can contribute a percentage of each month's earnings to cover estimated tax payments prior to their due date. It can be devastating when you wind up owing money you've already spent. Talk with your accountant to help you get set up. If you have employees, check with your accountant or the local IRS and state office of taxation to determine what tax requirements apply to your particular situation.

STAY OPEN TO NEW IDEAS

You are now armed with the nuts and bolts of managing and growing your home business. You can keep current in your field and stay ahead of the competition by constantly expanding your knowledge and skill base. The best way to do this is through professional organizations, publications, seminars, classes, and the Internet. Always remain open to new opportunities to learn and grow in your business, and you'll find that one success leads to another.

CHAPTER TWELVE

Pulling It All Together

Homeworker Hint

Working at home is about tuning in to your needs and the needs of your family. It's as simple as that. There is no cookie-cutter approach that works for everyone. It takes a lot of planning and the ability to advance and adjust quickly.

Beth, Accountant

Congratulations! You have completed the necessary steps to creating a successful work-at-home lifestyle suited to your needs. You have a master plan, and now it's just a matter of carrying it through. Most things are learned through trial and error, and you have to keep trying until you find systems and strategies that work. Don't be afraid to experiment. Just don't give up. It takes a while to get adjusted, so allow yourself a learning curve of at least six months to feel comfortable and productive in your new work arrangement.

Unlike people who work outside the home, your work and personal lives are blended together in one setting. They're right in front of you twenty-four hours a day. You can't easily use work to escape from family or vice versa, as those who commute have the option of doing. That's why strategies aimed at preserving your boundaries and schedule are absolutely vital.

The thinking and planning steps you took throughout this book will come back to you tenfold in terms of your well-being and success, and the quality of life you'll create for yourself and your family. You deserve to feel good because you are now armed with self-awareness, and that combined with a plan and the ability to advance and adjust are your keys to lasting happiness and success.

Everything in life has its ups and downs, and working at home is no exception. Homeworkers use a variety of strategies to overcome obstacles, allowing them to minimize internal conflict and maximize productivity. If they don't have obvious solutions, they create them. They don't just accept things as they are. Some turn what may be considered negative situations into positive experiences.

Val, a travel agent—who refers to herself as a "single mom" for four nights a week because her husband travels for business—tailored her arrangement entirely around her husband's absence and inability to contribute to child care and household duties. She teamed up with a partner in her business, and both work extralong days, alternating days of the week. They also share a nanny on the three days they each work, who takes care of their children and does the housecleaning. They developed family-friendly company policies that allow for ample paid vacations and maternity leave.

Val works at home in order to be close to her daughter, and she crams five workdays into three while her husband is away so that they can have concentrated time together as a family when he returns on weekends. Prior to creating this arrangement, she and her husband sat down and discussed the issues of managing the house and producing the income necessary to meet their needs, and arrived at a division they were both satisfied with. Val is extremely happy to be able to work at home in a business that challenges her potential and gives her the ability to see her daughter on breaks throughout her workday. She is also able to spend time with her family on the weekends free of household responsibilities.

Pat, a newspaper publisher, seemed to have everything working against her. Her husband offered little or no support in managing the household or taking care of the kids, and they couldn't afford to pay someone to help in these areas. As a result, she struggled in her business, feeling overwhelmed by the multiple roles she was entirely responsible for.

Pat used her skills and creativity to overcome the tremendous challenges she faced. She started a publishing business with a long-term goal of having a company in which her children could eventually have the opportunity to use their unique talents. She worked around the fact that she had no start-up capital by using the barter system. She found someone who would donate all her business equipment in exchange for her writing and editing services. She keeps a part-time day-care business going to help with cash flow, which is comprised of handpicked playmates for her children so they stay occupied while she works.

Pat generally ignores the housecleaning duties until she (or her husband) can no longer stand it. Eventually her kids help her with the housecleaning in short spurts of concentrated effort. In turn, she rewards them and herself during mini segments of time in the afternoons by taking them on little outings to the beach, library, or park while her clients are at lunch. In essence, Pat found solutions to her problems and implemented strategies in accordance with her needs so that she could continue to work at home and be close to her children.

Amy spun off a computer software distributing company from a previous company she had worked for, and built her business to the point where her husband could leave his job and come home to work with her. There is a real sense of teamwork among the husband-and-wife partnerships.

Most "copreneurs" use a hired housecleaner and rely on paid child care, with many having in-home care. They are adamant about hiring help in their home and in their business so they can put effective, concentrated time into their work and personal lives. Having the home business as their sole source of income causes them to be very disciplined about creating boundaries and establishing support systems that enable them to succeed and work well together.

Ron established a home business with his wife, and once the business was built up, he continued working in the business while his wife went to work outside the home to pursue a career in management. Ron is proud of the fact that he runs the household and takes care of his son while his wife is making leaps and bounds in her career. This illustrates some of the unique lifestyles—especially those involving a team spirit—that couples invent so they can be close as a family and foster growth in everyone—mom, dad, and the kids.

Like the homeworkers I interviewed, you also have a golden opportunity to take control and be the master of your own destiny in a work-at-home lifestyle. As technology continues to advance at a rapid pace, and corporations increasingly hire independent contractors to work on a per-project basis, work-at-home opportunities will continue to flourish.

New careers and business ideas are popping up daily. Planned telecommuting communities, featuring homes prewired for computerized offices, are on the drawing board in several parts of the country. Neighborhoods with several homeworkers are creating a network of support by exchanging child-care services, meal preparation, social support, and business strategies.

Working at home is beginning to take shape as the preferred work (and life) style of the future. Trend watchers estimate that by 2010 a home business will exist in every other household. It's not unlikely that one day most of the working population will be doing it. So what are you waiting for? You have your "homework" cut out for you, and now is the time to take action. Best of luck!

CHAPTER THIRTEEN

Recommended Resources

Homeworker Hint

Respect for home businesses is growing because there are more and more of us. There's serious business out there—not just pin money.

Ann, Personal Image Consultant

New information on the work-at-home movement is popping up daily in the form of books, magazines, and newsletters. Help is available from a vast array of organizations, agencies, and on-line services. Following is a multitude of resources relevant to topics covered in each chapter.

CHAPTER I.
WHY WORK AT HOME?

Books

The Artists Way: A Spiritual Path to Higher Creativity, by Julia Cameron and Mark Bryan, Jeremy P. Tarcher/Putnam, 1995.

Making It on Your Own: Surviving and Thriving the Ups and Downs of Being Your Own Boss, by Sarah and Paul Edwards, Jeremy P. Tarcher/Putnam, 1991.

CHAPTER 2. ARE YOU SUITED FOR WORKING AT HOME?

Books

The Survivor Personality, by Al Siebert, Ph.D., Practical Psychology Press, 1994.

CHAPTER 3. CHOOSING A FITTING LINE OF WORK

Books

The Best Home Businesses for the 90's, by Paul and Sarah Edwards, Jeremy P. Tarcher/Putnam, 1994.

Breaking Out of 9 to 5, by Maria LaQueur and Donna Dickinson, Peterson Publishers, 1994.

The Complete Guide to Buying a Business, by Richard Snowden, Amacom, 1994.

Do What You Love, The Money Will Follow: Discovering Your Right Livelihood, by Marsha Sinetar, Paulist Press, 1987.

Finding the Hat that Fits: How to Turn Your Heart's Desire into Your Life's Work, by John Caple, Plume, 1993.

Finding Your Perfect Work: The New Career Guide to Making a Living, Creating a Life, by Paul and Sarah Edwards, Jeremy P. Tarcher/Putnam, 1995.

Franchise Opportunities Guide, (800) 543–1038.

The Franchise Opportunities Handbook, (202) 512-1800.

Franchises You Can Run from Home, by Lynie Arden, John Wiley & Sons, 1990.

How to Buy and Manage a Franchise: The Definitive Resource Guide If You're Thinking of Purchasing a Franchise or Turning Your Business into One, by Joseph Mancuso and Donald Boroian, Fireside, 1992.

How to Form Your Own Corporation, by Anthony Mancuso, Nolo Press, 1993.

How to Start a Service Business: The Essential Tools for Success in the Fastest Growing Industry of the Future, by Ben Chant and Melissa Morgan, Avon, 1994.

I Could Do Anything If I Only Knew What It Was, by Barbara Sher, Delacorte Press, 1994.

Inc. Your Dreams: For Any Woman Who Is Thinking About Her Own Business, by Rebecca Maddox, Viking, 1995.

LifeLaunch: A Passionate Guide to the Rest of Your Life, by Frederic Hudson and Pamela McLean, The Hudson Institute Press, 1995, (800) 582-4401.

Making a Living Without a Job: Winning Ways for Creating Work that You Love, by Barbara Winter, Bantam, 1993.

MLM Magic: How an Ordinary Person Can Build an Extra-Ordinary Networking Business from Scratch, by Venus Andrecht, Ranson Hill Press, 1993.

199 Great Home Businesses You Can Start & Succeed in for Under $1,000, by Tyler Hicks, Prima Publishing, 1991.

1001 Businesses You Can Start from Home, by Daryl Hall, John Wiley & Sons, 1992.

Scams, Swindles and Rip-Offs: Personal Stories, Power Lessons, by Graham Mott, Golden Press, (800) 844-7532.

Shifting Gears: How to Master Career Change and Find Work That's Right for You, by Carole Hyatt, Simon & Shuster, 1990.

Teleworking Explained, by Mike Gray, Noel Hodson, and Gil Gordon, John Wiley & Sons, 1993.

Tips and Traps When Buying a Franchise, by Mary Tomzack, McGraw-Hill, 1994.

Wave 3: The New Era in Network Marketing, by Richard Poe, Prima Publishing, 1995.

What Color Is Your Parachute?, by Richard Bolles, Ten Speed Press, 1995.

The Work-at-Home Sourcebook: Over 1,000 Job Opportunities Plus Home Business Opportunities & Other Options, by Lynie Arden, Live Oak Publications, 1992.

Work of Her Own, by Susan Wittig Albert, Ph.D., Jeremy P. Tarcher/Putnam, 1992.

Agencies

Direct Selling Association, provides written guidelines on how to evaluate multilevel marketing organizations, 1666 K Street, NW, Suite 1010, Washington, DC 20006, (202) 293-5760.

International Franchise Association, 1350 New York Ave. NW, Suite 900, Washington, DC 20005, (202) 628-8000.

National Fraud Information Center, (800) 876-7060.

CHAPTER 4.
MANAGING CHILDREN

Books

The Babysitting Co-op Guidebook, by Patricia McManus, ordering address: 915 N. Fourth St., Philadelphia, PA 19123.

The Complete Guide to Choosing Child Care, by Judith Berezin, Random House, 1991.

The Complete Guide to the Best Summer Camp for Your Child, by Richard Kennedy and Michael Kimball, Times Books, 1994.

Home-Based Employment and Family Life, edited by Ramona Heck, Alma Owen, and Barbara Rowe, Auburn House, 1995.

Mompreneuers: A Mother's Practical Step-by-Step Guide to Work-at-Home Success, by Ellen Parlapiano and Patricia Cobe, Perigee, 1996.

The Working Parents Help Book: Practical Advice for Dealing with the Day-to-Day Challenges of Kids and Careers, by Susan Crites Price and Tom Price, Peterson Publishers, 1996.

Magazines and Newsletters

At-Home Dad newsletter, 61 Brightwood Ave., North Andover, MA 01845-1702.

Child magazine, P.O. Box 3167, Harlan, IA 51593, (800) 777-0222.

Nanny News, Childcare News Network Corp., 137 Wood Ave., Stratford, CT 06497, (800) ME-4-NANNY.

Parents magazine, P.O. Box 3042, Harlan, IA 51537, (800) 727-3682.

Working Mother and *Working Woman* magazines, 230 Park Avenue, New York, NY 10169, (800) 234-9675.

Agencies/Associations/Organizations

American Camping Association, 12 W. 31st Street, New York, New York 10001, (800) 777- 2267.

The American Council of Nanny Schools, Delta College, University Center, MI 48710, (517) 686-9417.

Child Care Aware, (800) 424-2246.

Entrepreneurial Mothers Association, P.O. Box 2561, Mesa, AZ 85204, (602) 892–0722.

Families and Work Institute, www.familiesandwork.org, (212) 465-2044.

Home-Based Working Moms, workhommom@aol.com, www.hbwm.com, (512) 918- 0670.

Mothers' Home Business Network, P.O. Box 423, East Meadow, NY 11554, www.mhbn.com, (516) 997-7394.

NannyTax Inc., 50 E. Forty-second St., Suite 2108, New York, NY 10017, (212) 867-1776.

National Association of Child Care Resource & Referral Agencies, 1319 F St., Suite 810, Washington, DC 20004, (202) 393-5501.

Safe Sitter, 1500 North Ritter Ave., Indianapolis, IN 46219, (800) 255-4089.

YMCA Child Care Resource Service, (800) 481-2151.

CHAPTER 5. DIVIDING AND CONQUERING THE HOUSEHOLD LOAD

Books

Dinntertime Dilemma, (FREE) from the National Potato Board, offers cooking tips and recipes for speedy results. To order, send an SASE to 5101 East Forty-first Ave., Dept MH, Denver, CO 80216.

Eating Well Is the Best Revenge: Everyday Strategies for Delicious, Healthful Food in 30 Minutes or Less, by Marian Burros, Simon & Schuster, 1995.

How to Avoid Housework: Tips, Hints, and Secrets on How to Have a Spotless Home, by Paula Jhung, Simon & Schuster, 1995.

Kitchen Express, by Dee Wolk with Marsha Palmer, Kitchen Express Publishers, (800) 770-4336.

Mr. Food's Quick & Easy Side Dishes, by Art Ginsburg, William Morrow and Co., 1995.

Nathalie Dupree Cooks Quick Meals for Busy Days, by Nathalie Dupree, Clarkson Potter, 1996.

Once-a-Month-Cooking, by Mimi Wilson and Mary Beth Lagerborg, Focus on the Family Publishing, Colorado Springs, CO 80995.

Organize Your Family!, by Ronni Eisenberg with Kate Kelly, Hyperion, 1993.

Organize Your Home!, by Ronni Eisenberg with Kate Kelly, Hyperion, 1994.

The Second Shift: Working Parents and the Revolution at Home, by Arlie Hochschild, Viking, 1989.

Smart Crockery Cooking, by Carol Munson, Sterling Publishing, 1996.

Stephanie Winston's Best Organizing Tips, by Stephanie Winston, Simon & Shuster, 1995.

Weekdays Are Quick Meals: From Speedy Stir-Fries to Soups to Skillet Dishes and Thirty Minute Stews, by the editors of Time-Life Books, Time-Life Books, 1996.

Videos

How to Organize Your Home: Secrets of a Professional Organizer, by Stephanie Schur, SpaceOrganizers, (800) 383-8811.

CHAPTER 6. WORKING AT HOME CAN ENHANCE YOUR RELATIONSHIP

Books

The Book of Love, Laughter and Romance: Wonderful Suggestions and Delightful Ideas for Couples Who Want to Stay Close, Have Fun, and Keep the Enchantment Alive, by Barbara and Michael Jonas, Games Partnership Ltd., 1994.

Conscious Loving: The Journey to Co-Commitment: A Way to Be Fully Together Without Giving Up Yourself, by Gay and Kathlyn Hendricks, Ph.D., Bantam, 1992.

Couple Skills: Making Your Relationship Work, by Matthew McKay, Ph.D., Patrick Fanning, and Kim Paleg, Ph.D., New Harbinger Publications, 1994.

Couples and Money: Why Money Interferes with Love and What to Do About It, by Victoria Felton-Collins, Ph.D., Bantam, 1990.

Courtship After Marriage: Romance Can Last a Lifetime, by Zig Ziglar, Ballantine, 1990.

Getting Past No: Negotiating Your Way from Confrontation to Cooperation, by William Ury, Bantam, 1993.

Getting Together: Building Relationships as We Negotiate, by Roger Fisher and Scott Brown, Penguin, 1989.

He and She Talk: How to Communicate with the Opposite Sex, by Laurie Schloff and Marcia Yudkin, Plume, 1993.

Honey, I Want to Start My Own Business: A Planning Guide for Couples, by Azriela Jaffe, HarperBusiness, 1996.

How to Stay Lovers While Raising Your Children, by Anne Mayer, St. Martin's Press, 1990.

Making It Through the Night: How Couples Can Survive a Crisis Together, by Pat Quigley and Marilyn Shroyer, Ph.D., Conari Press, 1992.

Men Are from Mars, Women Are from Venus: A Practical Guide for Improving Communication and Getting What You Want in Your Relationships, by John Gray, Ph.D., HarperCollins, 1992.

Money Demons: Keep Them from Sabotaging Your Relationships—and Your Life, by Dr. Susan Forward and Craig Buck, Bantam, 1994.

Money Harmony: Resolving Money Conflicts in Your Life and Relationships, by Olivia Mellan, Walker and Company, 1994.

Now That I'm Married, Why Isn't Everything Perfect? The Eight Essential Traits of Couples Who Thrive, by Susan Page, Little, Brown and Company, 1994.

1001 Ways to Be Romantic, by Gregory Godek, Casablanca Press, 1991.

Romance 101: Lessons in Love, by Gregory Godek, Casablanca Press, 1993.

Secrets About Men Every Woman Should Know, by Barbara DeAngelis, Ph.D., Dell, 1990.

The Seven Basic Quarrels of Marriage: Recognize, Defuse, Negotiate, and Resolve Your Conflicts, by William Betcher, M.D., and Robie Macauley, Villard Books, 1990.

That's Not What I Meant: How Conversational Style Makes or Breaks Relationships, by Deborah Tannen, Ph.D., Ballantine, 1986.

When Opposites Attract: Right Brain/Left Brain Relationships and How to Make Them Work, by Rebecca Cutter, Dutton, 1994.

Who's on Top, Who's on Bottom: How Couples Can Learn to Share Power, by Robert Schwebel, Ph.D., Newmarket Press, 1994.

You Just Don't Understand: Women and Men in Conversation, by Deborah Tannen, Ph.D., Ballantine, 1990.

CHAPTER 7. ESTABLISHING RULES, BOUNDARIES, AND SCHEDULES

Books

Boundaries, by H. Cloud, HarperCollins, 1996.

The Gentle Art of Communicating with Kids, by Suzette Elgin, John Wiley & Sons, 1996.

Good Behavior Made Easy Handbook: Over 1200 Sensible Solutions to Your Child's Problems from Birth to Age Twelve, by Stephen Garber, Marianne Daniels Garber, and Robyn Freedman Spitzman, Great Pond Publishers, 1992.

The Loving Parents' Guide to Discipline: How to Teach Your Child to Behave, with Kindness, Understanding, and Respect, by Marilyn Gootman, Berkley Books, 1995.

The New Dynamics of Goal Setting: Flextactics for a Fast Changing World, by Denis Waitley, William Morrow and Co., 1996.

Notes from a Friend: A Quick & Simple Guide to Taking Charge of Your Life, by Anthony Robbins, Fireside, 1995.

Parent & Child: Getting Through to Each Other, by Lawrence Kutner, William Morrow and Co., 1991.

Parents' Guide to Raising Responsible Kids: Preschool Through Teen Years, by Karyn Feiden, Prentice-Hall Press, 1991.

Positive Discipline, by Jane Nelson, Ballantine, 1996.

CHAPTER 8. DEALING WITH THE BIG THREE PSYCHOLOGICAL CHALLENGES (ISOLATION, MOTIVATION, STRESS)

Books

Attracting Terrific People: How to Find, and Keep, the People Who Bring Your Life Joy, by Lillian Glass, St. Martin's Press, 1997.

Big Book of Relaxation: Simple Techniques to Control the Excess Stress in Your Life, by Shakti Gawain, Relaxation Co., 1994.

The Confidence Course: Seven Steps to Self-Fulfillment, by Walter Anderson, HarperCollins, 1997.

Dancing with Fear: Overcoming Anxiety in a World Full of Stress and Uncertainty, by Paul Foxman, J. Aronson, 1996.

Dr. Nancy Snyderman's Guide to Good Health: What Every Forty-Plus Woman Should Know About Her Changing Body, by Nancy Snyderman, M.D., WilliamMorrow and Co., 1996.

Embracing Your Inner Critic, by Hal Stone and Sidra Stone, Harper San Francisco, 1993.

Food and Mood: The Complete Guide to Eating Well and Feeling Your Best, by Elizabeth Somer, Henry Holt & Co., 1995.

From Panic to Power: Proven Techniques to Calm Your Anxieties, Conquer Your Fears, and Put You in Control of Your Life, by Lucinda Bassett, HarperCollins, 1995.

Homecoming: Reclaiming and Championing Your Inner Child, by John Bradshaw, Bantam, 1992.

How to Win Friends and Influence People, by Dale Carnegie, Simon & Schuster, 1981.

Is Your "Net" Working?: A Complete Guide to Building Contacts and Career Visibility, by Anne Boe and Bettie Youngs, Ph.D., John Wiley & Sons, 1989.

Learned Optimism: How to Change Your Mind and Your Life, by Martin Seligman, Ph.D., Pocket Books, 1990.

Mastering the Winds of Change: Peak Performers Reveal How to Stay on Top in Times of Turmoil, by Erik Olesen, Harper-Business, 1993.

Maximum Achievement, by Brian Tracy, Simon & Schuster, 1995.

The New Dynamics of Winning, by Denis Waitley, William Morrow and Co., 1993.

The Pleasure Prescription: To Love, to Work, to Play—Life in the Balance, by Paul Pearsall, Hunter House Publishers, 1996.

Power Networking: 55 Secrets for Personal and Professional Success, by Donna Vilas and Sandy Vilas, Mountain Harbour Publications, 1992.

The Power of Optimism, by Alan McGinnis, HarperCollins, 1990.

60-Second Shiatzu: The Natural Way to Energize, Ease Pain, and Conquer Tension in One Minute, by Eva Shaw, Henry Holt & Co., 1995.

The Stress Solution: An Action Plan to Manage the Stress in Your Life, by Lyle Miller, Alma Smith, with Larry Rothstein, Pocket Books, 1993.

Toxic People: Ten Ways of Dealing with People Who Make Your Life Miserable, by Lillian Glass, Simon & Schuster, 1995.

Unlimited Power, by Anthony Robbins, Ballantine, 1987.

The Wellness Book, by Herbert Benson, M.D., and Eileen Stuart, R.N., M.S., Fireside, 1992.

Winning People Over: 14 Days to Power and Confidence, by Burton Kaplan, Prentice-Hall, 1996.

You Can Find More Time for Yourself Every Day, by Stephanie Culp, Betterway Books, 1994.

Audiotapes

Denis Waitley's Psychology of Motivation, by Denis Waitley, Simon & Schuster Audio, 1993.

Powertalk! On Creating Extraordinary Relationships, by Anthony Robbins, Audio Renaissance, 1996.

Psychology of Winning, by Denis Waitley, Simon & Schuster, 1995.

The Science of Self-Confidence, by Brian Tracy, Nightingale-Conant, 1991.

CHAPTER 9. ORGANIZING YOUR TIME AND WORK SPACE

Books

How to Survive Your Computer Workstation, by Julia S. Lacey, CRT Services Inc., (800) 256-4379

The Ninety-Minute Hour, by Jay Levinson, E.P. Dutton, 1990.

101 Secrets to Living an Organized Life, by Janet Taylor, P.O. Box 54091, Philadelphia, PA, 19105-4091, (215) 229-7232, Torganized@Aol.com.

Organize Your Office!, by Ronni Eisenberg and Kate Kelly, Hyperion, 1994.

Organizing Your Home Office for Success, by Lisa Kanarek, Plume, 1993.

Preventing Computer Injury: The Hand Book, by Stephanie Brown, Ergonome, 1993.

Time Management for Unmanageable People, by Ann McGee-Cooper with Duane Trammell, Bantam, 1994.

Time Shifting: Creating More Time to Enjoy Your Life, by Stephen Rechtschaffen, Doubleday, 1996.

Timelock: How Life Got So Hectic and What You Can Do About It, by Ralph Keyes, Ballantine, 1993.

Winning the Fight Between You and Your Desk, by Jeffrey J. Mayer, Harper Business, 1995.

Agencies

National Association of Professional Organizers (NAPO), 1033 LaPosada Dr., Austin, TX 78752-3880, (512) 206-0151.

The National Institute of Occupational Safety and Health, publishes a newsletter on how to avoid common home-business ailments related to heavy computer usage, (800) 356-4674.

CHAPTER 10. MAKING THE TRANSITION TO A WORK-AT-HOME LIFESTYLE

CHAPTER 11. MANAGING AND GROWING YOUR HOME BUSINESS

Books

The Business Planning Guide: Creating a Plan for Success in Your Own Business, by David Bangs, Upstart Books, 1993.

The Complete Work-at-Home Companion, by Herman Holtz, Prima Publishing, 1993.

The Credit Process: A Guide for Small Business Owners (FREE twenty-six-page booklet). Write to the Federal Reserve Bank of New York, Public Information Department, 33 Liberty Street, New York, NY 10045.

Dictionary of Occupational Titles, by the U.S. Employment Service, U.S. Government Printing Office, 1993.

Easy Financials for Your Home-Based Business, by Norm Ray, Rayve Productions, 1993.

Financial Essentials for Small Business Success, by Joseph Tabet and Jeffrey Slater, Dearborn Financial Publishing, 1993.

Financing Your Small Business, by Jeffrey Seglin, McGraw-Hill, 1990.

For Entrepreneurs Only: Success Strategies for Anyone Starting or Growing a Business, by Wilson Harrell, Career Press, 1994.

Getting Business to Come to You, by Paul and Sarah Edwards with Laura Clampitt Douglas, Jeremy P. Tarcher/Putnam, 1991.

Government Giveaways for Entrepreneurs II: Over 9,000 Sources of $$, Help & Information to Start or Expand your Business, by Matthew Lesko, Information USA, 1994.

Growing Your Home Based Business, by Kim Gordon, Prentice-Hall, 1992.

Guerrilla Marketing Excellence: The Fifty Golden Rules for Small Business Success, by Jay Levinson, Houghton Mifflin, 1993.

Home Based Entrepreneur: The Complete Guide to Working at Home (second ed.), by Linda Pinson and Jerry Jinnett, Dearborn Trade Publishing, 1993.

Home Business Big Business: How to Launch Your Home Business and Make It a Success, by Mel Cook, Collier Books, Macmillan Publishing Company, 1992.

Homemade Money (fifth ed.), by Barbara Brabec, Betterway Publications, 1994.

The Home Office and Small Business Answer Book, by Janet Attard, Henry Holt & Co., 1993.

How to Achieve Credit Card Merchant Status, by Paul Madjenovic, Todd Publications, 1995, (800) 747–1056.

How to Set Your Fees and Get Them, by Kate Kelly, Visibility Enterprises, 1994, (800) 784-0602.

How to Start, Finance, and Manage Your Own Small Business, by Joseph Mancuso, Fireside, 1992.

How to Write a Business Plan, by Mike McKeever, Nolo Press, 1993.

Insuring Your Business: What You Need to Know to Get the Best Insurance Coverage for Your Business, by Sean Mooney. Insurance Information Institute, 110 William Street, New York, NY 10038, (212) 669-9250.

Inventing and Patenting Sourcebook, by Richard Levy, Gale Research, 1992.

It's Not What You Make—It's What You Keep! How to Keep as Much After-Tax Money as the Law Allows, by Julian Block, Prima Publishing, 1995.

The Job/Family Challenge: Not for Women Only, by Ellen Bravo, John Wiley & Sons, 1994.

Keeping the Books, by Linda Pinson and Jerry Jinnett, Dearborn Financial Publishing, 1996.

Making Telecommuting Happen: A Guide for Telemanagers and Telecommuters, by Jack Niles, Van Nostrand Reinhold, 1994.

Managing by the Numbers, by David Bangs, Upstart Publishing, 1992.

Marketing Online, by Marcia Yudkin, Plume, 1995.

Marketing Your Services: A Step-by-Step Guide for Small Businesses and Professionals, by Anthony Putman, John Wiley & Sons, 1990.

The MITE Telecommuting Implementation Manual, by the Midwest Institute for Telecommuting Education (MITE), 1994, (612) 879-5409.

Money-Smart Secrets for the Self-Employed, by Linda Stern, Random House, 1997.

On Your Own, by Lionel Fisher, Prentice-Hall, 1995.

1,000+ Stationery Designs, by Val Cooper, Point Pacific Press, 1995.

The Online Marketing Handbook: How to Sell, Advertise, Publicize, and Promote Your Products and Services on the Internet and Commercial Online Systems, by Daniel Janal, Van Nostrand Reinhold, 1995.

The Partnership Book: How to Write a Partnership Agreement, by Dennis Clifford and Ralph Warner, Nolo Press, 1993.

Running a Family Business, by Joseph Mancuso, Prentice-Hall Press, 1991.

Selling Yourself: Be the Competent, Confident Person You Really Are!, by Joyce Newman, MasterMedia, Ltd., 1994, (800) 334-8232.

Six Steps to Free Publicity: And Dozens of Other Ways to Win Free Media Attention for You or Your Business, by Marcia Yudkin, Plume/Penguin, 1995.

The Small Business Guide to Advertising with Direct Mail: Smart Solutions for Today's Entrepreneur (FREE eighty-eight-page guide). Write to the U.S. Postal Service, Sales/Account Management Department, Room 5540, 475 L'Enfant Plaza SW, Washington, DC 20260-6300, (800) 238-3150.

Soft Selling in a Hard World: Plain Talk on the Art of Persuasion, by Jerry Vass, Running Press, 1993.

Surviving the Start-Up Years in Your Own Business, by Joyce Marder, Betterway Publications, 1991.

Telecom Made Easy: Money-Saving, Profit-Building Solutions for

Home Businesses, Telecommuters, and Small Organizations, by June Langhoff, Aegis Publishing Group, Ltd., 1995.

Telecommute! Go to Work Without Leaving Home, by Lisa Shaw, John Wiley & Sons, 1996.

The Telecommuter's Handbook: How to Earn a Living Without Going to the Office, by Debra Schepp, McGraw-Hill, 1995.

Telecommuting: How to Make It Work for You and Your Company, by Gil Gordon and Marcia Kelly, Prentice-Hall, 1986.

Trademark: How to Name Your Business and Product, by Kate McGrath and Stephen Elias, Nolo Books, 1993.

The Virtual Office Survival Handbook, by Alice Bredin, John Wiley & Sons, 1996.

What the IRS Doesn't Want You to Know: A CPA Reveals the Tricks of the Trade, by Martin Kaplan and Naomi Weiss, Villard Books, 1995, (800) 793-2665.

Working from Home, by Paul and Sarah Edwards, Jeremy P. Tarcher/Putnam, 1994.

Working Solo, by Terri Lonier, Portico Press, 1994.

Working Solo Sourcebook: Essential Resources for Independent Entrepreneurs, by Terri Lonier, Portico Press, 1995.

Working with the Ones You Love, by Dennis Jaffe, Conari Press, 1990.

Newspapers/Newsletters/Magazines

Bootstrappin' Entrepreneur, Suite B261-ND, 8726 S. Sepulveda Blvd., Los Angeles, CA 90045-4082.

Business Start-Ups, 2392 Morse Avenue, Irvine, CA 92614, (800) 274-8333.

Entrepreneur magazine, 2392 Morse Avenue, Irvine, CA 92614, (800) 274-8333.

Home Office Computing magazine, P.O. Box 53561, Boulder, CO 80322, (800) 678-0118.

Home PC magazine 150 N. Hill Drive, Brisbane, CA 95005, (800) 829-0119.

Inc.: The Magazine for Growing Companies, P.O. Box 51533, Boulder, CO 80323, (800) 234-0999.

Success: The Magazine for Today's Entrepreneurial Mind, P.O. Box 3038, Harlan, IA 51537, (800) 234-7324.

Telecommuting Review, Gil Gordon & Associates, 10 Donner Court, Monmouth Junction, NJ 08852, (732) 329-2266.

Working Solo, Portico Press, P.O. Box 190, New Paltz, NY 12561, (914) 255-7165.

Professional Associations/Organizations

American Association of Home-Based Businesses, P.O. Box 10023, Rockville, MD 20849, (800) 447-9710.

American Home Business Association, 4505 S. Wasatch Blvd., Salt Lake City, UT 84124, (801) 273-2350.

Center for Entrepreneurial Management, Inc., 180 Varick St., 17th floor, New York, NY 10014, (212) 633-0060.

Home Business Institute, Inc., P.O. Box 301, White Plains, NY 10605-0301, (914) 946-6600.

Independent Business Alliance, 111 John Street, 12th Floor, New York, NY 10038, (888) 670-8500.

Internal Revenue Service, Washington, DC 20224, (800) 829-3676.

National Association for the Cottage Industry, P.O. Box 14850, Chicago, IL 60614, (773) 472-8116.

National Association of Home-Based Businesses, P.O. Box 30220, Baltimore, MD 21270, (410) 363-3698.

National Federation of Independent Business, 600 Maryland Ave. SW, Suite 700, Washington, DC 20024, (800) 634-2669.

SCORE (Service Corps of Retired Executives), 409 3rd Street SW, 6th Floor, Washington, DC 20024, (800) 634-0245.

Small Business Foundation of America, Inc., 722 12th Street NW, Washington, DC 20005, (202) 628-8382.

Small Business Service Bureau, 554 Main Street, Worcester, MA 01608, (800) 343-0939.

Small Office Home Office (SOHO), 2121 Precinct Line Road, Hurst, TX 76054, (800) 495-SOHO.

U.S. Small Business Administration (SBA), 409 3rd Street SW, Suite 7000, Washington, DC 20416, (800)-8-ASK-SBA.

Agencies

American Institute of Certified Public Accountants, 1211 Avenue of the Americas, New York, NY 10036-8775.

Copyright Office, Library of Congress, 101 Independence Ave. SE, Washington, DC 20559, (202) 707-8350.

Council of Better Business Bureaus, 4200 Wilson Blvd., Arlington, VA 22203, (703) 276-0100.

Health Insurance Association of America, 555 13th Street NW, Suite 600E, Washington, DC 20004, (202) 824-1600.

Insurance Information Institute, 110 William St., New York, NY 10038, (212) 669-9200.

International Association of Financial Planners, (800) 945-4237.

IRS Taxpayer Education Office, (800) 829-1040.

Lawphone, (800) 255-3352.

National Insurance Consumer Help line, (800) 942-4242.

Patent and Trademark Office, U.S. Department of Commerce, Washington, DC 20231, (800) 786-9199.

Quotesmith (health insurance options), (800) 556-9393.

Support Services Alliance (group insurance for small business owners), (800) 322-3920.

Computer On-Line Services

America Online, (800) 827-6364.

AT&T Worldnet, (800) 809-1103.

CompuServe, (800) 848-8199.

Delphi, (800) 695-4005.

Genie, (800) 638-9636.

Microsoft Network, (800) 426-9400.

Prodigy, (800) 776-3449.

Computer On-Line Resources

AT&T Home Business Resources Web Site
http://www.att.com/hbr

Business at Home: Making a Life While Making a Living
http://www.gohome.com

Business Resources Center
http://www.kcilink.com/brc

Entrepreneur Small Business Square
http://www.entrepreneurmag.com

Gil Gordon's Web Page (Telecommuting)
http://www.gilgordon.com

The Home Office Home Page
http://www.bankamerica.com

The Home Office Hub
http//www.gohome.com

Homeworks
http://www.homeworks.com

MCI Small Business Center
http://www.mci.com/SmallBiz/

Small & Home-Based Business Links
http://www.ro.com/small business/homebased.html

Small Business Administration
http://www.sba.gov

Small Office Home Office (SOHO) America
http://work.soho.org/soho

Small Office Site
http://www.smalloffice.com

Small Office Site Work & Family Area
http://www.smalloffice.com/cooler/keep.htm

Smart Business Supersite
http://www.smartbiz.com

SOHO Central
http://www.hoaa.com

REFERENCES

Aburdene, P., and Naisbitt, J. *Megatrends for Women.* New York: Villard Books, 1992.

Ahrentzen, S. "Managing Conflict by Managing Boundaries: How Professional Homeworkers Cope with Multiple Roles at Home." *Environment and Behavior* 22 (1990): 723–52.

Alvarez, M. "The Best Home-Office Design Tips." *Home-Office Computing* (September 1990): 42–46.

Andrews, A., and Bailyn, L. "Segmentation and Synergy." In J. Hood, ed., *Men, Work and Family.* Newbury Park, CA: Sage Publications, 1993: 262–75.

Ball, A. "The Daddy Track." *New York* (October 23, 1989): 52–60.

Barnett, R., and Baruch, G. "Determinants of Fathers' Participation in Family Work." *Journal of Marriage and the Family* 49 (1987): 29–40.

Beach, B. *Integrating Work and Family Life: The Home-Working Family.* New York: State University of New York Press, 1989.

Benson, H., and Stuart, E. *The Wellness Book.* New York: Fireside, 1992.

Bergman, S., and Surrey, J. "The Woman-Man Relationship: Impasses and Possibilities." (Work in Progress No. 22). Wellesley, MA: Stone Center, 1992.

Berner, J. *The Joy of Working from Home.* San Francisco: Berrett-Koehler Publishers, Inc., 1994.

Betz, N., and Fitzgerald, L. *The Career Psychology of Women.* Boston: Academic Press, 1987.

Bredin, A. *The Virtual Office Survival Handbook.* New York: John Wiley & Sons, Inc., 1996.

Campbell, A., Converse, P., and Rodgers, W. *The Quality of American Life.* New York: Russell Sage Foundation, 1976.

Cavanah, C. "Getting Personnel." *Entrepreneur* (June 1996): 44–47.

Cheney, K. "You Can Make Six Figures Working at Home." *Money* (March 1996): 74–87.

Christensen, K. "White-Collar Home-Based Work—The Changing U.S. Economy and Family." In K. Christensen, ed., *The New Era of Homebased Work.* London: Westview Press, 1988: 1–11.

Coates, V. "Office Automation Technology and Home-Based Work." In K. Christensen, ed., *The New Era of Home-Based Work.* London: Westview Press, 1988: 114–25.

Edwards, P., and Edwards, S. *Working from Home.* Los Angeles: Jeremy P. Tarcher, Inc., 1990.

Ferree, M. "Beyond Separate Spheres: Feminism and Family Research." *Journal of Marriage and the Family* 52 (1990): 866–84.

Ferree, M. "The Gender Division of Labor in Two-Earner Marriages." *Journal of Family Issues* 12 (1991): 158–80.

Fisher, L. *On Your Own.* Englewood Cliffs, NJ: Prentice-Hall, 1995.

Fitzsimmons, B. "Happy Homemakers: Stay-at-Home Dads Find Real Job Satisfaction." *North County Times* (October 5, 1996): E-3.

Fowlkes, M. "The Myth of Merit and Male Professional Careers: The Roles of Wives." In N. Gerstel and H. Gross, eds., *Families and Work.* Philadelphia: Temple University Press, 1987: 347–60.

Giele, J. "Changing Sex Roles and Family Structure." In P. Voydanoff, ed., *Work and Family: Changing Roles of Men and Women.* Palo Alto, CA: Mayfield, 1984: 191–208.

Gilbert, L. *Men in Dual-Career Families: Current Realities and Future Prospects.* Mahwah, NJ: Lawrence Erlbaum Associates, 1985.

Gilbert, L., and Dancer, L. "Dual-Earner Families in the United States and Adolescent Development." In S. Lewis, D. Izraeli, and H. Hootsmans, eds., *Dual-Earner Families: International Perspectives.* Newbury Park, CA: Sage Publications, 1992: 151–71.

Gilbert, L. *Two Careers/One Family.* Newbury Park, CA: Sage Publications, 1993.

Griffin, C. "Kidding Around." *Entrepreneur* (September 1996): 55–59.

Griffin, C., and Page, H. "Home Improvement." *Entrepreneur* (September 1996): 108–12.

Heck, R. "The Effects of Children on the Major Dimensions of Home-Based Employment." *Journal of Family and Economic Issues* 13 (1992): 315–46.

Hochschild, A. *The Second Shift: Working Parents and the Revolution at Home.* New York: Viking, 1989.

Home Office Guide. *Consumer Reports* (September 1996): 26–27.

Horrigan, M., and Markey, J. "Recent Gains in Women's Earnings: Better Pay or Longer Hours." *Monthly Labor Review* (July 1990): 11–17.

Jaffe, A. *Honey I Want to Start My Own Business.* New York: Harper Business, 1996.

Jaffe, D. *Working with the Ones You Love.* Berkeley: Conari Press, 1990.

Levinson, J. *Ninety-Minute Hour.* New York: E.P. Dutton, 1990.

Lewis, R. "All the 'Comforts' of Home." *Bulletin* 2 (October 1996).

Longstreth, M., Stafford, K., and Mauldin, T. "Self-Employed Women and Their Families: Time Use and Socioeconomic Characteristics." *Journal of Small Business Management* 3 (1987): 30–37.

Lublin, J. "Rights Law to Spur Shifts in Promotions." *The Wall Street Journal* (December 30, 1991): B1.

Lynn, J. "Friendly Hire." *Entrepreneur* (June 1996): 36.

Lynn, J. "Hire Power." *Entrepreneur* (August, 1996): 33.

Madjenovic, P. *How to Achieve Credit Card Merchant Status.* West Nyack, NY: Todd Publications, 1995.

Malcolm, A. "A Day of Celebration for a More Active Kind of Dad." *The New York Times* (June 16, 1991): 14.

Maslow, A. *Toward a Psychology of Being.* New York: Van Nostrand, 1962.

McGarvey, R. "Ready, Set, 'Net!'" *Entrepreneur* (June, 1996): 143–49.

McHale S., and Crouter, A. "You Can't Always Get What You Want: Incongruence Between Sex-Role Attitudes and Family Work Roles and Its Implications for Marriage." *Journal of Marriage and the Family* 54 (1992): 537–47.

Michelozzi, B. *Coming Alive from Nine to Five.* Mountain View, CA: Mayfield Publishing Company, 1992.

Owen, A., Carsky, M., and Dolan, E. "Home-Based Employment: Historical and Current Considerations." *Journal of Family and Economic Issues* 13 (1992): 121–38.

Parker, L. *How to Open and Operate a Home-Based Writing Business.* Old Saybrook, CT: The Globe Pequot Press, 1994.

Parlapiano, E., and Cobe, P. *Mompreneurs.* New York: Perigee, 1996.

Perry-Jenkins, M., and Crouter, A. "Men's Provider-Role Attitudes: Implications for Household Work and Marital Satisfaction." *Journal of Marriage and the Family* 11 (1990): 136–56.

Pleck, J. "Men's Power with Women, Other Men, and Society: A Men's Movement Analysis." In R. Lewis, ed., *Men in Difficult Times: Masculinity Today and Tomorrow.* New York: Prentice-Hall, 1981: 234–44.

Pleck, J. "Are 'Family Supportive' Employer Policies Relevant to Men?" In J. Hood, ed., *Men, Work and Family.* Newbury Park, CA: Sage Publications, 1993: 217–37.

Price, S., and Price, T. *The Working Parents Help Book.* Princeton, NJ: Peterson's, 1994.

Rix, S. *The American Woman 1987–1988: A Report in Depth.* New York: Norton Press, 1987.

Schwartz, F. "Management Women and the New Facts of Life." *Harvard Business Review* 1 (January/February 1989): 65–76.

Sedney, M. "Development of Androgyny: Parental Influences." *Psychology of Women Quarterly* 11 (1987): 311–26.

Sekaran, U. *Dual-Career Families.* San Francisco: Jossey-Bass Publishers, 1986.

Severence, T. "Show Me the Money." *AHB In Touch* (Fall 1997): 1.

Shaw, L. *Telecommute!* New York: John Wiley & Sons, Inc., 1996.

Silverstein, L. "Fathering Is a Feminist Issue." *Psychology of Women Quarterly* 20 (1996): 3–37.

Solomon, B. "A Real Mom's Guide to Working at Home." *Parents* (May 1996): 45–46.

Stein, B., and Espindle, M. "How Home-Business Owners Balance Business and Family." *Home-Office Computing* (August 1991): 42–43.

Stern, L. "Organize!" *Home-Office Computing* (February 1991): 48–51.

Stoltz-Loike, M. *Dual-Career Couples: New Perspectives in Counseling.* Alexandria,VA: American Association for Counseling and Development, 1992.

Sullivan, N. "Escaping the Time Trap." *Home-Office Computing* (July 1993): 96.

Taylor, J. "Clear Out the Paperwork" (E-mail, April 8, 1997) Available: Torganized@Aol.com.

Thoits, P. "Negotiating Roles." In F. Crosby, ed., *Spouse, Parent, Worker: On Gender and Multiple Roles.* New Haven, CT: Yale University Press, 1987: 11–22.

Vannoy-Hiller, D., and Philliber, W. *Equal Partners: Successful Women in Marriage.* Newbury Park, CA: Sage Publications, 1989.

Wallace, D. "The Home Office High Wire." *Home-Office Computing* (October 1993): 69–74.

Wallace, D. "Overcoming Isolation." *Home-Office Computing* (March 1995): 59–65.

Wiley, M. "Gender, Work, and Stress: The Potential Impact of Role-Identity Salience and Commitment." *Sociological Quarterly* 32 (1991): 495–510.

Winter, M., Puspitawati, H., Heck, R., and Stafford, K. "Time-Management Strategies Used by Households with Home-Based Work," *Journal of Family and Economic Issues* 14 (1993): 69–92.

Witt, C. "Bad-Check Enforcement Program." *AHB In Touch* (Winter 1997): 2.